By
E. RAYMOND CAPT M.A., A.I.A., F.S.A. Scot

PUBLISHED BY
ARTISAN SALES
P.O. BOX 1497 • THOUSAND OAKS
CALIF. 91360 U.S.A.

ISBN: CLOTH 0 – 934666 –20–2   PAPER 0 - 934666– 21–0
LIBRARY OF CONGRESS CATALOG CARD NUMBER: 86–70103

THE AUTHOR

E. RAYMOND CAPT M.A., A.I.A., F.S.A. Scot.

At first glance one might think E. Raymond Capt must be an ordained minister. He quotes chapters and verses from the Scriptures and tells about Bible characters in a flowing narrative which would credit any pulpit. What he's been, for over forty years, though, is a practicing archaeologist — not always digging to unearth ancient remains but in recent years, sifting through known archaeological findings to shed new light on the history of the Bible.

Capt holds a Master of Arts degree in Christian History and Biblical Archaeology from Covenant College, Lake Wales, Florida, and California State teaching credentials in BIBLICAL Archaeology and History. He is also a member of the Archaeological Institute of America. In addition to writing, Capt has produced and presents slide and film lectures on Biblical Archaeology. These have been enjoyed by clubs, churches and schools in many states and in Great Britain.

In 1972 Capt was elected a Fellow of the Society of Antiquaries of Scotland and in 1976 received an honorary Doctorate of Literature, (Doctor Literarum Honoris Causa) from the Accademia Testina Per Le Scienze, (established A.D. 450) Pescara, Italy.

Robert J. Germain-Ller, Ph.D.,

Dean of the Graduate School
Covenant College

THE GREAT PYRAMID

CONTENTS

PAGE

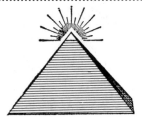

THE PYRAMIDS OF GIZA

MYCERINUS (MENKURE) - CHEPHREN (KHAFRE) - CHEOPS (KHUFU)

PREFACE

As I set about the task of writing a new study of the Great Pyramid of Giza, I am reminded of the words of John Taylor, one of the earliest students of Pyramidology: "Many must approve, before the thought will enter into the popular mind; and if that result ever takes place, I am only one among many who are entitled to a commendation; nay, there is no room for commendation to any one, for all do but impart what has been given."

I am only one in a long line of students who have expounded on the Great Pyramid. My original work on the subject, "The Great Pyramid Decoded" (first published in 1971) was only intended to be an introduction to the subject. It was to draw attention to other more comprehensive works. (Ex. "The Great Pyramid — Its Divine Message" by David Davidson and H. Aldersmith;" "Great Pyramid Passages" by John and Morton Edgar;" "Pyramidology" in four volumes, by Dr. Adam Rutherford)

All these writers have passed away and their works are out of print. Modern day writers on the Great Pyramid have brought out some excellent books, but, they all fail to present the most important feature of the Great Pyramid — God's plan for humanity architecturally embodied in its construction.

It was the desire to fill this 'void' that motivated me to produce a second book on the Great Pyramid, expanding my earlier work with additional details and illustrations, without weighing it down with complex and technical information available from past research. And, most important, to present the spiritual aspects and current theories concerning prophecy revealed in the design of the Pyramid, as an unbiased observer. I will let the reader choose what position he or she will take.

THE SPHINX

CHAPTER 1.

ISAIAH 19:19-20

"In that day shall there be an altar to the Lord in the midst of the land of Egypt, and a pillar (Hebrew "Matstsebah," correctly translated monument) *at the border thereof to the Lord. And it shall be for a sign, and for a witness unto the Lord of Hosts in the land of Egypt."*

According to the above passage, this altar-monument is to be found *"in the midst of the land of Egypt"* and yet *"at the border thereof."* There is only one spot on the face of the earth that complies with both of those conditions and that is the exact spot where the Great Pyramid stands. The Great Pyramid is situated on a line corresponding with the 30° North Latitude drawn just south of Cairo, dividing the country into Lower and Upper Egypt. To the immediate east of the Pyramid is highly cultivated and densely populated land in which stands the Metropolis of Egypt. To the immediate west of the Pyramid is the Great Sahara Desert — nothing but sand for many hundreds of miles.

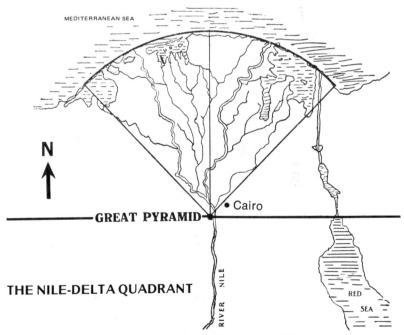

THE GREAT PYRAMID OF GIZA STANDS AT THE GEOMETRIC CENTER AND YET AT THE SOUTHERN EXTREMITY OF THE QUADRANT

Lines produced from the two diagonals of the Pyramid, to the northwest and northeast, enclose the Nile Delta, which resembles an open fan with a long handle. The Delta, or Lower Egypt, is the fan; the strip of cultivated land which borders the Nile is the handle. The Great Pyramid stands at the geometric center and southern extremity of this Nile-Delta Quadrant. Thus we see, the Great Pyramid is in the midst of the land of Egypt and yet at the border of it, both geometrically and geographically.

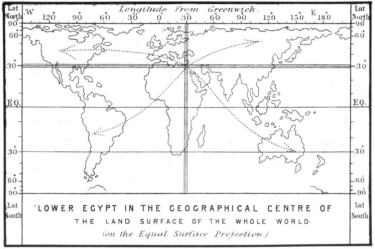

LOWER EGYPT IN THE GEOGRAPHICAL CENTRE OF THE LAND SURFACE OF THE WHOLE WORLD. *(on the Equal Surface Projection)*

The Great Pyramid was also placed in the exact center of all the land area of the earth. Lines drawn through the north-south and east-west axis of the Pyramid divide equally the earth's terrain. The north-south axis (31° 9' meridian east of Greenwich) is the longest land meridian, and the east-west axis, (29°58' 51" north) the longest land parallel.

It should be noted that the official name of the Great Pyramid is the "Great Pyramid of Giza," which means, in English, the "Great Pyramid of the Border." This gives additional proof that the "altar" of Isaiah 19:19-20 is the Great Pyramid of Giza. According to Isaiah, this altar was to be for a "sign" and a "witness." This indicates it was not an altar of sacrifice, in which case it could not have been built of hewn stone, for the law has never been rescinded that is given in Exodus 20: 25: *"If thou wilt make Me an altar of stone, thou shalt not build it of hewn stone; for if thou lift up thy tool upon it, thou has polluted it..."*

The Bible tells us of other altars of witness or pillars of covenant. Jacob set up a "witness" (at Bethel) of the oath which he

The Great Pyramid Text of Scripture

—— Isaiah 19: 19-20 ——

ביום ההוא יהיה מזבח ליהוה בתוך ארץ מצרים ומצבה
אצל־גבולה ליהוה : והיה לאות ולעד ליהוה צבאות
בארץ מצרים כי־יצעקו אל־יהוה מפני לחצים וישלח
להם מושיע ורב והצילם :

This Great Pyramid Text of Scripture, in the original Hebrew, contains 30 words. In Hebrew the letters of the alphabet were employed as arithmetical figures, consequently every word is also a row of figures and thus all Hebrew writing has numeric value. The above Hebrew Text as numbers is as shown below—the value of every letter is given and each line represents a word. **The total value is 5,449.**

(1)	2	+	10	+	6	+	40				=	58
(2)	5	+	5	+	6	+	1				=	17
(3)	10	+	5	+	10	+	5				=	30
(4)	40	+	7	+	2	+	8				=	57
(5)	30	+	10	+	5	+	6	+	5		=	56
(6)	2	+	400	+	6	+	20				=	428
(7)	1	+	200	+	90						=	291
(8)	40	+	90	+	200	+	10	+	40		=	380
(9)	6	+	40	+	90	+	2	+	5		=	143
(10)	1	+	90	+	30						=	121
(11)	3	+	2	+	6	+	30	+	5		=	46
(12)	30	+	10	+	5	+	6	+	5		=	56
(13)	6	+	5	+	10	+	5				=	26
(14)	30	+	1	+	6	+	400				=	437
(15)	6	+	30	+	70	+	4				=	110
(16)	30	+	10	+	5	+	6	+	5		=	56
(17)	90	+	2	+	1	+	6	+	400		=	499
(18)	2	+	1	+	200	+	90				=	293
(19)	40	+	90	+	200	+	10	+	40		=	380
(20)	20	+	10								=	30
(21)	10	+	90	+	70	+	100	+	6		=	276
(22)	1	+	30								=	31
(23)	10	+	5	+	6	+	5				=	26
(24)	40	+	80	+	50	+	10				=	180
(25)	30	+	8	+	90	+	10	+	40		=	178
(26)	6	+	10	+	300	+	30	+	8		=	354
(27)	30	+	5	+	40						=	75
(28)	40	+	6	+	300	+	10	+	70		=	426
(29)	6	+	200	+	2						=	208
(30)	6	+	5	+	90	+	10	+	30	+ 40	=	181

Height of the Great Pyramid in <u>Pyramid inches</u> = 5,449

(to the original Summit Platform)

RUTHERFORD

had sworn to God and another (at Mizpah) as a "witness" of the agreement between Laban and himself. These altars originated in the mind of man to meet the need of the moment. It would suffice if they only lasted a few generations and excited sufficient curiosity to ensure that the story which they embodied would be passed from father to son until the story became a part of the racial tradition.

But the Great Pyramid is a "witness" of quite another order. It has outlasted a hundred generations and its secrets remained a mystery during this period. It was intended to be as durable as anything human could be. With this purpose it was constructed with the greatest precision and of the most suitable and durable material. Acting on this hypothesis we may disregard the various theories (and they are many) which have been suggested to account for the colossal expenditure of labor and material involved in the construction, theories that fail to recognize its relationship with Isaiah 19: 19-20.

A remarkable mathematical relationship exists between the text of Isaiah 19:19-20 and the Great Pyramid. The total sum of the numerical value of the original Hebrew text of Isaiah 19:19-20 is 5,449. (See chart, page 12) The actual height of the Pyramid, as left unfinished by the builders, was 5,449 Pyramid inches. The distance from the Pyramid's entrance right through to the farthest extremity of the interior passages and chambers is also equal to 5,449 Pyramid inches. (Pyramid inches are explained in chapter 10)

Having shown that the Great Pyramid occupies a site which satisfies the exceptionally peculiar conditions of the Isaiah text, we have established a "prima facie" case for further inquiry into the secrets of this "altar of witness." And further, the word pyramid is

THE GREAT PYRAMID

a clue as to where the secrets of the Pyramid can be found. In the ancient Coptic language, the word pyramid is "Urim Middin." Urim means "revelation" and Middin means "measures," thus defining the Great Pyramid in the astronomical and geometrical term, Divine Revelations or Revelation Measures.

The theory that the Great Pyramid is the "witness" of Isaiah 19:19-20 and has a purpose other than a burial tomb may be somewhat startling and considered an extravagant fancy. However, on the other hand, the theory may be true. And if such is the possibility or even the probability, the matter is not only worthy of our examination, but it would seem our duty to test it in every possible field of inquiry.

To The Great Pyramid

Somber, mysterious, lofty, ancient pile,
Enigma of remotest history,
Who set thee here beside the storied Nile,
Eternal watch to keep?
What Master Architect conceived thy plan?
Thou baffling riddle of the centuries,
Standing where Egypt's delta, like a fan,
Spreads northward, lush and green.
What skilful workman wrought in ages past,
So long ago their tools, their books, their songs,
The echo of their speech are lost to us?
No puny folk were they who set these stones
With artful nicety each in its place,
To stand, while things like nations, kings and thrones
Grow old and crumble into dust.
Unlike the other buildings standing near,

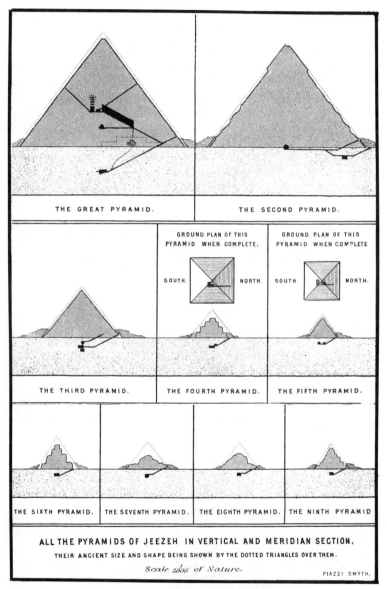

THE GREAT PYRAMID.

THE SECOND PYRAMID.

GROUND PLAN OF THIS PYRAMID WHEN COMPLETE.

SOUTH.   NORTH.

GROUND PLAN OF THIS PYRAMID WHEN COMPLETE

SOUTH.   NORTH.

THE THIRD PYRAMID.

THE FOURTH PYRAMID.

THE FIFTH PYRAMID.

THE SIXTH PYRAMID.

THE SEVENTH PYRAMID.

THE EIGHTH PYRAMID.

THE NINTH PYRAMID

ALL THE PYRAMIDS OF JEEZEH IN VERTICAL AND MERIDIAN SECTION,
THEIR ANCIENT SIZE AND SHAPE BEING SHOWN BY THE DOTTED TRIANGLES OVER THEM.

Scale $\frac{1}{5000}$ of Nature.

PIAZZI SMYTH,

THE NINE PYRAMIDS OF GIZA

16

CHAPTER 2.

PHYSICAL APPEARANCE

The Great Pyramid of Giza (Gizeh) is situated about ten miles to the southwest of Cairo, the capital of Egypt. Known as the Pyramid of Cheops (Khufu), it stands on the northern edge of the Giza Plateau, 198 feet above sea-level, in the eastern extremity of the Libyan section of the Great Sahara Desert. The Great Pyramid is the most northerly of a group of nine pyramids comprising the "Giza Complex." Near the Great Pyramid stand two notable pyramids, one slightly smaller, attributed to Chephren, (Khafre) the son of Cheops. The other, smaller still, is attributed to Mycerinus, (Menkure) the grandson of Cheops. The remaining six pyramids are relatively small and are in ruins. To the south-east of the Great Pyramid lies the Sphinx, carved out of the rock, with its gaze directed towards the rising sun.

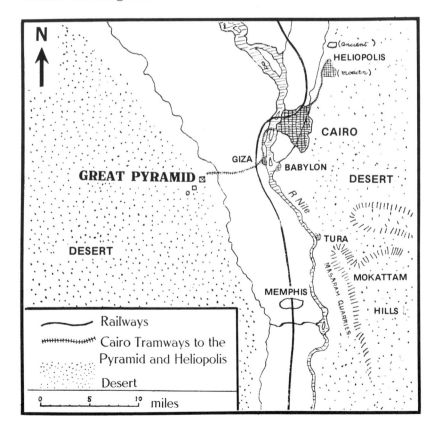

17

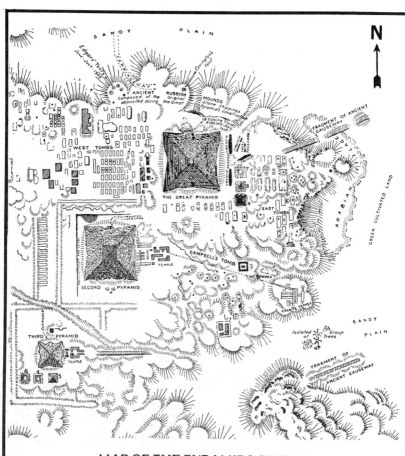

MAP OF THE PYRAMIDS OF GIZA

SHOWING THEIR POSITION ON THE FLAT-TOPPED HILL OF ROCK
WHICH RISES JUST SOUTH OF THE LOW DELTA LAND OF LOWER EGYPT

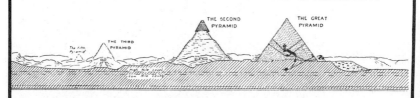

MERIDIAN SECTION THROUGH THE GREAT PYRAMID
AND ITS HILL (LOOKING WEST)

MYCERINUS — CHEPHREN — CHEOPS

19

STEP PYRAMID OF ZOSER AT SAKKARA

The total number of identified pyramids in Egypt is about 80. They are situated in an area of desert, on the west side of the Nile Valley, extending some 70 miles to the north from the Giza Plateau. They were built over a period of nearly one thousand years, from the 27th to the 18th centuries B.C. The most notable, outside the Giza Complex, are those of Abu Sir, Sakkara, Dahshur, Lisht and Meidun. The oldest pyramid is the Step Pyramid of Zoser at Sakkara, built around 2700 B.C. It rises in six unequal "steps" to a height of 204 feet.

The superior pyramids, however, were erected during the period of the Old Kingdom (during Dynasties III to VI — between 2700-2200 B.C.) and this is known as the "Pyramid Age." The largest and most famous of these pyramids are the Pyramids of Giza. The first of the Giza pyramids to be erected was the Great Pyramid of Cheops, (Khufu) around 2623 B.C. It has been referred to as marking the apogee of pyramid-building in respect to both size and quality. (The Pyramids of Egypt — I.E.S. Edwards, Head of the Dept. of Egyptian Antiquities in the British Museum)

Today, seen at a distance, the Great Pyramid looks like a great pile of rock. Nearer at hand, it is seen that the stones, composing the structure, are roughly cut and laid in even courses, one upon another. These courses, or layers, seen to form a series of gigantic steps, sloping back from the base on all four sides, to a level platform on top. Because it is the oldest building in the world and because of its immense size, the ancients conferred upon it the predominent distinction of being the first of the Seven Wonders of the World. They chose more wisely than they themselves realized. All the other Wonders of the Ancient World have passed into oblivion and any attempt to create another Seven Wonders of the World places the Great Pyramid of Giza at the top of the list.

Modern scientific investigations have shown, with the exception of the comparatively small space occupied by the passages and chambers, the Great Pyramid is a solid mass of stone blocks having a square base and four tapering sides that rise 454½ feet to a small platform on top. Its original designed height is 484 feet, equal to a modern 48 story skyscraper. The length of each side of the Pyramid's base is 755 3/4 feet and the entire structure covers slightly over 13 acres. In sheer bulk, the Great Pyramid is the largest man-made building in the world.

The yellow limestone (nummulitic) blocks making up the bulk of the Pyramid average 2½ tons each and are estimated to number about 2,300,000. This equals nearly 90,000,000 cubic feet of masonry and enough to build 30 Empire State buildings. To make another comparison, there is sufficient stone in the Great Pyramid to build a wall three feet high and one foot thick extending a distance of over 5,600 miles.

In its original state, each of the four sides of the Great Pyramid had an area of 5½ acres, thus totalling 22 acres of highly polished limestone blocks. In the brilliant sunshine of Egypt, the sides acted as gigantic mirrors, reflecting the sun's rays that could be seen for many miles around. Seen from the moon, the Great Pyramid would have been seen as a bright star on the earth. Appropriately, the ancient Egyptians called the Great Pyramid "Ikhet," meaning the "Glorious Light."

By means of its reflections and shadows, the Great Pyramid became the great sundial of Egypt, not only for the days and hours, but for the seasons of the year. Exactly as a modern chronometer gives the hours, say, of midnight, 6 a.m., noon, and 6 p.m., so the reflections from the Pyramid gave accurately the days upon which the Winter Solstice, the Spring Equinox, the Summer Solstice, and the Autumnal Equinox occurred. This precisely defined the Solar Astronomical Year.

Noon of the Summer Solstice was the point when the Great Pyramid's triangular reflections were most notable and the Pyramid cast no shadows. These are respectively the shortest noon reflections of the year from the South, East, and West faces of the Pyramid, and the longest noon reflection of the year from the North face of the Pyramid.

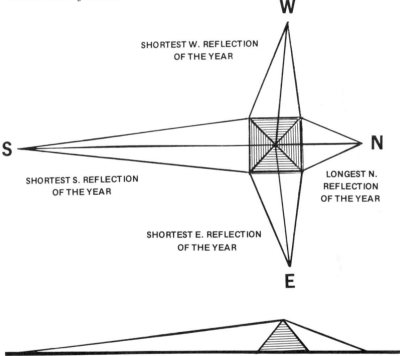

By contrast, at noon on the Winter Solstice, the Great Pyramid's northern face, in which the Entrance is located, was in the shade and a shadow was cast on the ground (at the north side) while the sun-light on the south side was reflected back into the air.

The solid beams of reflected light proceeding from the East and West slopes of the Pyramid at noon had a further remarkable property defining Winter as distinct from Spring, Summer, and Autumn. The East and West noon-reflected beams each had a surface seen from the North side of the Pyramid, and a surface seen from the South side of the Pyramid.

These noon-reflected beams each had a sharply defined ridge running from the Pyramid apex to the apex of each of the images projected on the ground, and as viewed from the South, always, throughout the year, appeared to be inclining away from the observer. The side of the East or West noon reflected beam, however, as viewed from the North side of the Pyramid, appeared inclining away from the observer during Spring, Summer, and Autumn, but appeared overhanging toward the observer during Winter, as shown on the following diagram.

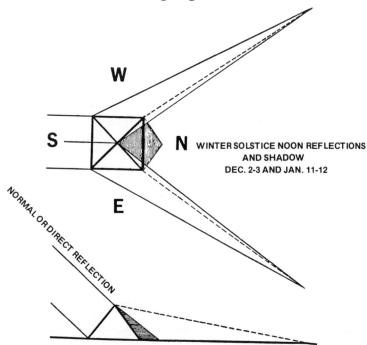

**WINTER SOLSTICE NOON REFLECTIONS
AND SHADOW
DEC. 2-3 AND JAN. 11-12**

UPPER LIMIT OF SOUTH SLOPE REFLECTION — UPPER LIMIT OF NORTH SLOPE SHADOW

The orientation of the Great Pyramid in relationship to true north is such as to cause it to be declared the "most accurately oriented edifice on earth." That is to say, its four sides are directed to the four cardinal points of the compass with less than 3 minutes of one degree off true north. By comparison, the Paris Observatory is 6 minutes of one degree off true north. It is possible that originally the Great Pyramid was absolutely perfectly orientated and the slight error measured today is the result of centuries of contraction or expansion of the earth's crust or from earthquakes, which seismography records as not being infrequent in the territory contiguous to the Great Pyramid.

Such nearly perfect orientation is exceedingly hard to secure, even with modern astronomical equipment, and seemingly impossible without it. If the knowledge of the magnetic needle was known, it would have been of little value. It points to the magnetic north, not to the true north. The magnetic north is also constantly moving. The celestial pole (true north) is a point, usually defined by a star, through which the polar axis of the earth would pass were it projected to the star sphere.

From its physical appearance, the Great Pyramid stands at the head of the world in vastness of dimensions. For over forty centuries it has been enshrouded in the deepest mystery but now it is beginning to yield up its secrets. Modern research is finding it to have been constructed in perfection of workmanship and in the practical mastery of problems that would tax the ingenuity of modern engineers. It was built for permanence and for surviving all the commotions of nature and all the vandalism of men. Signally, the builders succeeded. Not a stone necessary to its ulterior purpose has been lost.

Old Time

> Old Time, himself so old, is like a child,
> And can't remember when these blocks were piled
> Or caverns scooped; but, with amazed eye,
> He seems to pause, like other standers-by,
> Half thinking how the wonders here made known
> Were born in ages older than his own.

Anonymous

ENTRANCE AS SEEN IN THE NINETEENTH CENTURY A.D.

26

CHAPTER 3

HISTORICAL RECORD

Our earliest record of the Great Pyramid of Giza is found in the writings of the Greek historian, Herodotus, who is often referred to as the "Father of History." He was born around 484 B.C. at Halicarnassus, a Greek colony on the coast of Asia Minor, and died around 425 B.C. Herodotus visited Egypt to gather information from the scholar-priests for his books. From an Egyptian priest, through an interpreter, Herodotus gathered traditional accounts of the erection of the Great Pyramid. Although evidence goes to show he accurately recorded what he saw and heard, he did believe some things that were not true. In Herodotus's day, the Pyramid was already very ancient so it is not surprising, therefore, that all sorts of legends and fanciful theories had grown up around the Great Pyramid.

Herodotus, in addition to writing about the Great Pyramid, also recorded that the actual burial vault that Cheops constructed for himself was an "underground apartment" on an "island formed by drawing water from the Nile by a channel." The underground vault described is believed to be the subterranean vault tomb some three hundred yards from the Pyramid's Mortuary Temple, known as "Campbell's Tomb." Running around this vault is a deep trench (73 feet deep by 5 feet-four inches wide) which could be filled with water at High Nile. The vault itself, is above high water level of the Nile, so it could be said to fit the description as an "underground apartment on an island."

Homer (the traditional epic poet of Greece — dates vary from 685 B.C. to 830 B.C.) does not seem to make any allusion to the Great Pyramid, perhaps for the reasons that it had no connection with mythology, or with any of his heroes. Eratosthenes, (236 B.C.) Strabo and Pliny, (about the beginning of the Christian Era) all wrote about it. The Egyptian historian Manetho (born at Sebenithe in the Nile Delta about 200 years after Herodotus' visit to Egypt) mentions the Great Pyramid, but only fragments of his writings exist and they come second-hand from Flavius Josephus. (cira. A.D. 37-100) Other historians who wrote about the Great Pyramid are Julius Africanus (circa. A.D. 300) and Eusebius of Caesarea. (circa. A.D. 254-340)

Diodorus Silculus, who lived during the first century before Christ, also wrote that Cheops was not buried in the Great Pyramid; "Although these kings (Cheops and Cephren) intended these (pyramids) for their sepulchres, yet it happened that neither of them

Pyramidographia:

OR A
DESCRIPTION
OF THE
PYRAMIDS
IN ÆGYPT.

By IOHN GREAVES, Professor
of Astronomy in the University
of OXFORD.

*Romanorum Fabrica, & antiqua opera (cum veniâ
id dictum sit) nihil accedunt ad Pyramidum splendo-
rem, & superbiam.* Bellon. lib. 2. Observ. cap. 42.

LONDON,
Printed for *George Badger*, and are to be sold at
his shop in St *Dunstans* Churchyard
in Fleet-street 1 6 4 6.

TITLE PAGE OF "PYRAMIDOGRAPHIA" PUBLISHED A.D. 1646

was buried there." (Liber I, 63) Diodorus adds that their burials were "in an obscure place." In confirmation of the statement that these two monarchs were buried elsewhere, the sarcophagi in these two Pyramids — the Great Pyramid and Second Pyramid of Giza — are both undecorated and uninscribed, thus indicating that no royalty was ever placed in them. There are indications, however, that at some time later, someone else used Cephren's sarcophagus, for the lid shows that it had been fixed down and then forced off.

Several Arab writings are extant that comment on the Great Pyramid. The most outstanding is the report of Edrisi, (Idrisi) who died around A.D. 1166. Edrisi entered the Pyramid by way of Al Mamoun's forced entrance and describes the interior of the Great Pyramid. From his records, we know that there was an empty coffer in the Queen's Chamber, similar to that of the one found in the King's Chamber, in that it was also uninscribed and undecorated. (Nuzhat-el-Mushtak — "Description of the World")

During the Renaissance and Reformation periods, a long list of travelers visited the Great Pyramid. The list included Breydenbach. (A.D. 1484) Martin Baumgarten, (A.D. 1507) Dr. Pierre Belon, (A.D. 1546) Johannes Helferich, (A.D. 1565) Jean Palerme, (A.D. 1581) Laurence Aldersey, (A.D. 1586) Prosper Alpin, (A.D. 1591) George Sandys, (A.D. 1610) and John Greaves. (A.D. 1638-9)

JOHN GREAVES

John Greaves (Professor of Astronomy at the University of Oxford, England) was the earliest scholar to make a truly scientific study and investigation of the Great Pyramid. He visited Egypt in 1637 in order to explore its pyramids. He afterwards wrote the first book devoted entirely to the Great Pyramid. The book was published in London in A.D. 1646 under the title, "Pyramidographia: A

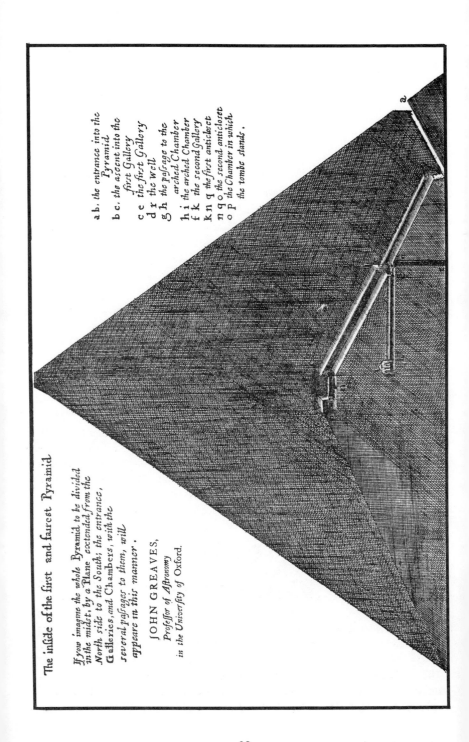

The inside of the first and fairest Pyramid

If you imagine the whole Pyramid to be divided in the midst, by a Plane extended from the North side to the South; the entrance, Galleries, and Chambers, with the several passages to them, will appear in this manner.

JOHN GREAVES,
Professor of Astronomy
in the University of Oxford.

a b. the entrance into the
        Pyramid
b c. the ascent into the
        first Gallery
c e the first Gallery
d r the well
g h the passage to the
        arched Chamber
h i the arched Chamber
f k the second Gallery
k n q the first anticloset
n q o the second anticloset
o P the Chamber in which
        the tombe stands.

30

Description of the Pyramids in Egypt." (This author has a copy printed in 1737 by J. Hughs, London)

Greaves was followed by M. de Monconys, (1647) M. Thevenot, (1657-8) M. de Chazelles, (1693) Cassini, (1702) and others, all making measurements of the Great Pyramid. Perhaps the most important measurements were made by Mr. Nathaniel Davison (1763) the British Consul at Algiers. His measurements gave confirmation to the work of the French scholars, further establishing the fact that the Pyramid was constructed so that its sides should face the cardinal points of the compass.

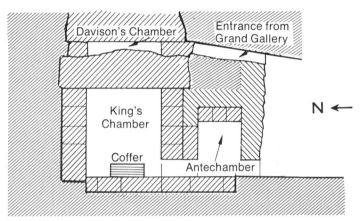

Davison discovered the first of the relieving chambers over the roof of the King's Chamber, which was named "Davison's Chamber," after him. In a letter, written in 1779, Davison makes a conjecture which was later verified. He wrote: "From some of the original covering still remaining at the top of the second great one, (Khafre's Pyramid) it is more than probable that the steps of the sides of the other (Cheops Pyramid) which now exists, were covered in the same manner, with stones of such a form as to make a smooth surface from top to bottom..."

In 1798 the French army defeated the Ottoman Turks at the "Battle of the Pyramids" and Napoleon became the master of Egypt. During the French occupation of Egypt, the engineers of Napoleon's army explored the ancient ruins of Egypt, including the Great Pyramid. While making measurements they uncovered much valuable information. It was they who first discovered the corner sockets of the Great Pyramid, peculiar to no other pyramid. They also discovered the relationship of the Pyramid's structure and dimensions to astronomical science.

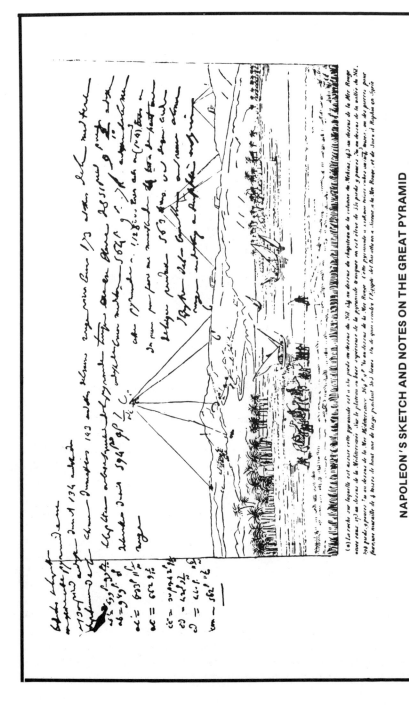

NAPOLEON'S SKETCH AND NOTES ON THE GREAT PYRAMID

32

In 1817 Caviglia, a bold but illiterate and fanciful seaman, became intrigued by the mystery of the Great Pyramid. He became convinced that there were still undiscovered passages in the interior of the Pyramid. Giving up the sea, he settled down to explore the Great Pyramid and other neighboring monuments. Although Caviglia never found any "secret" passages, his efforts in cleaning out the known passages elicited new facts regarding the interior of the Pyramid.

COLONEL HOWARD-VYSE
(IN 1830)

Colonel Howard Vyse, in 1830, was the next to make significant progress toward lifting the veil of mystery from the Great Pyramid. With the help of a hundred hired laborers, he exposed the Pyramid's Casing Stones and Pavement and then made observations and measurements. It was Vyse's investigations that interested Sir John Hershel, the great English Astronomer Royal, in making a careful study of the Great Pyramid. John Hershal, along with Professor Piazzi Smyth, became convinced that the Great Pyramid, in its design and construction, evidenced a wonderful knowledge of astronomy, applied mathematics and other scientific information, predating our recorded knowledge by several thousand years. Vyse's research is incorporated in three volumes (Operations at the Pyramids of Gizeh) published in London in 1840-42.

Mr. Robert Menzies, of Leith, Scotland, is given credit for being the first to attract general attention to the assertion that the Great Pyramid was a treasury of Divinely given wisdom embodying chronological, meteorological, astronomical, mathematical, historical and Biblical truths. He also contended that this storehouse of wisdom remained sealed by Divine appointment, to be revealed to those now living; to whom these truths would bear witness, at a time when they would be most needed.

John Taylor, a London publisher, gifted mathematician and amateur astronomer, began a study of the measurements of the Great Pyramid in order to analyze the results from a mathematician's point of view. His conclusion was that the architect of the Great Pyramid was not an Egyptian, either by race or religion. He believed it would be found, eventually, that the measurements and contours of the Pyramid passage system, as its chambers, were intended to indicate and symbolize a prophetic and historical record, especially in relationship to Biblical revelation. Taylor's work was published in 1859 under the title, "The Great Pyramid: Why was it built?"

Taylor made models to scale of the Great Pyramid and began to analyze results from a mathematician's point of view. He was puzzled as to why the builders of the Pyramid should have chosen the particular angle of 51° 51' for the Pyramid's faces instead of the regular equilateral triangle of 60°. Taylor concluded they had been designed to be equal in area to the square of the Pyramid's height. This unique geometric construction was found in no other pyramid in Egypt. Taylor also established a number of facts with regards to the mathematical features of the Pyramid, which once was ridiculed, but are now generally admitted as demonstrably true. The greatest contribution made by Taylor was linking the astronomy and mathematics of the Great Pyramid with a study of the Bible.

C. PIAZZI SMYTH

It remained, however, for Professor Piazzi Smyth, Astronomer Royal of Scotland, to lift the investigation and study of the Great Pyramid into the realm of applied science. Smyth had carefully studied Taylor's findings and decided that the only way to definitely confirm or refute Taylor's theories would be to go to Egypt himself and carefully measure the Pyramid. With his wife, this astronomer spent several months (winters of 1864-5) at the Great Pyramid, directing a large group of assistants and laborers, making scientifically accurate measurements and observations.

The results of Smyth's work were published in three large volumes in 1867, in Edinburgh, Scotland. (Our Inheritance in the Great Pyramid) for which Smyth received a gold medal from the Royal Society of Antiquaries of Scotland. Smyth summed up his investigation: "...(the Great Pyramid) revealed a most surprisingly accurate knowledge of high astronomical and geographical physics... nearly 1500 years earlier than the extremely infantine beginning of such things among the ancient Greeks."

Smyth's publications were discussed in many academic societies of the day and resulted in new investigators entering upon the subject. The increasing number of reports of studies made on the Great Pyramid confirmed and enlarged the theories that had previously been deduced, fully supporting the scientifically grounded and growing belief that the ancient pillar of stone had about it something more than a mere tomb for a rich and ambitious Pharaoh — something infinitely more than was ever in the power of the Egyptians to originate, or even to understand.

The next important contributor to our knowledge about the Great Pyramid was a mechanical engineer by the name of William Flinders Petrie. Petrie, who became fascinated by the writings of both Taylor and Smyth on the Great Pyramid, determined to re-survey and measure the entire structure. With steel tapes and special chains 1200 inches long, as well as self-compensating accessory appliances, Petrie set about measuring with a far finer accuracy than Smyth could accomplish. Most of Petrie's instruments allowed him to measure to within 1/100 of an inch, and in some cases, for really carefully work, enabled him to do so within 1/1000 of an inch.

Petrie summed up his investigations in a book entitled "The Pyramids and Temples of Gizeh." (1883) Although Petrie belittled Smyth's basic contention about the Pyramid's perimeter incorporating the length of the solar year, it was Petrie's meticulously careful measurements that observed a definite hollowing of the core masonry on each side of the Pyramid and led to the discovery of the astronomical features of the Great Pyramid, thereby confirming Smyth's conclusions.

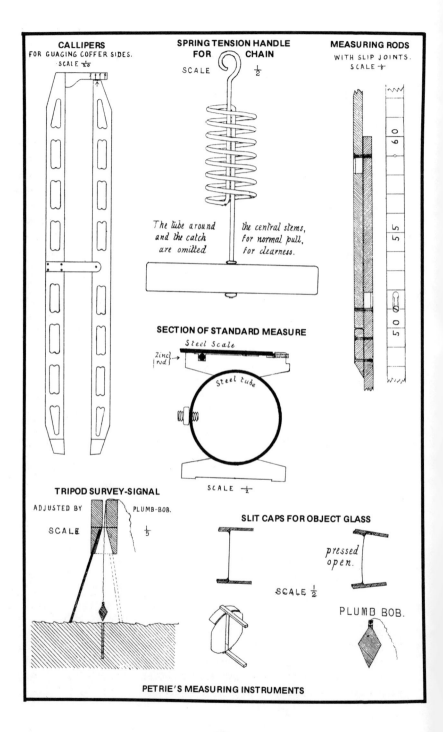

CALLIPERS
FOR GUAGING COFFER SIDES.
SCALE $\frac{1}{10}$

SPRING TENSION HANDLE
FOR CHAIN
SCALE $\frac{1}{2}$

MEASURING RODS
WITH SLIP JOINTS.
SCALE $\frac{1}{1}$

The tube around and the catch are omitted *the central stems, for normal pull, for clearness.*

6 0
5 5
5 0

SECTION OF STANDARD MEASURE

Steel Scale

Zinc rod

Steel tube

SCALE $\frac{1}{2}$

TRIPOD SURVEY-SIGNAL
ADJUSTED BY   PLUMB-BOB.
SCALE $\frac{1}{5}$

SLIT CAPS FOR OBJECT GLASS

pressed open.

SCALE $\frac{1}{2}$

PLUMB BOB.

PETRIE'S MEASURING INSTRUMENTS

36

It was the mixing of Biblical prophetic conclusions with sound scientific discoveries made on the Great Pyramid that brought scholars of the day to publicly ridicule and attempt to discard Smyth's and Menzies' theories about the Pyramid. Such skepticism didn't end in Menzies' day; it is continuing today by scholars who are reluctant to acknowledge a Supreme Being Who deals with mankind.

In 1891 Charles T. Russell produced his great theological work, "Thy Kingdom Come." The final section included a study of the Great Pyramid entitled "The Corroborative Testimony of God's Stone Witness and Prophet, The Great Pyramid in Egypt." With a circulation of several million copies, a renewed interest was generated in the Pyramid. In this study the reader is taken on a step by step visit through the Great Pyramid as Russell presents a school of thought concerning the symbolism of the passageways and chambers. In his treatise, Russell made the following statement (on page 319) regarding the Great Pyramid: "This witness of the Lord in the land of Egypt will bear such testimony as will honor Jehovah and fully correspond with His written Word. We thus introduce this 'Witness' because the inspiration of its testimony will doubtless be as much disputed as that of the Scriptures, by the prince of darkness, the true god of this world and those whom he blinds to the truth."

It has been pointed out that this remarkable forecast by Russell has been strikingly fulfilled in the works of Joseph F. Rutherford, (popularly known as Judge Rutherford) the founder of the Jehovah's Witnesses sect, as the following extract from his writings states: "it is certain that the Pyramid of Gizeh was not built by Jehovah God; nor was it built at His command...the Devil himself superintended the building of the Pyramid of Gizeh." (The Watch Tower, November 1928)

Another writer to bring out a book on the Great Pyramid was Professor Charles Lagrange, Astronomer at the Royal Observatory in Brussels, Belgium. His book, published in French in 1892, was followed by an English translation under the title "The Great Pyramid." Lagrange's contribution to the 'deciphering' of the Great Pyramid of Giza was the discovery of the so-called "Displacement Factor" (covered in chapter 21) in the construction of the Pyramid.

The next great investigator to make a study of the Great Pyramid was David Davidson, a structural engineer from Leeds, England. An agnostic, Davidson's object was to destroy and dispose of the theories that prophetic revelations were embodied in the construction of the Pyramid. Ironically, his studies of the measurements of the Pyramid confirmed the Divine nature of the Pyramid and caused him to write that the Great Pyramid was "an expression of the Truth in structural form" and that it "establishes the Bible as the inspired work of God."

Davidson claimed that the builder of the Great Pyramid was more highly skilled in the science of gravitational astronomy, and therefore in the mathematical basis of the mechanical arts and sciences, than modern civilization. He added "that it has taken man thousands of years to discover by experiment what he knew originally by a surer and simpler method," and "it means that the whole empirical basis of modern civilization is a makeshift collection of hypotheses compared with the Natural Law basis of the civilization of the past."

As to why the Great Pyramid was built and its passages carefully secreted, Davidson surmised that the builder intended to monumentalize the science he knew for another civilization far in the future, much as we go about burying time capsules. Like Menzies and Smyth before him, all that Davidson managed to accomplish was to antagonize the agnostic scientific world with his insistence upon the record-preserving nature of the Pyramid. However, Davidson's conclusions, published in a voluminous book of detailed mathematical analyses and computations, (The Great Pyramid — Its Divine Message — D. Davidson & H. Aldersmith-1924) reopened the entire subject of Pyramid measurements and spawned a whole new school of "Pyramidologists."

In 1903 another Scotsman, James Rutherford, became intensely interested (through Russell's writings) in the Great Pyramid and in turn interested his son, Adam Rutherford, who was then a boy of 9 years old. The son began to draw charts and read all the books available on the subject. By 1939 father and son were lecturing together, far and wide, on the Great Pyramid. James Rutherford died on January 12, 1945 and Adam kept on lecturing and writing until his death in 1975.

Adam Rutherford's exhaustive research and writings on the Great Pyramid are recognized today as a classic source of information on the Great Pyramid and will remain so for many years to come. In this present generation none has succeeded Adam Rutherford to the list of the "greats" in Pyramidology.

Pyramidology is the science which co-ordinates, combines and unifies science and religion, and is thus the meeting place of the two. When the Great Pyramid is properly understood and universally studied, false religions and erroneous scientific theories will alike vanish, and true religion and true science will be demonstrated to be harmonious.

Adam Rutherford

**DR. ADAM RUTHERFORD STANDING IN DOORWAY
OF THE QUEEN'S CHAMBER**

AL MAMOUN'S MEN DISCOVERING THE GRAND GALLERY
OF THE GREAT PYRAMID

CHAPTER 4.

PYRAMID OPENED BY AL MAMOUN

No record has been found to indicate the upper chambers of the Great Pyramid were penetrated before A.D. 820, when Caliph Al Mamoun of Bagdad came to Egypt to seek the wealth reportedly hidden within its secret recesses. From his youth, in his father's (Caliph Naroon al Rasheed) court, Al Mamoun had listened to the tellers of enchanted tales about mysterious Egypt, with allusions to fabulous treasure buried in the stone sepulchers of their kings. The largest (the Great Pyramid) was reported to contain everything of value that the story-tellers could think of; secret medicines, books of hidden sciences, jewelry worth a king's ransom and a "large hall where a quantity of golden coins were put up in col-umns, every piece of which was the weight of one thousand dinars."

Al Mamoun was determined to ascertain what was really hidden in the greatest of all the pyramids, and he did so, with the aid of a band of Arabian laborers. When Al Mamoun directed his workmen to begin excavating near the base of the middle of the north side of the Great Pyramid, he was guided by an indistinct rumor. The Romans had once entered the Great Pyramid through a cleverly concealed doorway on the north side of the structure.

Evidence that the Romans knew of the hidden entrance to the Great Pyramid is found in the writings of Strabo (Greek geographer born 63 B.C.) about the time of the birth of Christ. In his "Geographica," Strabo states that the Great Pyramid, "a little way up one side, has a stone that may be taken out, which being raised up, there is a sloping passage to the foundation." That the Romans did find this secret entrance is noted by the blackened Roman letters found by M. Caviglia, in 1920, upon the roof of the Subterranean Chamber. However, at the time of Al Mamoun, knowledge of the location of the original outside entrance to the Great Pyramid was lost and unknown.

The records of Al Mamoun's forced entrance into the Great Pyramid are extant today. With the crude implements which the time afforded they laboriously excavated a tunnel about 40 yards into the structure, not knowing the real entrance was about 25 feet away to the east. But one day, when the exhausted workers were about to quit in despair of finding any treasure, they heard a dull thud of a stone falling in some hollow space; within no more than a few feet on one side of them. Energetically, they started digging anew, in the direction of the strange noise. Hammering away, they finally

41

burst into a narrow passage sloping upward and downward from their point of entry.

Here was exposed what had been hidden from the Egyptians for centuries; for the falling of that stone revealed the chief secret of the building. The large angular fitting stone fitted into the ceiling of the inclining and narrow passage, quite undistinguishable from the other part of the ceiling, had now dropped on to the floor before their eyes. Revealed in the space from where the stone had fallen was the beginning of another passage, clearly ascending from the descending passage they had discovered. However, a series of huge granite plugs or square wedge-like shapes were immovably jammed in the passage, blocking access.

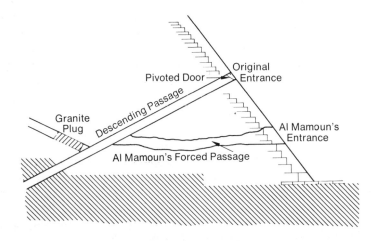

First, the exuberant workers, following the open and downward sloping passage to its end, found a deep cavernous chamber in the natural rock under the Pyramid's foundation. Here, to their disappointment, they found nothing but the unfinished, roughly hewn chamber containing in the floor a square cut well shaft leading nowhere. On the far side of the chamber, an even narrower horizontal passage led some 50 feet to a blank wall.

Returning some 276 feet up the downward sloping passage, the Arabs turned their attention to the peculiar granite plug blocking the upward sloping passage. To break it in pieces within the confined entrance passage space seemed quite out of the question. The plug was of indeterminate length and evidently weighing several tons, so they began cutting away the ordinary softer masonry along the west side of the granite.

As the Arab's chisels penetrated the limestone blocks, they found that the granite plug was actually three separate stones totalling about 15 feet in length. Beyond the third plug they found themselves in a passage sloping upward but again blocked - but this time the filling material was only limestone which could be cracked with chisels and removed piece by piece. It was only a matter of time before the passage above the granite plug was free from obstruction.

Continuing upwards, the Arabs found themselves in a tall gallery about 28 feet high and 7 feet wide. At the beginning of the gallery was a low, narrow (horizontal) passage. Following this passage they entered a rectangular limestone chamber with a rough floor and a gabled limestone roof. The room, about 18 feet long and nearly square, had an empty niche in the east wall. Al Mamoun, thinking the niche might conceal the entrance to another chamber, had his men hack their way into its solid masonry for a few feet before deciding there was, behind it, only limestone core masonry.

Returning to the entrance of the horizontal passage, the Arabs examined the tall gallery-chamber. This new passage continued upward at the same slope as the preceeding passage. On each side was a narrow bench or shelf, slotted at regular intervals. At the top of this gallery they came upon a huge solid stone (level on the top) raised about three feet above the sloping floor of the gallery. Beyond this step, or platform, the floor continued level through another low passage. A third of the way along this passage, it widened and heightened into a sort of ante-chamber, allowing Al Mamoun's men to raise their heads before again being obliged to stoop along the short passage which led to yet another chamber.

The torches of the Arabs revealed this new chamber to be a great and well proportioned room; the walls, floor and ceiling were all of beautifully squared and polished red-granite blocks. So finely jointed were the stones that the point of a pen knife could not be made to penetrate the joints. Because of its comparable large size and flat ceiling, the Arabs named it the "King's Chamber" — a name that remains today. Because of its smaller size and gabled roof, the limestone chamber with the niche was named the "Queen's Chamber."

To the amazement and disappointment of the Arabs, there was no sign of treasure. They searched frantically but could find nothing of interest or value. All the room contained was a large coffer or sarcophagus of highly polished granite, which, when struck, gave off a bell-like sound. In their fury they ripped up part of the

THE "COFFER" IN THE KING'S CHAMBER

floor and hacked at the walls in a vain attempt to find another hidden passage.

Legend has it the Caliph was astonished. His quarriers, infuriated over their deception into such enormous, unrequited and fruitless labors, began to murmur threats against Al Mamoun. The Caliph, regardless of his exalted station as their leader, was in dire jeopardy and he realized it. Pleading for just one more day, he promised he would surely reward them for their work. That night while his men were asleep, Mamoun secretly buried some gold coins in a spot adjacent to the Pyramid. The next day, he confronted his men and in a grandiose manner announced that in a vision during the night, Allah had revealed to him where the wealth that they had been seeking really lay. The men dug at the spot directed by the Caliph and soon recovered the cache of gold. The sum of gold, miraculously exactly equalled the wages claimed for their work. The men praised Allah mightily because He, many centuries ago, had placed in that spot, in gold coin that was now genuine Arabian money, an amount that was exactly equal to the sum due the crew of men for their several weeks of toil, and in the wage scale prevalent at the time of their labors!

It is highly probable that at very long intervals, both before the Romans and after the Romans (before Al Mamoun) various visitors to Egypt "re-discovered" the hidden entrance. It is also quite possible that the builders of the Pyramid anticipated the concealed entrance to be "discovered" and access gained into the sloping passage and the chamber below. They conveniently left this passage free of rubble and filling, unlike the passage above the plug which was blocked up with stone fragments. Perhaps this was part of the planning — that intruders would find the empty subterranean chamber (the customary burial location) and would not be inclined to search further, their curiosity satisfied.

In short, the subterranean chamber was exactly where it "ought" to have been, underground at the end of a long sloping passage, fulfilling the well known Egyptian "Lepsius' Law" governing ancient Egyptian-Pyramid building. The only exception to the Lepsius Law was that the subterranean chamber "ought" to have been finished first before the start of the construction of a stone pyramid on the surface above. However, the chamber being unfinished, without the customary sculptured sarcophagus, wall paintings and inscriptions, was indicative (at the time) that the king had not as yet been buried in his burial chamber. Any idea that the burial place might be in the upper masonry of the pyramid would never have entered one's mind.

Fanatical zeal and greed for greater riches had now opened the mysterious structure. Although the Pyramid itself had yielded no slightest vestige of the reward faithfully promised the men by their ruler, they had found one of the greatest treasure-vaults on earth, an intellectual and spiritual bonanza beyond all monetary reward. However, they and those who followed them for centuries were unaware of the Great Pyramid's true wealth.

At the time of Al Mamoun's forced entry into the Great Pyramid, the building still was protected by its limestone covering, but in the thirteenth century A.D. a great earthquake is reported to have hit the area and dislodged some of the casing-stones. These were taken for use in other buildings and for nearly 200 years the Pyramid was periodically stripped of its casingstones. A considerable quantity of the 100-inch thick blocks was transported to Cairo, to be used in the erection of mosques and other buildings. Many more of the stones were burned to extract the lime they contained. As a consequence of these depredations only a few of the casing-stones now remain (in situ) on the Pyramid, saved by sands drifting deeply over them, concealing them from the view of the vandals.

Drawn by K. Vaughan

46

CHAPTER 5.

CONSTRUCTION DETAILS

Herodotus, in his "History, Book II, Enterpe, pgs. 124-125, wrote: "...one hundred thousand men worked at a time and were relieved every three months by a fresh party. It took ten years arduous toil by the people to make the causeway for the conveyance of the stones, a work, in my opinion, not much inferior to the Pyramid itself, for its length is five stadia (over a half mile) and its width ten orgyae (about 60 feet 8 inches) and its height where it is highest, eight orgyae: (48 feet 6 inches) it is built of polished stone with carvings of animals on it. It took ten years then to make this causeway, the works on the eminence where the Pyramid stands and the underground apartments which Cheops had made as a burial vault for himself, in an island formed by drawing water from the Nile by a channel. The Pyramid itself took twenty years to build. It is square, each side is eight plethra (800 feet — as close as he professes it to be) and the height is the same; it is composed of polished stones and jointed with the greatest exactness; none of the stones are less than 30 feet." (Herodotus probably meant cubic feet, not linear feet)

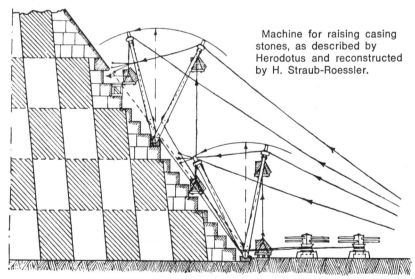

Machine for raising casing stones, as described by Herodotus and reconstructed by H. Straub-Roessler.

"This Pyramid was built thus, in the form of steps which some call crossae, others bomides. When they had laid the first stones in this manner, they raised the remaining stones by machines made of short planks of wood: having lifted them from the machine that

47

THE FIVE SOCKETS OF THE GREAT PYRAMID
AT THE BASE

SHOWING THEIR RELATIVE POSITIONS

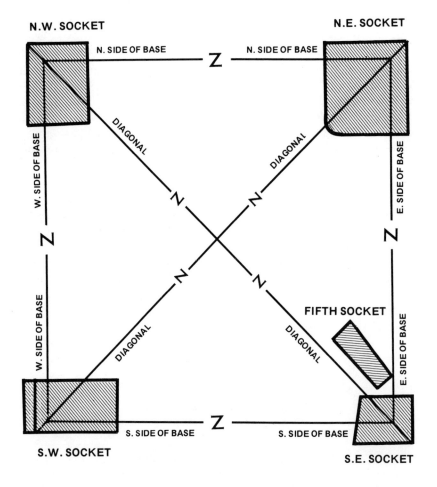

N.W. SOCKET

N. SIDE OF BASE

N

N. SIDE OF BASE

N.E. SOCKET

DIAGONAL

DIAGONAL

W. SIDE OF BASE

N

E. SIDE OF BASE

N

N

N

N

W. SIDE OF BASE

DIAGONAL

FIFTH SOCKET

DIAGONAL

E. SIDE OF BASE

S.W. SOCKET

S. SIDE OF BASE

N

S. SIDE OF BASE

S.E. SOCKET

N.T.S.

stood ready on the first range; and from this it was drawn to the second range on another machine; for the machines were equal in number to the range of steps; or they removed the machine, which was only one, and portable, to each range in both ways, as it is related. The upper portion of the Pyramid was finished first; then the middle and finally the part that is lowest and nearest to the ground."

Diodorus, in contradiction to Herodotus, says that the Great Pyramid was constructed by means of "mounds." (ramps) Most modern Egyptologists believe that this method was employed. Probably four ramps, of brick and earth, were made, one on each side, as roads upon which the stones were taken up to each layer of construction, by means of sledges pulled over rollers. Perhaps one ramp was used to take the empty sledges back down.

The actual construction of the Great Pyramid began with the preparation of the ground level of the site. Around a natural outcropping of rock, a surface was leveled. The outcropping of rock was terraced around and left as an "anchor" to ensure stability against internal earth pressures. All who are knowledgeable in modern engineering are aware of the ingenious devices used to compensate for shocks, stresses and strains caused by expansion and contraction of the materials of which a structure is composed. These devices consist of roller-bearings, expansion joints, of ball and socket arrangements which take care of these stresses and strains without communicating them to the main structure.

An amazing, scientifically engineered feature of the Great Pyramid, distinguishing it from all other pyramids, was a method they used to safeguard the structure against earth movements. At each corner of the base of the Great Pyramid, the builders cut mortises, some eight feet by fifteen feet in size, into the natural rock. Into the mortises they placed heavy, carefully chiseled stones, to act as anchors for the four sloping corner-edges of the Pyramid. These anchorage-blocks were so placed as to allow a space between the sides of the mortises and the corner stones, thus allowing for expansion caused by changes of temperature or earthquakes — serving the purpose of ball and socket joints. This safety innovation was not to be used again for over 4000 years.

These socket-bedded corner-stones demonstrate that over forty-six hundred years ago the builders of the Great Pyramid understood the workings of natural laws and also how to allow for their effects. They also give evidence of the foresight and engineering skill on the part of the Pyramid's Architect which characterize every detail of the edifice, and awaken the admiration and wonder of all engineers and scientists who have visited and examined the structure.

These corner-sockets (and Casing-Stones) still remaining in place, make possible the reconstruction of the Pyramid as originally completed. This reconstruction of design is absolutely essential in restoring original dimensions and measurements upon which the interpretation of the Great Pyramid's passage-system is based. However difficult this may seem to the reader, these details are easily determined by a skilled engineer or architect, having these few stones remaining in place, from which to determine exact measurements and angles.

Before commencing to lay the core masonry, an inclined passage, about four feet high and three and a half feet wide, was bored downward at an angle of 26° 18' 9.7", (with a north-south axis) running some 350 feet through the solid rock. As constructed, the mouth of the bore, viewed from the bottom, gave a sky range of rather less than one-third of a degree, or about one-fourth more than the moon's apparent diameter. This opening could be easily reduced by using a diaphragm covering up all the mouth of the bore except a small opening near the center, and another corresponding diaphragm occupying the lower part of the bore from which observations of the Pole-star could be made.

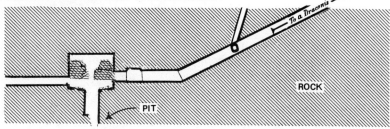

At the time of the building of the Great Pyramid, the then Pole-star Alpha, of the constellation of the Dragon, (known as Draconis or Dragon Star) was in true north. For hundreds of years before and after the building of the Pyramid no other star could be seen by any one looking up the boring. Therefore, the boring, when first made, must have been directed towards this star. The slow motion of a star very near the Pole would made it ideal for alignment purposes; any movement would be of little importance when sighted from earth. Obviously the inclined passage was intended to establish the true direction of the Pole-star at its lower culmination in order to align the foundation of the Pyramid on a true north-south axis.

Knowing the purpose of the slanting passage, we can use the observed direction of the passage to determine what was the position of the Pole-star at the time when the foundation of the Pyramid was laid, and confirm which Pole-star it may have been. The Pole-star (Polaris) that appears so unchanging in the north at present, has not always been the Pole-star nor will it continue to be. There is a shift of the Pole so slight that it cannot be observed in the space of one, or even two or three lifetimes, but in the course of many centuries it begins to be noticeable. This is due to a gradual change in the direction of tilt of the Earth's axis because of the gravitational attraction of the Sun and Moon, which tend to pull Earth's equatorial bulge into line. This double attraction causes the Earth to wobble slightly, like a spinning top. The axis completes one rotation in about 25,800 years, which causes the exact location of the Pole to move in a slow circle around the north sky. This movement is called "the precession of the equinoxes."

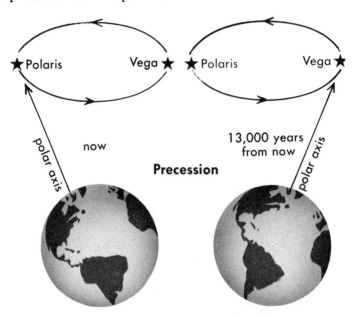

This movement causes the location of the Pole to move and different stars appear as the Pole-star. The circle shifts from Alpha Draconis, (the Dragon Star) which was the Pole-star five thousand years ago, to our present Polaris (in the tail of Ursa Minor), then on to Alderamin in the constellation of Cephus, to Deneb, to Vega, and so back again to the Dragon Star. This whole cycle of the Pole-

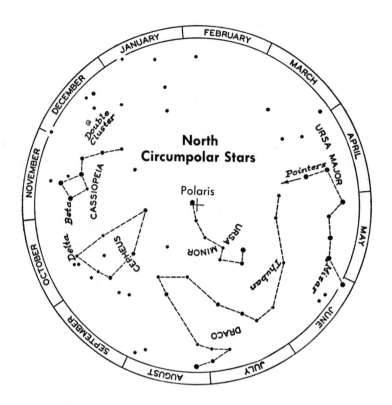

North Circumpolar Stars

Polaris

JANUARY · FEBRUARY · MARCH · APRIL · MAY · JUNE · JULY · AUGUST · SEPTEMBER · OCTOBER · NOVEMBER · DECEMBER

Double Cluster

CASSIOPEIA

Delta Beta

CEPHEUS

URSA MINOR

DRACO

Thuban

URSA MAJOR

Pointers

Mizar

stars takes about 25,800 years. Polaris is a comparative newcomer to its present position. Only within the last two thousand years has it come near enough to the axis of the skies to be used in determining true north. It still has some one hundred and twenty-five years to go before reaching the point at which it comes nearest to the Pole. Then it will appear to us on earth as the one fixed and focal point of the heavens for many hundreds of years. There are, of course, gaps between the various Pole-stars, long periods of time when no star is near the exact north and the so-called "circumpolar stars" all seem to be in motion.

With regards to its astronomical position, it seems the builders of the Pyramid intended to place the Pyramid as close as possible to latitude 30°, or in other words, in that latitude where the true Pole of the heavens is one-third of the way from the horizon to the point overhead (the zenith) and where the noon sun at true spring or autumn (when the sun rises almost exactly in the east, and sets almost exactly in the west) is two-thirds of the way from the horizon to the point overhead. Star observations, made from this position, would simplify many problems in the geometrical construction of the Pyramid.

At the bottom of the sloping passage (about 100 feet vertically under the center of the base of the Pyramid site) a horizontal passage was cut for a short distance southward and a "Subterranean Chamber" was begun to be carved out of the heart of the rock with admirable skill. After cutting a passage southward for the necessary length of the chamber, the builders commenced dressing the ceiling, which they made exquisitely flat and smooth, though 46 feet long by 28 feet wide. Then the workers began sinking down vertical cuts to form the walls, apparently to complete a rectangular chamber whose walls, ceiling and floor would be perfect pattern planes.

After cutting downwards from the ceiling of this Subterranean Chamber to a depth of about 4 feet at the west end and 13 feet at the east end, they stopped in the midst of their work. A small bored passage was extended horizontally, into the rock a few feet further toward the south. This passage was also left unfinished. In the low eastern area of the large chamber a pit was dug to a depth of about 80 feet and near the north end of the west wall a small recess was cut into the ceiling. It is unknown why the Subterranean Chamber was left unfinished.

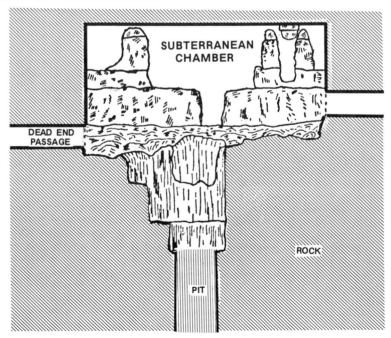

OLD ENGRAVING SHOWING PAVEMENT AND CASING STONES "IN SITU"

54

A limestone "pavement" was laid upon the cut rock surface and in places a basalt pavement has been found showing magnificent workmanship. The blocks of basalt were sawn and fitted together and laid upon a bed of limestone, which in turn was of such fine quality that the Arabs later destroyed a large part of the work in order to extract the limestone for burning. The pavement originally covered a third of an acre, however only about a quarter of this pavement remains "in situ."

The placing of the core stones started in the center, around the rocky "anchor" and positioned so as to form a small square inside a larger designated square marked out on the surface of the leveled site. Blocks were added to all sides of the small square, keeping the shape of a square, stopping only when the layer of stones was almost as large as the designated size. These core stones required only the top and bottoms to be smooth, so as to stand steadily on the smooth level base and support the blocks above. The sides were left somewhat rough and uneven, except when the outer edge of the planned square had been reached. Then the core stones were made to fit tightly. These stones were called "backing-blocks," and completed the core-layer of that level.

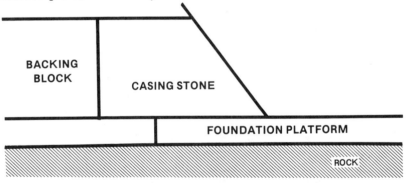

The second layer of stones was laid over the first, again commencing from the center and working out, being careful to maintain a square shape, a little smaller than the one below. This was repeated, layer after layer, until the last layer formed a very small square on top and ready to receive the capstone. The top piece, or "capstone," according to tradition, was never placed, having been rejected by the builders. It should be pointed out that the capstone (or headstone) is also the "chief cornerstone," since all the four corners of the building converge in that one stone at the top. Thus, it alone, of all the stones in the structure, is the only one that is over all the four corners.

THE PYRAMID OF DAHSHUR SHOWING CONSTRUCTION OF CASING STONES

THE BENT PYRAMID OF DAHSHUR

57

As each layer of core blocks was laid, the passage sloping down to the Subterranean Chamber Passage was extended upward through each layer of core stone, at the same angle and size as below the Pyramid base, until it reached the outer edge of the core layer. This opening terminated about 55 feet (perpendicular) above the base level of the Pyramid. (This upper portion of the Descending Passage and the other interior passages and chambers will be described in the following chapter) It is noted that although each layer of core stones were uniform in thickness, the courses varied one with another, ranging from the 15th course of 28 Pyramid inches to the thickest, the 35th course of stone, which was 50 Pyramid inches. (A Pyramid inch is explained in chapter 10)

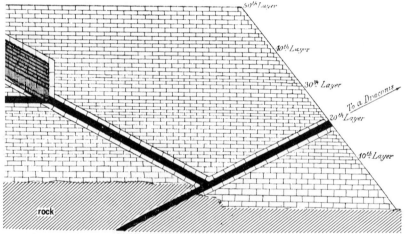

VERTICAL SECTION
SHOWING SUBTERRANEAN CHAMBER PASSAGE EXTENDED UPWARD

Now came the time to cover the core masonry with the smooth dense, marble-like limestones known as "Casing-Stones." From several indications, it seems that the masons planned the Casing-Stones, course by course, on the ground. For on all the Casing-Stones and on the core stones upon which each Casing-Stone was to be placed, there are lines drawn on the horizontal surfaces, showing where each stone was to be placed on those below it. If the stones were merely trimmed to fit each other as the building progressed, there would be no need to have so carefully marked the place of each block in this particular way; and it shows that they were probably planned and fitted together on the ground below.

The bottoms of the stones which would rest on the base, both sides of the stones which rested against other Casing-Stones, and the backs of the stones which rested against the backing-blocks had to be made perfectly smooth. The front surfaces of the backing-blocks would already have beem made smooth. The front angle of the Casing-Stone would be cut roughly to the same angle as the Pyramid design. Before these casing-blocks were laid the builders spread a thin layer of mortar on the stones into which a casing-block would fit. The sledge then brought the stone up and it was carefully levered into position with crowbars and rollers. The watery mortar helped the stone to slip into place.

When the final Casing-Stone had been wedged into its place in the first layer or square, the builders were careful to check that the casing-blocks formed a perfect square. This was particularly important in the lower courses of the Pyramid as a very small error at the bottom could grow into a very large error by the time the top was reached. When they were satisfied the first layer was correctly positioned, the builders started on the next course of Casing-Stones, proceeding as before.

When the Casing-Stones reached the outer opening of the Descending Passage, a "doorway" was constructed of fine-grained limestone, with a swivel stone door. While no remains of the door has been found, Stabo's description of such a door on the Great Pyramid fits the conditions, and a similar swivel door was found on the South Pyramid of Dashur.

PIAZZI SMYTH

59

EXAMPLE of the CASING-STONES of a PYRAMID, SUPER-POSED.
ON THE RECT-ANGULAR MASONRY COURSES: FROM A PHOTOGRAPH BY P.S. OF THE SUMMIT OF THE 2° PYR.

The placing of the Casing-Stones required the greatest skill in fitting each stone against the rough backing stones in their individual position; the sides and face of each Casing-Stone having already been smoothed. On each course of Casing-Stones a thin layer of mortar was spread on the sides, top and bottom where it rested against other Casing Stones. The sloping face of each Casing-Stone was cut to the exact angle of 51° 51' 4.3". It is believed (as Josephus reported) that the finished cutting of the face of the Casing-Stones started at the top and went downward, the ramp being removed as the workers progressed downward.

In 1837, Colonel Howard Vyse, Egyptologist, discovered a few of the original Casing-Stones "in situ." His discovery revealed the amazing accuracy in the fitting of the stones one to another, work that has been considered to equal the most modern optician's skill. Sir Flinders Petrie, (English Egyptologist 1853-1942) in his account of the Casing-Stones records, "The mean thickness of the joints is one-fifth part of an inch. The mean variation of the cuttings

REMNANT OF THE ORIGINAL CASING-STONE SURFACE OF THE GREAT PYRAMID.
NEAR THE MIDDLE OF ITS NORTHERN FOOT. AS DISCOVERED BY THE EXCAVATIONS OF COL. HOWARD VYSE IN 1837.

of the stone form a straight line, and from the true square, is but one-hundredth part of an inch in the length of 75 inches up the face." That the masons were able to maintain these tolerances despite the area and weight of the stones to be moved — some 16-29 tons each, is seemingly almost impossible. This feat was duplicated in all the Casing-Stones, which are estimated to have numbered approximately 144,000.

Colonel Vyse, speaking of the mortar used in the joints, says, "...such is the tenacity of this cement...that a fragment of a stone that had been destroyed remains fixed in its original alignment, notwithstanding the lapse of time and the violence to which it has been exposed." Modern chemists have analyzed the mortar (part goat milk and bird eggs) but have been unable to compound one with such fineness and tenacity as that exhibited in the Great Pyramid.

The Great Pyramid retained its marble-like covering until the 13th century A.D., when a great earthquake shook the structure, cracked its face, and dislodged some of the Casing Stones. It didn't take much imagination for local builders to realize the labor saved in using stones already cut and polished for their buildings. They began to use the Pyramid as a quarry, with the result that in two centuries, all but a few Casing-Stones, hidden in the sand, were stripped from the face of the Pyramid. Exposure to the elements left the core masonry as we see it today.

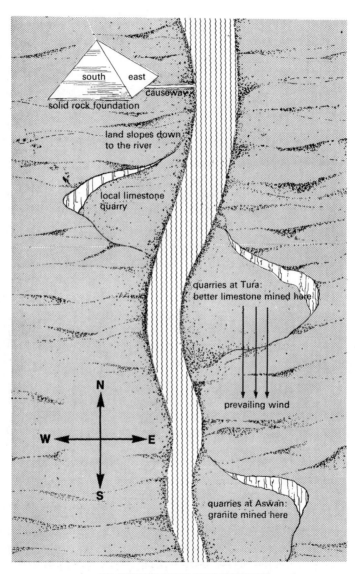

NILE RIVER VALLEY QUARRIES

CHAPTER 6.

QUARRYING AND TRANSPORTING THE STONE

How the ancient Egyptians cut and moved the stone from the quarries to the Pyramid being built has been the subject of much speculation. As we know, the Great Pyramid used millions of tons of stone, most of which were in 2½ ton blocks. This was no easy undertaking, yet the Egyptians managed to accomplish this task. If we look at a map of ancient Egypt we will see how they did it.

The Great Pyramid, as well as all the other pyramids, lie near the Nile River. Most of the stone quarries of Egypt are also located near and up the river from the pyramids. The obvious solution was to carry the stone in boats down the Nile. By means of petrological identification, the location of the quarries that supplied the material in the construction of the Great Pyramid have been located.

The methods used by the ancient Egyptians to quarry stone were probably similar to the methods used today. The main difference being the better quality of modern tools, such as the use of steel and carboloy bits for drilling. The Egyptians used copper, a softer metal that blunts easily. They did possess a type of iron and some authorities believed they had discovered a special way to make copper harder. So far, no examples of such a copper have been found in Egypt. However, saws of copper showing evidence of having had hard gem-stones embedded in the edges have been discovered. Such saws would have been used to make a cut into the stone (Ex. granite) and then drive dry wooden wedges into the cuts. Water poured over the wooden wedges would cause the wood to swell, thus splitting the stone along the cuts. This method of cutting stone was used by Solomon's quarrymen when building the Temple at Jerusalem.

The poorer-quality limestone found near the Pyramid site was taken from the quarry by means of surface stripping (open-cast method). Fortunately for the builders of the pyramids, this local area had an abundant supply of exposed limestone. The better type of limestone found at Tura required mining. There they cut away the side of a cliff to expose an even face of limestone. Then they constructed a ramp of earth that reached the upper portion of the exposed limestone. This would enable them to quarry the first stones at the top and work down. By examining tools and unfinished stones at the quarries, we can describe how the Egyptians may have proceeded in removing the limestone blocks.

LONG COPPER QUARRYMAN'S CHISEL FROM GEBELEIN

COPPER MASON'S CHISEL FROM GHORAB (NEW KINGDOM)

COPPER MORTISE CHISEL

COPPER MASON'S CHISEL

MASON'S MALLETT FROM SAQQARA

POUNDING BALL OF DOLERITE FROM ASWAN

POLISHING STONE OF BLACK GRANITE FROM SAQQARA

WEDGE FOR SPLITTING STONE FROM SAQQARA

64

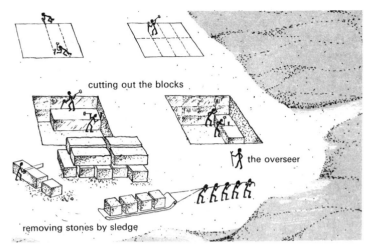

cutting out the blocks

the overseer

removing stones by sledge

The quarrymen first cut a hollow in the limestone large enough for a man to work in. The floor of the hollow would be the top of the stone the men wished to remove. A quarryman then crawled into this hollow and, using long copper chisels, cut down the back and sides of the stone block. They used wooden mallets to hammer down the chisels. When the block was free on all sides except the bottom, they would cut holes or a long cut on the exposed face along the bottom of the block. Wedges driven into the holes or cut would cause the block to split away from the rock to which it was joined.

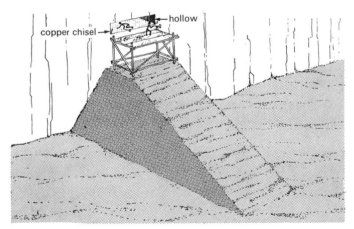

copper chisel —

hollow

When the block was levered up and out of the hollow, and removed, the ramp was lowered and work started on the next block of stone. This time the workmen had plenty of head-room.

When the lowest stone level with the floor of the quarry had been removed, another ramp was constructed so they could start at the top of the limestone face and at the same time go farther into the cliff. This type of quarry left huge holes in the cliffs which can still be seen today.

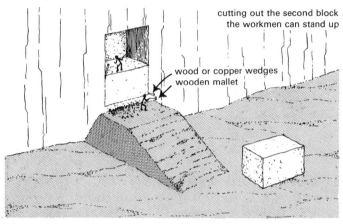

cutting out the second block
the workmen can stand up

wood or copper wedges
wooden mallet

The method of quarrying the granite was much the same as for the limestone, except it must have taken much longer to remove each block. Where poorer quality granite overlay better grade, fire was used to heat the covering rock. When the rock became hot enough, it would crumble and become easy to remove. When water was thrown on the hot rock, the surface would flake off, facilitating removal of the inferior rock. Usually, with granite, balls of dolerite (a very hard round green stone found near the Red Sea) were used to cut around the blocks of granite as well as to surface dress them.

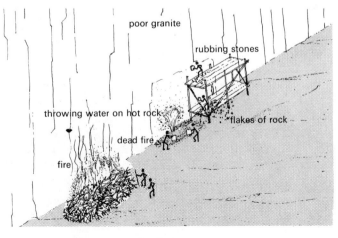

poor granite

rubbing stones

throwing water on hot rock

flakes of rock

dead fire

fire

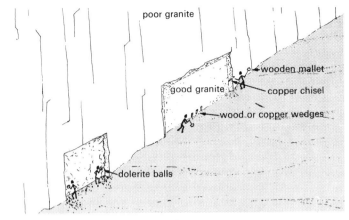

Cut blocks were taken from the quarries by means of wooden sledges. Ropes attached to the front of the sledges were pulled by gangs of men to the waiting boats on the bank of the Nile. In areas where sand had to be traversed, a bed of logs could have been laid and rollers placed under the sledge as it was pulled, using the "house-movers" technique of continually taking the rollers from back to front as they came out from under the sledge.

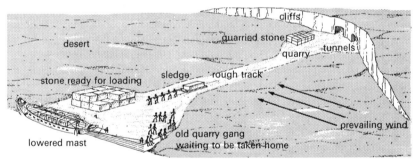

Egyptian tomb drawings show such sledges having water or some other liquid poured on the ground in front of them to help the sledges slide along the ground. When the river was reached, the stones were levered and dragged on board a boat. Perhaps the sledge with the stone was loaded onto the boat together to save unloading and reloading for carrying from the boat to the Pyramid building site. Moving the stone from the boats to the construction site would have been a more difficult task, because unlike the quarries usually above the river banks, (allowing gravity to assist in the pulling of the sledges) the pyramids were uphill from the river docking sites. However, each pyramid had a causeway connecting it to the Nile.

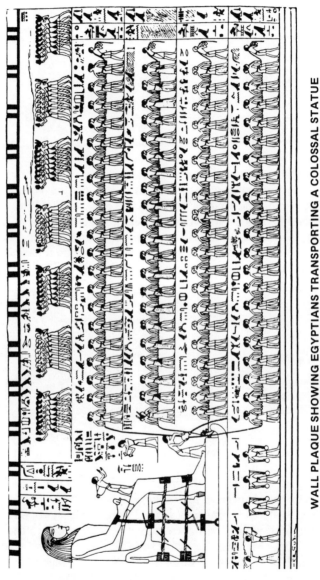

WALL PLAQUE SHOWING EGYPTIANS TRANSPORTING A COLOSSAL STATUE
NOTE THE TIMEKEEPER STANDING ON THE STATUE'S KNEE AND A MAN
POURING LIQUID ON RUNNERS TO DECREASE FRICTION

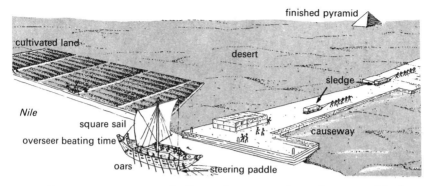

cultivated land
desert
finished pyramid
sledge
Nile
square sail
causeway
overseer beating time
oars
steering paddle

The causeways were built at the same time the pyramid site was being prepared. They were cut out of the rock with walls on either side and were used as a road for the sledges bringing the stone from the boats to the construction site. Upon completion of the pyramid they were roofed over and used for the funeral procession when it traveled from the river to the pyramid.

The boats used in transporting the stones down the Nile River were probably barge-type flat-bottomed drafts that had a large square sail attached to a single mast in the center of the boat. This was to take advantage of any wind which might arise, but sails were not the main means of moving the boat. On either side of the boat was a row of oars which would have been used whenever a prevailing wind was encountered. At the rear of the boat was a large, paddle-shaped rudder which the helmsman used to steer the boat. On the return voyage from the Pyramid site to the quarries, the oarsmen would have to row to make headway against the swollen river. If there was a favorable breeze, the sail would be hoisted to aid them.

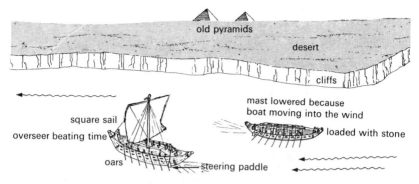

old pyramids

desert

cliffs

mast lowered because
boat moving into the wind

square sail

loaded with stone

overseer beating time

oars

steering paddle

The great amount of labor expended in quarrying and transporting such a mass of masonry as required in the construction of the Great Pyramid in the time span reported by Herodotus has always been a cause of astonishment.   But an examination of Herodotus's statement and a consideration of the internal economy of the country (even up to a century ago) would explain it.   In describing the transport of the stones, Herodotus expressly states that 100,000 men worked at one time, "each party during three months."   Since the inundation of the Nile lasted somewhat more than three months, during which time the farming land was covered with water, the cattle were left to wander on the barren desert or fed on dry fodder, and most of the inhabitants were almost idle. Only a few hands were needed to regulate the flow of water into the dammed-up basins in the country, and the greater part of the population would turn willingly to any employment they could get. Here then, is the explanation of the vast amount of labor from a country of limited area.

It was during the three months of inundation by the Nile that the non-working hands were set to unskilled labor. While the Nile was at its full height, barges were busily employed in floating the masses of hewn stone across the five mile width of the Nile from the causeways at the quarries to the causeway at the Pyramid site, about 9 or 10 miles down the stream. It is noticeable that the period of three months is only mentioned in connection with the removal of the stones, not with the actual quarrying or building.   These latter activities must have been done by a large staff of skilled masons, helped by an abundance of unskilled laborers, to do the heavy work of lifting and transport during the three months when the general population was out of work.

The actual course of work during the building of the Pyramid would have been somewhat as follows: At the end of July when the Nile was flooding, the levy of 100,000 men would assemble for the transportation of the stones. Not more than eight men could work well together on an average block of stone estimated at 40 cubic feet, (2½ tons) so the workers would probably be divided into working parties of about that number. If, then, each of these parties brought over 10 average size blocks of stone in their three month's period of labor, the required quota for that year would be met. This assumption is based on allowing each party two weeks to bring their stones down the causeway at the quarry, a day or two of good wind to take them across and down the Nile, six weeks to carry them up the Pyramid causeway and four weeks to raise them to the required position in the Pyramid.

To recapitulate, the Great Pyramid contains about 2,300,000 blocks of stone averaging 50″ x 50″ x 28″ or 2½ tons each. If 8 men brought 10 stones — 100,000 men would bring 125,000 stones each season, or the total number needed to complete the Pyramid in less than 20 years. Thus, Herodotus's time period would be feasible. And after the three months of high Nile, the workers would be free to return to their own occupations in the beginning of November, when the land was again accessible.

Of course, the actual distribution of labor would have been more specialized, and there must have been a smaller body of masons permanently employed in quarrying the stones and trimming them at the Pyramid. Also, there was no doubt that a year's supply of stone from the precious three months inundation period was kept at the Pyramid on which the masons could work, while another crew could be placing stones that had been trimmed and arranged during the previous nine months.

The number of skilled masons used on the Great Pyramid can be estimated from the accommodations provided for them in the "barracks" behind the Second Pyramid. These barracks were used by the workmen of Khafra, but those of Khufu must have been equally numerous and have occupied a similar space, perhaps these identical buildings. The barracks excavated by the archaeologists would hold from 3,600 to 4,000 men easily. Since about 120,000 average blocks were required to be prepared every year, this would only be one block of stone prepared each month by a party of four men. Hence, this accommodation is really more than enough. However, most likely a good deal of lifting and building work would be going on throughout the year by unskilled laborers.

Thus we see that the traditional accounts of the construction of the Great Pyramid fulfill the requirements of construction — both as to manpower and time. The conditions of labor-supply were quite practical in such a land, and would not be ruinous to the prosperity of the country, or oppressive to the people.

CHAPTER 7.

INTERIOR PASSAGES

There are two systems of passages and chambers in the interior of the Great Pyramid — a downward system and an upward system. The upward system embraces two separate systems; (1) an ascending series made up of the Ascending Passage, Grand Gallery, King's Chamber Passages, Anti-Chamber and the King's Chamber itself; and (2) a horizontal series comprising the Queen's Chamber Passage and the Queen's Chamber. In addition to the two main systems, there is one strange, well-like passage, known as the "Well Shaft," common to both systems.

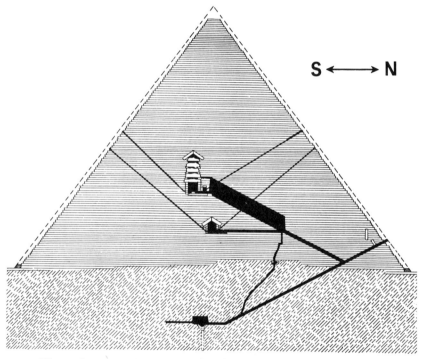

S ← → N

The only true entrance to the Great Pyramid from the outside is located on the north side of the Pyramid, 286.1 P. inches (nearly 24 feet) east of the north-south axis end at a point 668.4841 P. inches (about 55 feet) above the base-level of the structure. Its swivel stone door was constructed and hung so perfectly that it was indistinguishable from the other Casing-Stones. From the entrance, the Descending Passage — 41.2132 P. inches wide (about 3½ feet) by 52.7452 P. inches high (about 4½ feet) — slopes down at an angle of 26° 18'

Drawn by K. Vaughan

**WEST SIDE OF PLUG EXPOSED BY CALIPH AL MAMOUN
NEARLY TWELVE HUNDRED YEARS AGO**

10″, through both the core masonry and the solid rock, until it reaches a short horizontal passage leading to the Subterranean Chamber and the Pit, known as the "Bottomless Pit." (The Subterranean Chamber and the Pit were described in the preceeding chapter)

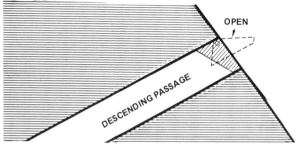

The First Ascending Passage is usually considered to begin at the intersection Point with the Descending Passage. Actually, however, it begins where its floor meets the Descending Passage roof. This point is 1169.7702 P. inches (about 97½ feet) from the original entrance. (The original length of the Descending Passage is calculated from the position of existing Casing-Stones and the similar entrances of the Third Pyramid and the South Pyramid of Dashur, both of which retain their original casing-stones) The Ascending Passage, however, is blocked by a granite plug only 14½ inches from the entrance. This granite plug is 15 feet long and is composed of three blocks of red granite, cut square and tapered and tightly wedged in the passage, allowing no play. Therefore, it can be concluded that they were placed in the passage during the construction of the passageway itself, before the structure reached a higher level.

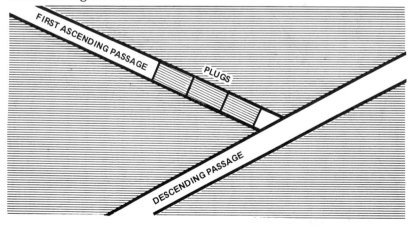

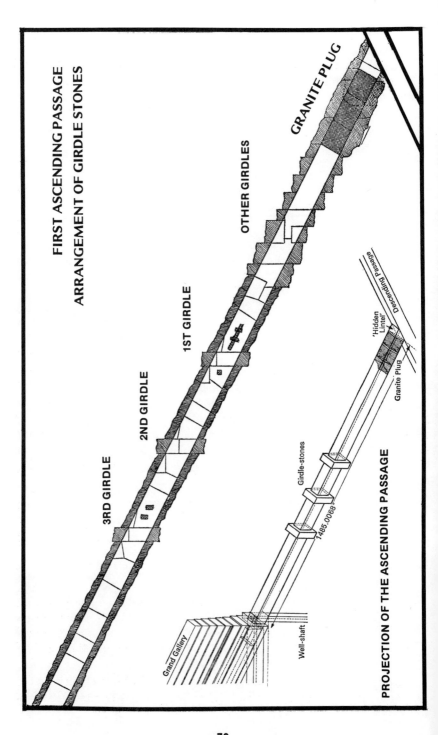

FIRST ASCENDING PASSAGE
ARRANGEMENT OF GIRDLE STONES

3RD GIRDLE

2ND GIRDLE

1ST GIRDLE

OTHER GIRDLES

GRANITE PLUG

PROJECTION OF THE ASCENDING PASSAGE

Grand Gallery

Well-shaft

Girdle-stones

1485.0068"

'Hidden Lintel'

Descending Passage

Granite Plug

76

The First Ascending Passage has the same width and height as the Descending Passage and slopes upward at the same angle (26° 18' 10") that the Descending Passage slopes downward. The length of the passage is 1485.0068 P. inches (about 123-¾ feet) and ends abruptly where it opens into the Grand Gallery. Although the limestone blocks lining the First Ascending Passage are now much decayed and exfoliated, they were magnificently executed as to arrangement. Piazzi Smyth, commenting on the masonic arrangement of the limestone blocks of the passage, wrote: "a most admirable order pervading the apparent disorder, tending also to hyper-excellence masonic construction."

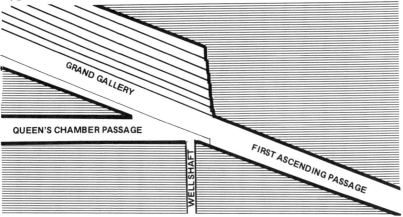

Another special feature of the masonry in the First Ascending Passage is what is called "Girdle Stones." The Girdle Stones are formed of limestone blocks between 31.5 to 32.9 P. inches in width. They are usually a single block which forms the roof, floor and side walls of the Passage. In other words, the Passage is bored through the single block or in some cases, one block forms the roof and top part of the side walls and the other comprises the lower part of the side walls and the floor. Whereas the stones forming the Passage (and all sloping passages of the Great Pyramid) lie at the same angle, (26° 18' 10") the Girdle Stones are the exception. They are built in vertically. (see chart, page 76)

Encircling the Granite Plug and for about 24 feet beyond it, the Girdle Stones are clustered together touching each other. Beyond the last, or southerly one, are three more, all 10 Royal Cubits (206.06539 P. inches) apart. Accompanying each of the last three Girdle Stones, farther up the Passage, are inset stones, resembling pointers, set into the side wall just in front of each Girdle Stone. In the case of the central, or Second Girdle, the pointer is

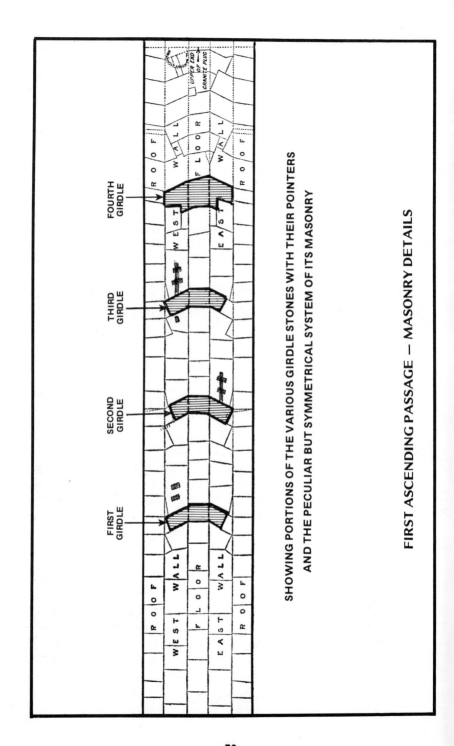

SHOWING PORTIONS OF THE VARIOUS GIRDLE STONES WITH THEIR POINTERS
AND THE PECULIAR BUT SYMMETRICAL SYSTEM OF ITS MASONRY

FIRST ASCENDING PASSAGE — MASONRY DETAILS

on the east wall, while in the case of the other two, (First and Third Girdles) the pointers are on the west wall.

The Grand Gallery that the First Ascending Passage opens into is a magnificent chamber, extending upward at the same angle at a distance of 1881.2223 P. inches. (about 157 feet) It has two ramps, one on each side, running the full length of the Gallery. On the surface of each ramp, at regular distances, (41.2132 P. inches) oblong holes are cut vertically down — against the side walls. There are 28 such niches on each ramp, however, one of the west wall is missing due to the forced opening from the Well Shaft into the Grand Gallery, made after the completion of the Pyramid.

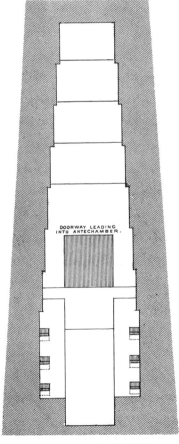

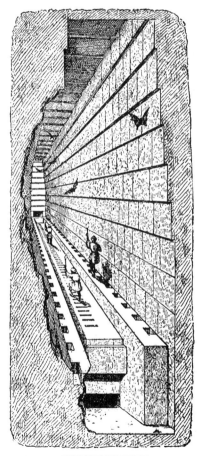

VERTICAL CROSS SECTION   PERSPECTIVE VIEW

GRAND GALLERY

79

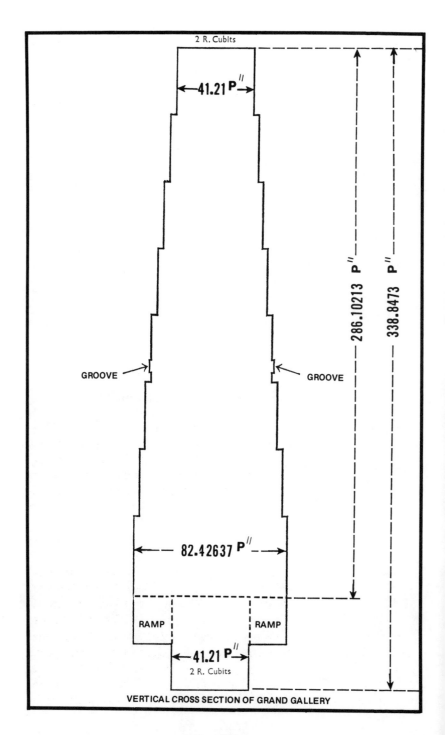

2 R. Cubits

41.21 $P^{//}$

GROOVE   GROOVE

286.10213 $P^{//}$

338.8473 $P^{//}$

82.42637 $P^{//}$

RAMP   RAMP

41.21 $P^{//}$

2 R. Cubits

VERTICAL CROSS SECTION OF GRAND GALLERY

The height of the Grand Gallery is 338.8473 P. inches (about 28 feet) which is 286.1 P. inches (about 22 feet) in excess of that of the Ascending Passage. The width of the Grand Gallery, above the tops of the side ramps is 82.4264 P. inches (about 7 feet) and the space between the ramps, at the floor level, is 41.2132 P. inches. (about 3½ feet) By means of seven overhanging courses of masonry, the ceiling width of the Grand Gallery is reduced to 41.2132 P. inches, the same as the floor between the ramps. The projected masonry, averaging three inches beyond the course on which it rests, forms a corbelled vault of unparalleled dimensions.

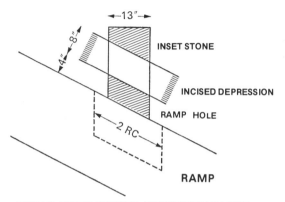

DETAIL OF FEATURES ABOVE THE RAMPS

A groove runs the entire length of the Gallery on both sides. (east and west walls) The lower edge of these grooves is 5¼ inches above the third overlap from the bottom and is approximately midway between the floor and roof with which the grooves are parallel. Each of the two grooves has a mean depth of ¾ of an inch and is 6 inches wide. These grooves do not appear to have any structural purpose, although it has been suggested they may have been designed to support a wooden "decking" dividing the Grand Gallery into two sections, an upper and lower part.

The Grand Gallery is considered one of the greatest and finest examples of corbelled architecture extant. Perret and Chipiez, renowned architects, in their work, "Ancient Egyptian Art," state, "The glory of the workmen who built the Great Pyramid is the masonry of the Grand Gallery...The faces of the blocks of limestone of which the walls are composed have been dressed with such care that it is not surpassed even by the most perfect example of Hellenic architecture on the Acropolis at Athens." The excellent workmanship is somewhat obscured today, due to the condition of the lime-

GRAND GALLERY AND QUEEN'S CHAMBER PASSAGE

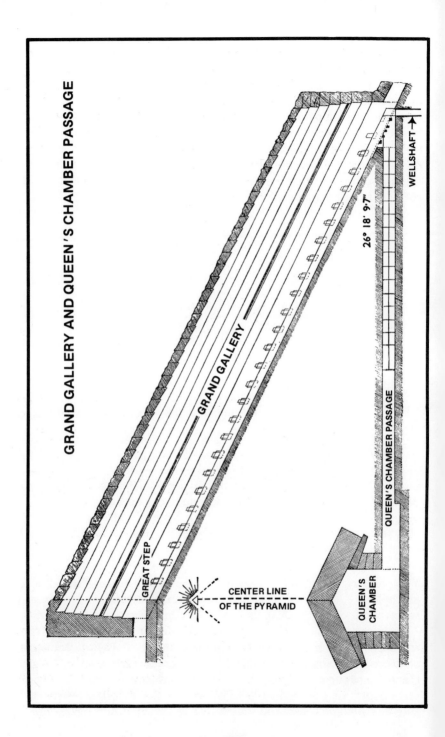

82

stone walls that are much decayed and exfoliated from exposure to the air and the fumes from torches through many long centuries.

The roof stones of the Grand Gallery are set at a steeper slope than the passage. Each stone is separately upheld by the side walls across which it lies. Thus no stone can press on the one below it, so as to cause a cumulative pressure all down the roof. There is no way of ascertaining the shapes of the ceiling masonry without actually removing one. However, the commonly accepted theory is the supposition that the roof is formed of slabs laid "title fashion." In most drawings of the ceiling it is represented as follows:

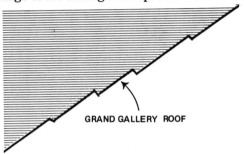

GRAND GALLERY ROOF

For the slabs to be laid "title fashion" the bottom end of the higher slab must be inserted under the top end of the lower slab. (as shown below) While it is not impossible, it is highly unlikely that the builders would have selected so laborious a system whereby the tendency to displacement of the stones is ever present during construction.

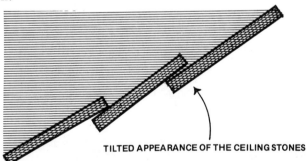

TILTED APPEARANCE OF THE CEILING STONES

In keeping with the perfection of workmanship apparent throughout the Grand Gallery's interior, it is most logical the shape of a ceiling stone is a seven-sided one. The following sketch shows how the uniform levels of the course are preserved and no hollow spaces are formed that would require being filled up. This theory is in keeping with the structural principle carried out in the con-

83

struction of the floor of the Grand Gallery: the stones made to rest on steps formed by the Pyramid's courses, or half courses.

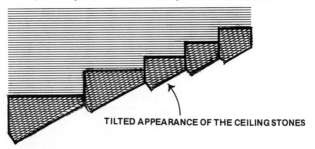

TILTED APPEARANCE OF THE CEILING STONES

Originally covered over by the floor stones of the Grand Gallery is a horizontal passage starting from the lower end of the Grand Gallery and terminating in the Queen's Chamber. The passage is divided into two parts; the first portion extends northward for 1305.2246 P. inches (about 108 ¾ feet) at a height of 46.9880 P. (about 3¾ feet) The second portion continues an additional 216.5668 P. inches (about 18 feet) with a height of 67.5946 P. inches (about 5½ feet) due to a drop of 20.6066 P. inches — an exact Egyptian Royal Cubit. (a little over 1½ feet — An Egyptian Royal Cubit will be explained in chapter 10) The total length of the combined portions of the Queen's Chamber Passage is 1521.7914 P. inches (about 126¾ feet) and terminates at the beginning of the Queen's Chamber.

LOOKING FROM GRAND GALLERY INTO QUEEN'S CHAMBER PASSAGE

The Queen's Chamber is beautifully constructed in polished limestone with its floor resting on the 25th course of core masonry, from the base of the Pyramid. The Chamber is 226.6725 P. inches (about 19 feet) in length and 206.0659 P. inches (about 17 feet) in width. The height of the north and south walls is 184.2642 P. inches. (about 15⅔ feet) The east and west walls are gabled, the apexes extending 243.7504 P. inches (about 20¼ feet) above the floor. The floor of the Queen's Chamber was left rough, however, all around the chamber is a footing of fine stone that projects out to four inches from the base of the walls. It is from this level footing that measurements for the heights are taken.

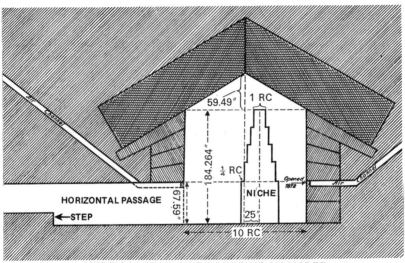

VERTICAL SECTION OF QUEEN'S CHAMBER
SHOWING NICHE IN THE EAST WALL

The air-channel openings are found in the Queen's Chamber, one in the north wall and one exactly opposite in the south wall. Both ventilation openings are on the same level as the top of the entrance doorway and are approximately 8½ inches high and 8 inches wide. As originally constructed, the builders stopped the air-channels short by 5 inches from coming into the chamber. The openings were only discovered in 1872 by Mr. Waynman Dixon, in company with a friend, Dr. Grant doing research on the Queen's Chamber. Perceiving a crack and investigating it by slipping a wire into the opening, Dixon found the crack appeared to be quite long and wider than what showed on the surface of the wall. Applying a chisel to the area resulted in the tool soon slipping into the opening — and fresh air entering the chamber. Further excavating proved

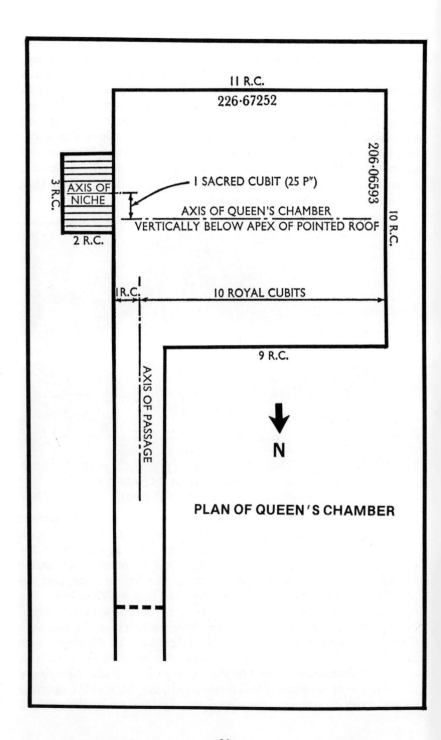

PLAN OF QUEEN'S CHAMBER

11 R.C.
226·67252
206·06593
10 R.C.
1 SACRED CUBIT (25 P")
AXIS OF NICHE
AXIS OF QUEEN'S CHAMBER
VERTICALLY BELOW APEX OF POINTED ROOF
3 R.C.
2 R.C.
1 R.C.
10 ROYAL CUBITS
9 R.C.
AXIS OF PASSAGE
N

86

the cavity to be the inner end of a nearly squared air-channel extending to the outer surface of the Pyramid.

Investigating the opposite wall, Dixon discovered a second air-channel similar to the first. The conclusion can only be that the builders purposely planned for the ducts to stop short 5 inches from entering the room. There was no jointing or plugging of the opening. To quote Professor C. Piazzi Smyth, (who recorded the discovery of the air-channels) "...the thin plate was 'left' and a very skillfully, as well as symmetrically left, part of the grand block composing that portion of the wall on either side."

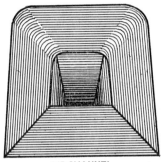

AIR CHANNEL

Another feature peculiar to the Queen's Chamber is a large corbelled recess 184.26425 P. inches (about 15⅔ feet) high, in the east wall, known as the Niche. The Niche extends eastward for a distance of 41.21319 P. inches — exactly 2 Egyptian Royal Cubits, (nearly 3½ feet) terminating in a dead end. The center line or vertical axis of the gable end of the Queen's Chamber to the south wall is a distance of 25 P. inches — an exact Pyramid Sacred Cubit. (25.0265 English inches)

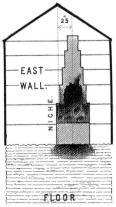

Al Mamoun reported having found a plain, lidless and empty sarcophagus in the Queen's Chamber and as late as the 12th century A.D. it remained in existence. In A.D. 1136 the famous Arab writer, Edrisi, who visited Egypt that year, describes seeing it. Since that date no record of its existence has been found. It is possible that some of the limestone fragments now filling many holes and corners of the chamber, caused by excavations, may have come from the Coffer.

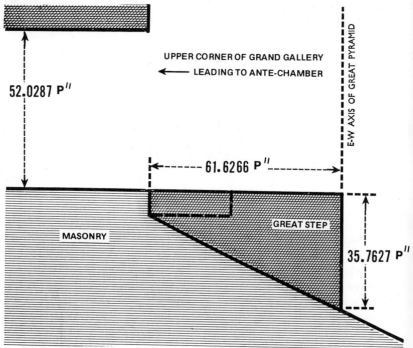

At the upper end of the Grand Gallery is the Great Step, having a height of 35.76277 P. inches (nearly 3 feet) and the face of it is lying exactly on the east-west axis of the Pyramid; that is to say, it is exactly half way through the Pyramid from north to south. The top of the Great Step, which extends across the full width of the Grand Gallery, is horizontal and level with the passage leading to the King's Chamber. The Great Step protrudes back from the end or top of the Grand Gallery 61.62660 P. inches (little over 5 feet)

The horizontal passage leading to the King's Chamber is divided into three sections: (1) First Low Passage (2) Anti-Chamber (a high central section) (3) Second Low Passage. The First Low Passage is 52.0287 P. inches. (about 4⅓ feet) The southern end of the First Low Passage emerges into what is commonly called the "Ante-Chamber." The Ante-Chamber's two side walls and south end wall (except for one foot at the top) are of red granite. Each of the two side walls have a wainscot of approximately a foot thick. Thus the width between the wainscot is 41.2132 P. inches (same as the First Low Passage) and increases to 65.2560 P. inches width above the wainscot.

A CROSS-SECTION OF THE HORIZONTAL PASSAGE SYSTEM SHOWING:-
(1) THE GREAT STEP   (2) THE FIRST LOW PASSAGE   (3) THE ANTE-CHAMBER
(4) THE SECOND LOW PASSAGE   (5) THE KING'S CHAMBER

The floor of the Ante-Chamber is in two parts: (1) a limestone portion of 13.2273 P. inches (an extension of the limestone floor of the First Low Passage) and (2) a granite portion of 103.0330 P. inches. Thus the total length of the Ante-Chamber is 116.2603 P. inches. (about 9⅔ feet) The sidewall wainscots dip down a few inches below the floor, indicating that the floor was laid after the wainscots were positioned.

Each wainscot is characterized by four broad vertical grooves, 3¼ inches deep. The grooves on the side walls (east and west) are exactly opposite one another. Three of these grooves run from top to bottom of the wainscot and sink 3 inches below the floor-level.

**PERSPECTIVE VIEW OF ANTECHAMBER
SHOWING GRANITE LEAF REMOVED**

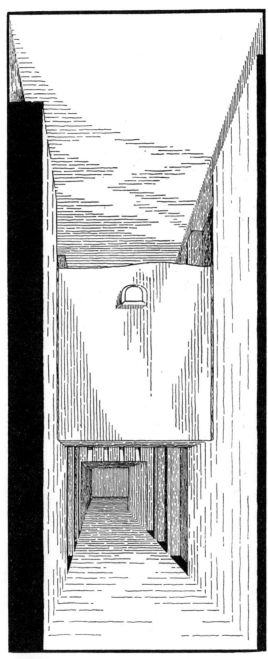

**PERSPECTIVE VIEW OF ANTECHAMBER
SHOWING GRANITE LEAF IN POSITION**

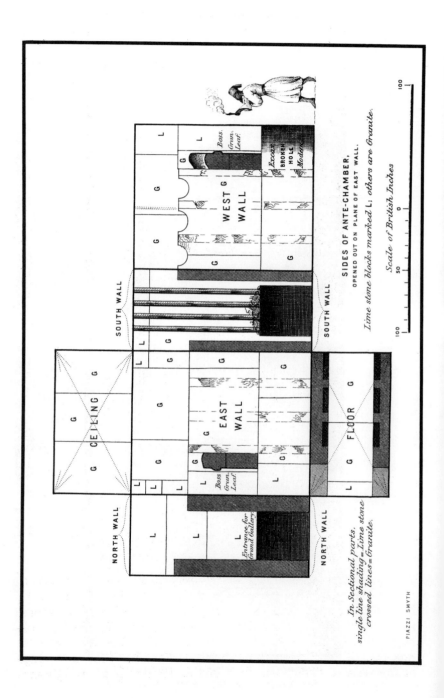

SIDES OF ANTE-CHAMBER,

OPENED OUT ON PLANE OF EAST WALL.

Lime stone blocks marked L: others are Granite.

Scale of British Inches

In Sectional parts,
single line shading = Lime stone
crossed lines = Granite.

PIAZZI SMYTH

One, the most northerly groove, runs from the top down to the bottom of two granite slabs, one over the other, extending across the passage from wall to wall. These slabs together are known as the "Granite Leaf." The whole height of the Ante-Chamber from floor to ceiling measures 149.4407 P. inches. (nearly 12½ feet) The ceiling of the chamber is formed of three large blocks which lie east-west.

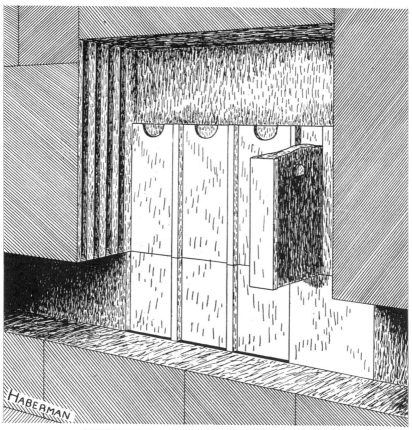

PERSPECTIVE VIEW OF THE ANTE-CHAMBER

The object of interest in the Ante-Chamber is a raised Boss or Seal in the shape of a horseshoe, on the south side of the Granite Leaf. The center of the Boss is filled in solidly and measures precisely 5 P. inches across its face. It is exactly 1 P. inch from the center line (or the north-south axis) of the chamber and protrudes precisely 1 P. inch from the face of the Granite Leaf. From the edge of the Boss to the Eastern end of the Granite Leaf the distance

93

VERTICAL SECTION (*LOOKING WEST*) OF KING'S CHAMBER: ANTE-CHAMBER AND HOWARD VYSE'S "CHAMBERS OF CONSTRUCTION" SHOWING "QUARRY MARKS"
SINGLE SHADE LINES INDICATE LIMESTONE   CROSSED LINES INDICATE GRANITE

KING'S CHAMBER AND CONSTRUCTION CHAMBERS
(LOOKING WEST)

is exactly 25 P. inches or 1 Pyramid Sacred Cubit.

THE BOSS ON THE GRANITE LEAF
1/11 real size.

For many years the significance of the Boss could not be deciphered. From its prominence, it was suspected to bear some important function. Today, there is little doubt but that the little projection was placed there to indicate the Great Pyramid's "standard unit of measurement" — the "Pyramid Inch" and the correct length of the unit known as the "Ancient Sacred Hebrew Cubit," which is exactly 25 P. inches in length. (Details of the Sacred Cubit are explained in Chapter 10)

The Second Low Passage is constructed entirely of red granite (as is the King's Chamber) and extends in length 101.0463 P. inches. (nearly 8½ feet) Its width and height are the same as the first Low Passage. The total length of both Low Passages and the Ante-Chamber is 269.3353 P. inches. (little over 22¼ feet)

The King's Chamber has been described as "the chief triumph of the Pyramid builder's architectural skill." It is built of red granite, in five courses of stone, all trimmed to exactly the same height, with an error not exceeding 1/10th on an inch. Unfortunately, it has been severely shaken by earthquakes over the long centuries since it was built. The injury which it has received can best be realized from the diagram on page 114, which illustrates the resulting displacement of its horizontal and vertical surfaces. Nevertheless, in spite of the damage done, we can know its intended dimensions, for theory confirmed by its geometric design defines the measurements which are supplied us by careful surveying.

The King's Chamber is 412.1319 P. inches in length (about 34 ⅓ feet), 206.0659 P. inches in width (little over 17 feet) and 230.3887 P. inches in height. (about 19¼ feet) Its roof is constructed of 43 massive granite beams, each 27 feet long and weighing from 50 to 70 tons. They are set joint-wise in five cushioned tiers and extend five feet beyond the walls. Above these are 24 great limestone rafters, forming a gabled roof.

The King's Chamber has two air-channels or ventilators; one in the north wall and the other directly opposite in the south wall. Both have a bore of about 9 inches square. Unlike the air-

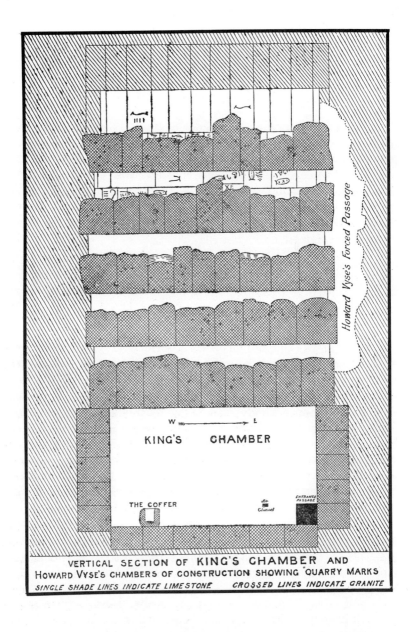

VERTICAL SECTION OF KING'S CHAMBER AND
HOWARD VYSE'S CHAMBERS OF CONSTRUCTION SHOWING "QUARRY MARKS
SINGLE SHADE LINES INDICATE LIMESTONE   CROSSED LINES INDICATE GRANITE

KING'S CHAMBER AND CONSTRUCTION CHAMBERS
(LOOKING NORTH)

channels left unopened in the Queen's Chamber, the ones in the King's Chamber were cut through to the surface of the inner wall masonry. Each air-duct was cut through each separate core stone and laid throughout their slanting length out to the outer surface of the structure. These afforded a supply of fresh air to those parts of the Pyramid.

In the masonry of the south air-channel of the King's Chamber was found (in 1837 by J.R. Hill, an assistant of Col. Howard Vyse) a small piece of wrought iron. The piece of sheet iron was discovered embedded in the cement of an inner joint when masonry was being removed in preparation for the clearance of sand and debris from the air-channel. This is regarded as the oldest specimen of wrought iron in the world. Sir Flinders Petrie commented: "That sheet iron was employed, we know, from the fragment found by Howard Vyse in the masonry of the south air channel; and though some doubt has been thrown on the piece, merely from its rarity, yet the vouchers for it are very precise; and it has a cast of a nummulite on the rust of it, proving it to have been buried for ages beside a block of nummulitic limestone, and therefore to be certainly ancient. No reasonable doubt can therefore exist about its being really a genuine piece used by the Pyramid masons; and probably such pieces were required to prevent crowbars biting into the stones, and to ease the action of rollers." (The Pyramids and Temples of Gizeh, pg. 212 -1st ed.)

The piece of iron can be seen today in the British Museum in London. It should be noted that there has been doubt cast on the iron as to its antiquity. It has been suggested that since the piece was found in the core masonry near to the position of the original casing-stones it is possible that it slipped down through a crack in the core masonry at the time the robbers of the Middle Ages were removing the outer casing stones of fine limestone for their own use in Cairo. Most present-day Egyptologists accept this viewpoint.

The five cushioned tiers above the King's Chamber are actually a series of five shallow Chambers of Construction. These spaces are appropriately termed, "relieving chambers" by the Egyptologists since the spaces have successfully prevented the collapse of the King's Chamber from the tremendous weight of the superincumbent masonry above the Chamber — amounting to several million tons. The horizontal granite beams that form the floor of each of the Chambers of Construction are dressed on the under side but wholly unwrought above. These successive floors are blocked apart along the north and south side; by blocks of granite in the lower, and of limestone in the upper chamber. The supporting blocks are from two to three feet high, regulating the ceiling heights of the chamber, and allowing each chamber to stand unbonded and capable of yielding freely to settlement. The use of limestone in the upper chambers would allow those chambers to take up the shock or subsidence caused by the great mass of masonry above them, by the crushing and "plastic" flow of the limestone. In other words, the higher chambers were purposely built weaker than the lower chambers and ceiling beams of the King's Chamber, to act as a succession or "buffer" between the superimposed mass of the Pyramid and the King's Chamber during expected subsidence movement.

To permit the "buffer" effect to be more effective, the beams or slabs of the Chambers of Construction were not built into the East and West walls, from which, as shown by the adhering plaster, the upper Chamber has subsided as much as 3 inches. Hence, instead of indicating bad workmanship — as has been supposed by some authorities not conversant with the design of constructional devices for counteracting the effects of subsidence movement that cannot be prevented — the workmanship seen in these Chambers is indicative of good design. An entirely rigid system of construction, with uniform workmanship from the lowest to the highest Chamber, would have proven disastrous, and unable to prevent the collapse of the King's Chamber.

That the design has proven successful is borne out by the fact that, even as it is, every one of the nine great granite beams forming the ceiling of the King's Chamber is cracked right across. Some of the granite beams above are also fractured and the huge sloping limestone rafters have been forced apart at the apex to the extent of 1 to 1½ inches.

The Chambers of Construction are entered from a small passage which starts in the East wall of the Grand Gallery, close under the roof, and leads into the lowest space. The other four spaces above can only be entered by the forced ascent cut by Col. Howard Vyse in 1830. This latter passage is not so easy to go up, as it is nearly one continuous height with no foot-holes. A slip at the top chamber would mean a fall of thirty feet. One would be required to use a rope ladder or similar device.

In the second upper Chamber of Construction are seen interesting mason's lines, drawn in red and black, that show to some extent, the methods used by the workers. Some of the lines are drawn in red on the granite, some over ancient plaster, while others are under

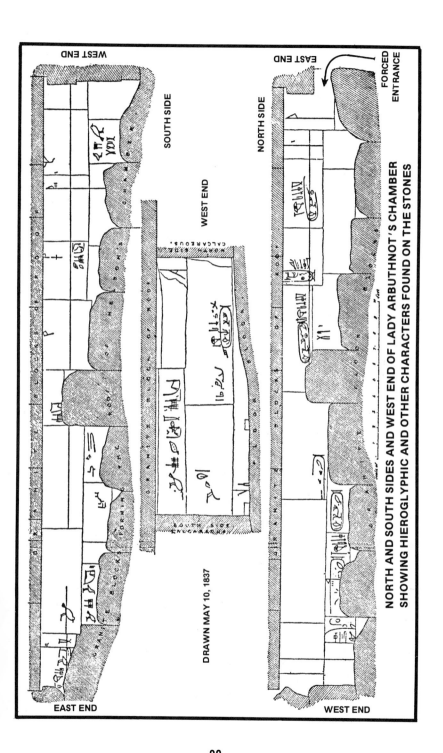

NORTH AND SOUTH SIDES AND WEST END OF LADY ARBUTHNOT'S CHAMBER
SHOWING HIEROGLYPHIC AND OTHER CHARACTERS FOUND ON THE STONES

DRAWN MAY 10, 1837

99

the plaster. These lines show they were drawn during the building, while it was being plastered, and slopped like whitewash into the joints. The third, fourth and fifth chambers also show red and black mason marks; one stone showing clearly a mark exactly a Sacred Cubit in length.

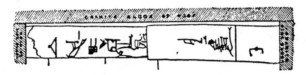

MARKS IN RED PAINT ON STONE
WEST END OF NELSON'S CHAMBER

The rough tops of the beams spanning the Chambers of Construction show the interesting method of quarrying them. On the top of each stone is a hollow or sink running along one edge. Branching from this cutting, at right angles across the stone, are grooves 20 to 25 inches apart, about 4 inches wide and 1½ inches deep. These seem to show that in cutting out a block of granite, a long groove was cut at the quarry to determine the trend or strike of the cleavage; and then, from this, holes were roughly bored about 4 inches in diameter and 2 feet apart to determine the dip of the cleavage plane. This method would have avoided any danger of skew fractures, and is the hallmark of old Egyptian masonry.

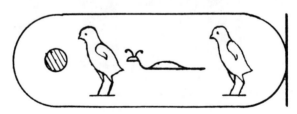

CARTOUCHE OF KHUFU

In the second Chamber of Construction is a large cartouche of Khufu (Cheops) nearly all broken away by Vyse's forced entrance. Vyse had copies of it, and other oval markings and quarry marks, sent to Samuel Birch of the British Museum in London. There the markings were translated and the oval markings identified. One was the cartouche of Khufu (King Suphis or Shofo) and one set of markings were hieroglyphics signifying the "year 17" which Egyptologists have deduced to mean the building had reached that stage of construction in the seventeenth year of Khufu's reign. All the original

100

**Stela of Khufu (Cheops), the reigning Pharaoh
at the time of the erection of
THE GREAT PYRAMID**

(now in Cairo Museum)

markings were subsequently examined by Egyptologists and their antiquity confirmed.

Other cartouches of Khufu (Cheops) were found in various places. One was discovered in the quarries of Wadi Magharah Hills, from where some of the stone for the Great Pyramid was derived. Another was found in one of Khufu's Boat-pits on the east side of the Pyramid. It was on wood which was subsequently carbon-dated to 2700 B.C. ± 50 years. This ended speculation that there might have been a far earlier king with a similar cartouche, quite unknown to Egyptologists.

VERTICAL CATOUCHE OF KHUFU
(FROM A ROCK IN THE SINAITIC PENINSULA)

**Ivory statuette of Khufu (Cheops) of the IVth Dynasty
in whose reign was built
THE GREAT PYRAMID**

(This statuette is now in the Egyptian Museum, Cairo)

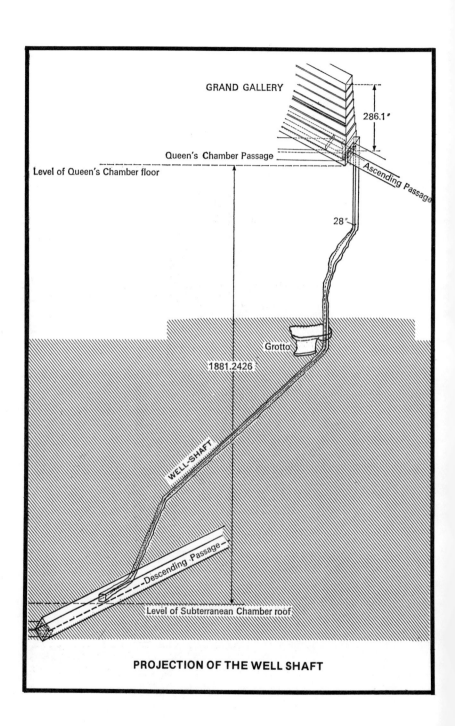

GRAND GALLERY

286.1″

Queen's Chamber Passage

Level of Queen's Chamber floor

Ascending Passage

28″

Grotto

1881.2426

WELL-SHAFT

Descending Passage

Level of Subterranean Chamber roof

PROJECTION OF THE WELL SHAFT

CHAPTER 8

WELL SHAFT

There is one strange, well-like passage, known as the "Well Shaft," common to both systems of passages. Starting from a point in the west side of the Descending Passage (about 86½ feet below the base line of the Pyramid) it irregularly and tortuously slants upward in a northerly direction until it reaches a large natural water-worn cavity (known as the Grotto) formed, in part, by a fissure in the rock. From there, the passage continues upward until it opens into the floor at the beginning of the Grand Gallery.

Opinions differ as to when, how and for what purpose the Well Shaft was tunnelled. David Davidson holds that it was made quite some time after the Great Pyramid was built. The lower part, under the Grotto, constructed first, ending in the Grotto. Then the upper portion was bored upward through the core masonry to open into one side of the Grand Gallery. The purpose of the tunnel was so the "keepers" of the Great Pyramid could make an inspection of the upper chambers for subsidence over the years or perhaps after some relatively strong earthquake to see what damage it may have caused. Davidson believed the investigators decided to enter the Pyramid from the Descending Passage instead of trying to carve their way around the Plug, as was later done by Al Mamoun. At a point nearly at the bottom of the Descending Passage they bored a short horizontal passage before starting their excavation upwards toward the Grotto and eventually the Grand Gallery.

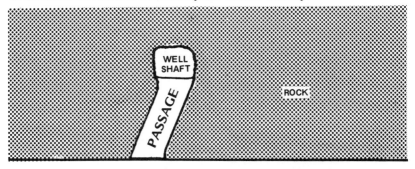

DESCENDING PASSAGE

PLAN OF LOWER OPENING OF WELL-SHAFT

The reason for starting so far down, says Davidson, instead of taking a shorter way, was to cut their way through an area that contained several fissures in the bedrock, noticeable from the Descending Passage. These fissures were nearly directly under the Grotto itself, originally formed by a large fissure. That fissure had been found and shored up, during the leveling of the site prior to the actual building of the Pyramid. Digging in a gradual upward slope, the workers cut through both fissures, finding them in not as bad condition as they had expected. At the level of the Grotto, before boring into the core masonry above, they enlarged the Grotto area for the purpose of by-passing workers and material.

From the Grotto, the excavators continued upward toward the Grand Gallery, and when sufficiently advanced, made an accurate survey from a fixed point of the Great Pyramid's construction to determine the exact location reached in azimuth (distance in angular degrees from the north star) altitude and distance. To have done so, says Davidson, shows the excavators must have known the precise internal arrangement and measurements of the Great Pyramid. Anyone boring blindly could have missed the few feet of the Grand Gallery and could have been boring for hundreds of feet without finding the upper chambers.

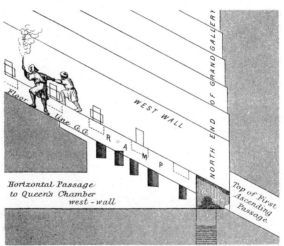

Once the workers had reached the Grand Gallery, they removed a section of the lower portion of the floor of the Grand Gallery and uncovered the hidden passage to the Queen's Chamber. This they inspected carefully, but found little or no sign of failure. Proceeding to the King's Chamber, the inspectors found indications of possible

106

instability due to movement. Inside the King's Chamber they found the ceiling beams uniformly cracked along the south ends. The cause of these fractures had been from subsidence. (see chart page 114) To enable them to monitor the fractures for further movement, according to Davidson, the keepers smeared the fractures and open joints with cement and plaster.

Flinders Petrie, in his report of his examination of the ceiling-beams in the King's Chamber, states, "Round the S.E. corner, for about 5 feet on each side, the joint is daubed up with cement, laid on by fingers. The crack across the eastern roof-beam has also been daubed up with cement, looking as if it had cracked before the chamber was finished. At the S.W. corner, plaster is freely spread over the granite, covering about a square foot altogether."

To gain access to the important Chambers of Construction over the King's Chamber, Davidson believed, the custodians, drove an opening into the east wall of the Grand Gallery at its upper or south end. (See chart page 89) Tunnelling clear of the wall blocks of the Grand Gallery, they bored a small passage toward the mouth and entered the First Chamber of Construction immediately above the roof of the King's Chamber. Here they found that the indications of instability were not so serious as they had feared, for they did not proceed higher than the first Chamber with their inspection. In all instances of forced entry, the excavators were careful not to destroy or interfere with the purpose of any essential feature of the Pyramid's passage construction. According to Davidson, the keepers then climbed back down the well, the bottom end of which they camouflaged, and left by the swivel-stone entrance on the north face.

A French professor of architecture, J. Bruchet, who visited the Great Pyramid and made measurements of the Well Shaft, disagrees with Davidson that the Shaft could have been dug from the bottom up, giving as his reason the fact that the bottom of the Well Shaft goes slightly below the level of the Descending Passage, which he claims would not have been so if the shaft had been started from below. And for the Well shaft to have been dug from above indicates it could only have been completed before the Ascending Passage was plugged, or after the opening of "Al Mamoun's hole." In a closed upper Pyramid there would have been no place to store the carloads of rubble from the digging of the Well Shaft. The King's and Queen's Chambers and the passages would not have been sufficient to contain the debris. Bruchet also points out that the Well Shaft could not have been dug after Al Mamoun, because the lower end of the Descending Passage was filled by him with the refuse of broken limestone plugs, which were not cleared out till 1817 by Caviglia.

✳ ✳ ✳ ✳

This writer, after visiting the Great Pyramid on several occasions and having read most of the writings of the early Pyramidologists concerning the problem of the Well Shaft, would like to offer the following explanation, as a possible answer to the questions raised about the Well Shaft.

I accept Davidson's theory that the Well Shaft was dug from the bottom up, in spite of the rock fragments constantly falling in the face of the chiselers and those workers below — BUT, only as far as the Grotto. The fact that the lower end of the Well is a little lower than the level of the Descending Passage is of little consequence. The extra depth could have been to receive the rock chippings being dug out overhead and falling down the shaft. When the area was filled up and perhaps overflowing with debris, it was cleaned out to receive another batch of rubble.

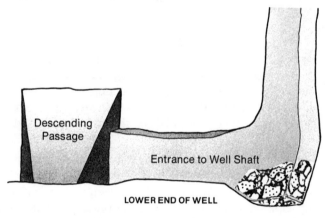

From the Grotto upward, the shaft was left as an opening between the core blocks as the masonry was laid. In other words, the passage from the Grotto to the Grand Gallery was not an excavation, but rather just a hole left between the core blocks as each layer of stone increased in height. This accounts for the irregularity of the shaft, with parts of the core blocks sometimes projecting into the shaft area. Such projections actually provided foot rests for climbing up and down the shaft.

Evidence that this upper portion of the Well Shaft was a feature

108

of the original structure is seen by the fact that the walls of the Well Shaft upward from the Grotto are built of cut and positioned lime-stones till the first layer of core blocks was encountered. The top portion of the Well Shaft (near the Grand Gallery) is also constructed of stones, carefully cut to size and arranged as to position. The stones forming the opening of the Well Shaft itself, were specially cut and arranged with direct reference to the open mouth of the Well Shaft. Immediately over the opening (on the west side of the Grand Gallery) is an unusually large wall stone, spanning the Ramp-stone (now missing) that obviously was placed there to further strengthen the masonry surrounding the open mouth of the Well. This special architectural arrangement is not found on the east side of the Grand Gallery.

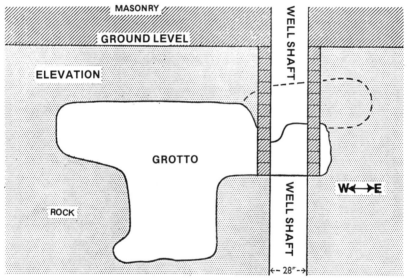

The purpose of having a passage between the Grotto and the Grand Gallery was to allow inspection of the base foundation of the Pyramid during construction. The Grotto was a large natural fissure in the weakest part of the base site. It was found when the site was leveled and instead of being filled in to provide a smooth building site, it was left, shored up, and a vertical shaft constructed the few feet upward to the first layer of core masonry. The opening left in the core masonry, as the Pyramid progressed higher and higher, allowed periodical inspections, from time to time, of the foundation which was receiving ever increasing weight from the masonry above. It was a simple matter for a master mason to climb down to the Grotto and back.

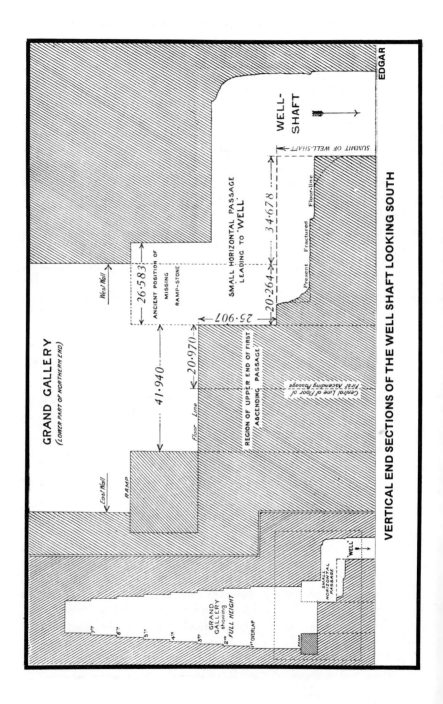

VERTICAL END SECTIONS OF THE WELL SHAFT LOOKING SOUTH

EDGAR

WELL-SHAFT

GRAND GALLERY
(LOWER PART OF NORTHERN END)

West Wall

26·583

ANCIENT POSITION OF MISSING RAMP-STONE

SMALL HORIZONTAL PASSAGE LEADING TO 'WELL'

34·678

20·264

SUMMIT OF WELL-SHAFT

Floor-line

Present Fractured

25·907

East Wall

RAMP

41·940

20·970

Floor Line

REGION OF UPPER END OF FIRST ASCENDING PASSAGE

Central Line of Floor of First Ascending Passage

GRAND GALLERY
showing
FULL HEIGHT

7TH
6TH
5TH
4TH
3RD
2ND OVERLAP
1ST OVERLAP

RAMP

SMALL HORIZONTAL PASSAGE

'WELL'

When the Pyramid reached the height of the roof of the King's Chamber, a final inspection would have been made. As all seemed well, the ramp stone on the west wall of the Grand Gallery was placed, covering up the mouth of the Well Shaft. At this point of construction, once the ceiling beams of the Kings Chamber were laid, the workers would be unable to re-enter the Grand Gallery. They could, however, enter the Descending Passage through the swivel stone entrance and continue to check on the fissures noticed on the side wall of the Descending Passage, near the Subterranean Chamber Passage.

Davidson's theory that an inspection was made by "keepers" of the Pyramid, many years later, is quite logical. If my suggestion is correct, that the Well Shaft from the Grotto upward to the Grand Gallery was already there; the inspectors only had to know where the Grotto was located. They were helped by following the fissures they knew intersected the Grotto. Once the Grotto was reached, they had ready access to the Grand Gallery without having the difficulty of boring through the many courses of masonry and locating the very small area (and the exact spot) of the Grand Gallery. At the top of the Well Shaft they only had to break or force out the stone covering the opening (the stone work around the opening of the Well Shaft shows signs of having the stone forced up from below) and enter the Grand Gallery.

R A M P

ENLARGED
PERSPECTIVE
VIEW
OF THE
BROKEN OUT
RAMP STONE
AND
THE ENTRANCE
TO THE
WELL,
so called.

PIAZZI SMYTH

111

After the keepers had made their inspection, they departed by way of the Well Shaft, unable, of course, to conceal their forced opening at the top, since the stone forced out, could not be replaced from below as they were leaving. The lower opening of the bore they had excavated from the Descending Passage to the Grotto, however, they could conceal by blocking it up with cut stones, to appear as a fissure shored up. This had been done to other fissures near their opening. It is noted that, although the lower opening is exposed today, a level cut above the opening indicates that squared stones did once cover the opening.

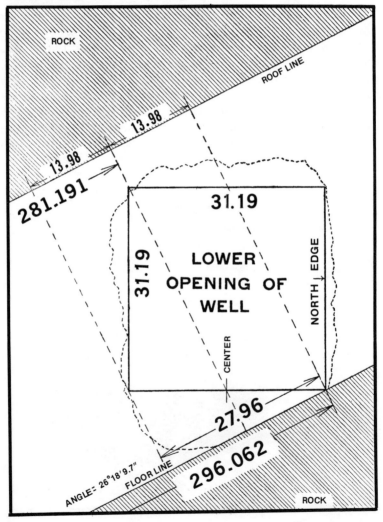

I believe that if Al Mamoun had not first noticed the exposed plug of the First Ascending Passage, he would have eventually torn out all the shoring stones in the Descending Passage, in a desperate search for the treasure he had promised to his workers. In such an event he would have undoubtedly found the Well Shaft. However, since the plug obviously hid another passage, he first forced an opening around it. Then after finding the main chambers of the Pyramid empty there should be no doubt but that he would have noticed the now open mouth of the Well Shaft in the Grand Gallery. His men would have explored it and, coming to the bottom blocked with stones, would have broken them out (which accounts for the edges of the opening appearing to have been broken as by a pry-bar) and found themselves back in the Descending Passage.

Thus the discovery of the upper passage system and the Well Shaft were both made by Al Mamoun and his men. In time, rubble removed by Al Mamoun from the First Ascending Passage settled down the Descending Passage, hiding both the lower opening of the Well Shaft and the Subterranean Chamber. This condition remained for centuries until re-discovered by Caviglia.

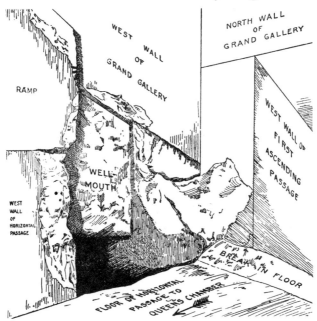

SHOWING THE SMALL HORIZONTAL PASSAGE LEADING FROM THE GRAND GALLERY
WESTWARD TO THE WELL

113

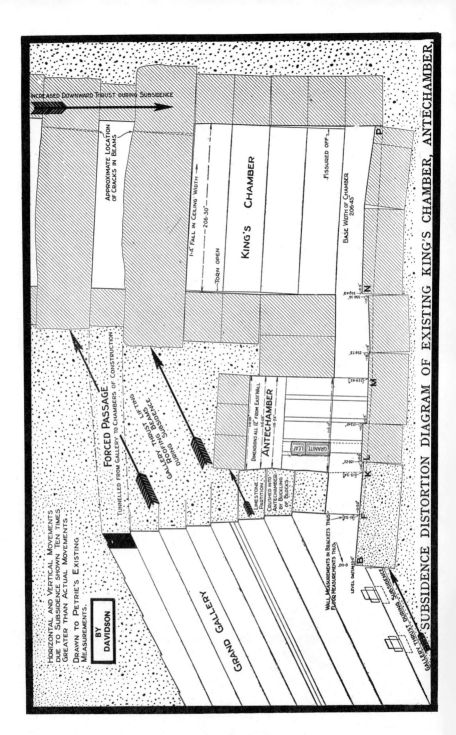

SUBSIDENCE DISTORTION DIAGRAM OF EXISTING KING'S CHAMBER, ANTECHAMBER,

INCREASED DOWNWARD THRUST DURING SUBSIDENCE

APPROXIMATE LOCATION OF CRACKS IN BEAMS

1·4" FALL IN CEILING WIDTH
206·30"
TORN OPEN

KING'S CHAMBER

FISSURED OFF

BASE WIDTH OF CHAMBER 206·45"

P

N

230·36" 229·03"

257·75"

[229·42]

ANTECHAMBER

116·05"
116·75"

DIMENSIONS ALL 12" FROM EAST WALL

GRANITE LEAF

[11·94"]

[103·34"]

[126·22"]

M

L

K

LIMESTONE PARTITION

CRUSHED INTO ANTECHAMBER BY BUCKLING OF BLOCKS.

[61·36"]

F

B

FORCED PASSAGE
TUNNELLED FROM GALLERY TO CHAMBERS OF CONSTRUCTION

GALLERY THRUST LIFTING BEAMS ROOFING SUBSIDENCE DURING

HORIZONTAL AND VERTICAL MOVEMENTS DUE TO SUBSIDENCE SHOWN TEN TIMES GREATER THAN ACTUAL MOVEMENTS.

DRAWN TO PETRIE'S EXISTING MEASUREMENTS.

BY
DAVIDSON

GRAND GALLERY

WALL MEASUREMENTS IN BRACKETS THUS [ ]
EXISTING MEASUREMENTS THUS

LEVEL DATUM 0·00"

GALLERY TILTED DURING SUBSIDENCE

114

CHAPTER 9.

TRIAL PASSAGES

The question is often raised if the Architect of the Great Pyramid employed some kind of a "blueprint," and if so, what kind? No doubt some form of a blueprint was used, just as they are used in building construction today. If they could be found, it would prove that the Great Pyramid did not just "grow," as was the fashion for pyramids built as tombs. The Egyptian Law (known as Lepsius' Law) of pyramid building called for each king, when he came to the throne, to start excavating a subterranean chamber with an inclined passage, said chamber intended for his tomb. Each year, the area over the chamber was covered with a few squared blocks of stone, until he died, leaving his successor to finish and close the edifice. Hence the size of each pyramid would depend upon the accident of the duration of the king's life. (Exceptions have been found where some long-lived kings have only small pyramids)

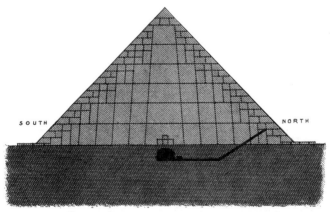

THE "LAW OF EGYPTIAN- PYRAMID BUILDING,"
AFTER LEPSIUS, WILD, BONOMI & GLIDDON.
IN MERIDIAN SECTIONAL ELEVATION.

Two such forms of "blueprints" have been found that show the whole character of the Great Pyramid was calculated and determined beforehand. One is in the form of a plan of the Pyramid's passage system cut into the solid rock of the Giza Plateau. It is located about a hundred yards east of the Pyramid and about 60 yards north of the little Seventh Pyramid of Giza. Known as the Trial Passages, it was obviously cut into the rock prior to the beginning of construction of the building proper. With a single exception of the position of the Well-Shaft, the passages are an exact model of the Great

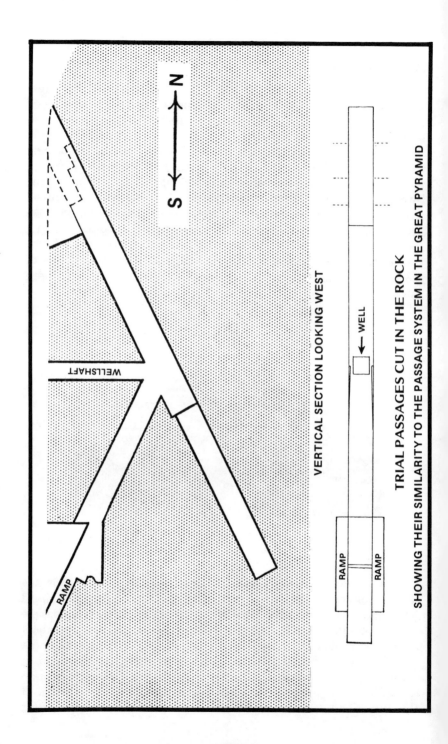

VERTICAL SECTION LOOKING WEST

TRIAL PASSAGES CUT IN THE ROCK

SHOWING THEIR SIMILARITY TO THE PASSAGE SYSTEM IN THE GREAT PYRAMID

Pyramid's Passage system, with full width and height but shorter in length. The Trial Passages could have been used by the masons as guides or templates in laying out the complete Passage System.

The resemblance of the Trial Passages to the actual passages in the Great Pyramid is striking, even to the beginning of the Horizontal Passage to the Queen's Chamber, the Ramps at the side of the Grand Gallery, and the contraction at the lower end of the First Ascending Passage to hold the Granite Plug. (except that in the Trial Passages, this contraction occurs additionally in the height, as well as in the width of the First Ascending Passage) Although the vertical bore of the Well-Shaft is in a different position in the Trial Passages, it is undoubtedly intended as a model of the Well-Shaft in the Great Pyramid; the bore of each being the same. The total lengths of the Descending and Ascending Passage (in the Trial Passages) are 66 feet and 50 feet respectively.

What could be the second set of "plans" for the Great Pyramid is a system of inclined tunnels cut into the rock of a hill, on the Plateau, which was once thought to be the remains or commencement of another pyramid of small size. However, Piazzi Smyth found they were arranged on the exact principles contained in the Great Pyramid. Smyth wrote concerning the tunnels: "There is a long descending entrance passage, an upward and opposite rising passage from the middle of that like the Great Pyramid's first ascending passage, then the beginning of a horizontal passage like that to the Queen's Chamber, and finally the commencement of the upward rising of the Grand Gallery with its remarkable ramps on either side. The angles, heights, and breadths of all these are almost exactly the same as obtained in the Great Pyramid."

The rock cut tunnels were evidently an experimental model, cut beforehand, to give the plan to which the Great Pyramid was to be constructed. Thus, the Trial Passages and the tunnels provided working plans or models from which the ancient masons worked, both of the outside angles and the inside arrangements. Such "plans" indicate that the Great Pyramid was not built under the Lepsius's law of pyramid building, since its plans provided for the buildings as a whole, pursued from commencement to completion without consideration of the lifespan of a king. And further, all the searchings into the Great Pyramid have failed to reveal any sign of the patching of one year's work to that of another, or any arrangement for such a contingency as the possible death of the king before the work was complete.

THE SACRED CUBIT AND THE ROYAL CUBIT

Their interrelation as revealed by the Great Pyramid

1 Sacred Cubit $= \dfrac{10^3\sqrt{\pi}}{4y}$ Royal Cubits $= 1.213204$ Royal Cubits

$\qquad\qquad = 25 \qquad$ Pyramid inches $= 25.0266$ British inches.
$\qquad\qquad\qquad\qquad$ (i.e., thumb-breadths)

1 Royal Cubit $= \dfrac{4y}{10^3\sqrt{\pi}}$ Sacred Cubits $= 0.8242637$ Sacred Cubits

$\qquad\qquad = 20.606593$ Pyramid inches $= 20.62852$ British inches.
$\qquad\qquad\qquad\qquad$ (i.e., thumb-breadths)

ADAM RUTHERFORD

118

CHAPTER 10.

SACRED CUBIT

Sir Isaac Newton (1642-1727) is credited with the discovery that the Great Pyramid was constructed on two different units of measurements called cubits. One he called "profane" and the other he called "sacred." Based on Greaves and other investigators' measurements of the King's Chamber, Newton computed that a cubit of 20.63 British inches produced a room with an even length of cubits: 20 x 10. This cubit Newton called the "profane" or Memphis cubit.

The other cubit (sacred) Newton derived from Josephus's description of the circumference of the pillars of the Temple at Jerusalem. Newton estimated this cubit to be between 24.80 and 25.02 British inches but believed the figure could be refined through further measurements of the Great Pyramid and other ancient buildings of the Hebrew pre-monarchy period. In the later monarchial period, in Palestine, the so-called "common cubit" of 18 inches was in general use. After the Babylonian captivity of Judah, the legal cubit of the Talmudists was 21.85 English inches.

Newton's research is recorded in a report titled "A dissertation upon the Sacred Cubit of the Jews and the Cubits of several nations; in which, from the Dimensions of the Greatest Pyramid, as taken by John Greaves, the ancient Cubit of Memphis is determined." Unfortunately, Newton's calculations were based on inaccurate measurements by Greaves of the base of the Pyramid. Due to insufficient clearance of the debris around the Pyramid's base, Greaves' figures were slightly in error.

Further research did find that Newton's "profane" cubit was equal to 20.6284 British inches and is now known as the "Egyptian Royal Cubit." This Royal Cubit was the unit of measurement employed by the workers in the actual construction of the Great Pyramid. The other and longer "sacred" cubit was found to equal 25.0265 British inches and is called today the "Sacred Cubit." This cubit predominates in the design of the Great Pyramid and through its application the Pyramid reveals its scientific features.

The Sacred Cubit is designated in the form of a horseshoe projection, known as the "Boss" on the face of the Granite Leaf in the Ante-Chamber of the Great Pyramid. By application of this unit of measurement it was discovered to be subdivided into 25 equal parts, the subdivisions being known as "Pyramid inches." (P. inches) One Pyramid inch equals 1.00106 British (and American) inches.

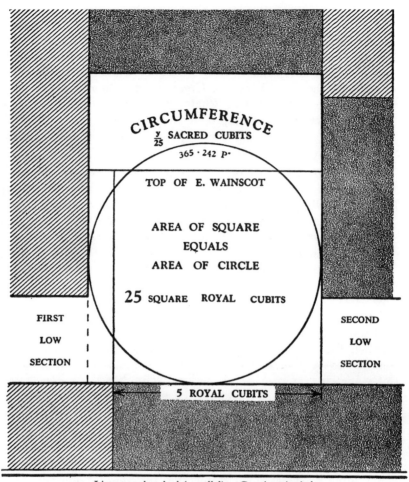

CIRCUMFERENCE

$\frac{y}{25}$ SACRED CUBITS

365·242 P·

TOP OF E. WAINSCOT

AREA OF SQUARE
EQUALS
AREA OF CIRCLE

25 SQUARE ROYAL CUBITS

FIRST
LOW
SECTION

SECOND
LOW
SECTION

5 ROYAL CUBITS

Limestone hatched (parallel): Granite stippled

GEOMETRICAL RELATIONSHIP
OF THE
SACRED CUBIT AND ROYAL CUBIT

RUTHERFORD

**RELATIONSHIP BETWEEN SACRED CUBIT AND ROYAL CUBIT
IS EXPRESSIBLE MATHEMATICALLY AS FOLLOWS:**

1 SACRED CUBIT =

$$10^3 \sqrt{\pi} / (4 \times 365.24235$$

ROYAL CUBITS

To convert an English inch measurement to its corresponding value in Pyramid inches one must deduct one-thousandth part of the English inch measure from itself. Therefore, a round 1000 English inches equal 999 Pyramid inches. Then to convert a Pyramid inch measure to its corresponding value in English inches, divide the Pyramid inch measure by .999.

There is an interrelationship between the Egyptian Royal Cubit and the Pyramid Sacred Cubit that allows for conversion of one measurement to the other.

This geometric relationship can be seen in the Ante-Chamber of the Great Pyramid. The length of the Ante-Chamber is equal to the diameter of a circle having a circumference of 365.242 Pyramid inches. This "year circle" is converted into a square of precisely equal area; the granite portion of the floor constituting the base of the square and the end of the granite wainscot forming the side-length of the square. The sides of this square are each found to measure exactly 5 Egyptian Royal Cubits of 20.60659 Pyramid inches. (see chart page 120) Thus, because of this mathematical relationship between the Sacred and the Royal Cubits, all measurements of the Great Pyramid are readily expressible in both Cubits, for the Royal Cubit is precisely 1/5 of the square root of the area of the Year Circle.

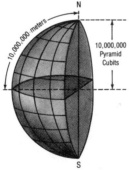

In 1859 John Taylor proposed that the Pyramid inch was also a Polar Diameter inch. The theory was adopted by Piazzi Smyth in 1864-5. Subsequent scientific calculations confirmed that the Pyramid inch is the 500,000,000 part of the earth's Polar Diameter. According to the results of the latest geodetic research in the International Geophysical Year (1957-8), the polar radius of the earth, as deduced from observations from the orbits of artificial satellites, is approximately 3949.89 miles. Dividing this figure by 10,000,000, the result is 1 Sacred Cubit (25 Pyramid inches) or 25.0265 British (and American) inches. Thus, the earth's Polar radius measures 10,000,000 Sacred Cubits or 250,000,000 Pyramid inches; hence, the Pyramid inch is the 500,000,000 th part of the earth's Polar Diameter.

If this method of arriving at a measure of distance seems unusual, consider the French meter, conceived as a unit of linear measure based also upon the size of the earth. The French meter was arrived at by taking the 10,000,000 part of the so-called "quadrant of the earth," as calculated from the North Pole to the equator, along a meridian passing through Dunkirk. As the earth is not a perfect sphere, the said distance is not a true quadrant, hence it is not truly scientific to determine a unit of straight measure from such a surface.

The calculations upon which the French meter are based were subsequently found to be slightly in error. Scientifically, a unit of straight measure should be based on the straight distance corresponding to the curved semi-meridian, namely the semi-axis or polar radius of the earth, as was done by the builder of the Pyramid.

Obviously, at the time the Great Pyramid was built, over 4500 years ago, no man on earth knew the precise dimensions of the oblate spheroid called the Earth. So the question is naturally raised, how was that knowledge incorporated in the measure of the Sacred Cubit? The answer will be forthcoming in another chapter of this book.

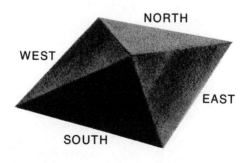

CHAPTER 11.

COFFER

Near the west end of the King's Chamber is located a flat-sided box of red granite known as the Coffer. It is the only moveable article of furniture found in the Great Pyramid. One corner has been broken off. This is attributed to Jean Palerme, a Frenchman, who recorded visiting the Pyramid in 1581 and taking a piece of the coffer home. It is noted that the Coffer could not have been placed in the King's Chamber after the Pyramid was finished because the Coffer is nearly an inch wider than the beginning of the First Ascending Passage. The only conclusion, then, is that the Coffer was placed in the King's Chamber before the roof was put on.

In its original position, the Coffer sat midway between the north and south walls of the King's Chamber with its sides parallel to the respective sides of the Chamber and its axis coinciding with the Pyramid's own north-south axis. That is to say that the Coffer's axis, which was due north and south, would be geometrically 286.1 P. inches west of the axis of the passage system.

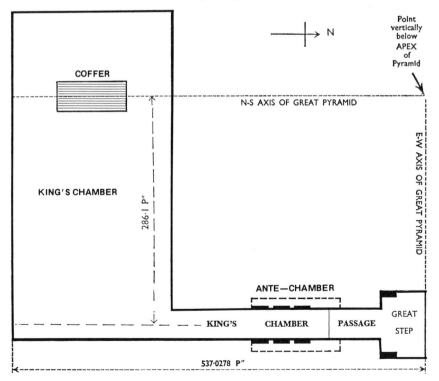

THE COFFER IN THE KING'S CHAMBER

124

The Coffer is formed from a single piece of red Aswan granite and exhibits an amazing feat of workmanship. Its sides were cut by a jewelled bronze saw (probably nine feet long) and its interior hollowed out as a carpenter might hollow out a block of wood with an auger. The spiral markings on the inner sides can still be discerned. Engineers have estimated that to accomplish this feat it would have required an overhead pressure of from one to two tons and the bits would have to have been of very hard and tough material, likely some precious stone.

The top of the Coffer is grooved around its inner edges, as though to receive a lid. However, there is no evidence that it ever had one. Although the Coffer is sometimes referred to as a "sarcophagus" by those who hold to the "tombic" theory for the Great Pyramid, it is neither inscribed nor decorated, as was the custom of the times. When discovered, it was found empty and there is no record of a body (mummy) ever having been placed in it.

The fact that the King's Chamber was vented with ventilators certainly indicates that the chamber was never intended for a tomb, which would have required an "air-tight" room. That it was not used as a tomb is confirmed by the statements of the classical historians, Herodotus and Diodorus, that Cheops (Khufu) was buried elsewhere. The strongest evidence for a tombic theory for the Great Pyramid lies in the Coffer, similar to the ordinary coffers of early Egyptian times. But, a close examination of it shows evidence that it was constructed for a purpose other than receiving and safeguarding a body. They are:

1. The Coffer is unusually deep. (nearly 3½ feet)
2. No lid has ever been seen or reported.
3. In no other case has a coffer been devoid of ornament or inscription.
4. The Coffer had no protection built around it, as was the custom.
5. Its location in chambers above the ground level is contrary to Egyptian burial procedure.
6. It had to be built and placed before the Pyramid was finished.
7. Its location was well defined by the passage system which would lead an intruder straight to it instead of concealing its resting place.
8. Its location in an air-conditioned chamber instead of an air-tight chamber required for preservation of a body.

In addition to the preceding evidences that the Coffer was not

The Coffer, in the King's Chamber,

South   North

Elevation, looking West.

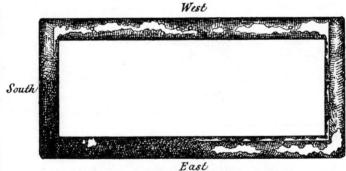

West

South   North

East

Plan, looking from above;
the shading in proportion to the deviation
from a horizontal plane.

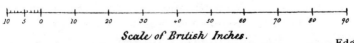

10   5   0   10   20   30   40   50   60   70   80   90

Scale of British Inches.

Edgar

intended for a burial vault is the great care and design of certain cubic proportions that would hardly have been incorporated into its construction had it been expected to just receive a body. Geometrically, the Coffer's measurements are:

	external	*interior*
Length	89.80568 P. inches	78.1 P. inches
Width	38.59843 P. inches	26.7 P inches
Height	41.21319 P. inches . Depth .	34.31 P. inches

Interior capacity — 78.1 x 26.7 x 34.31 = 71,545.6 cubic inches

From these measurements we find various proportions which include the following:

1. The cubic volume of the Coffer's walls (approximately 6 inches thick) and the bottom of the Coffer (approximately 7 inches thick) equals the cubic contents (volume) it could hold.
2. The length of the Coffer plus its width equals Pi (3.14159) times its height.
3. The diagonal of the inside bottom of the Coffer is double its height. (or 4 cubits)
4. The diagonal of the inside bottom of the Coffer rises parallel to the Pyramid's face. (51° 51' 14.3")
5. The sum of the length, width and height of the Coffer is equal to 1/5 of the sum of the length, width and height of the King's Chamber itself.
6. The Coffer's depth times 2 Pi equals the area of its two long sides. (East and West sides)
7. The Coffer's internal floor has a boundary whose length equals the circumference of a circle of equal area to the Coffer's outer floor or base.

Several investigators of the Great Pyramid have noticed other unique factors about the capacity of the Coffer. John Taylor, in 1859, wrote (The Great Pyramid: Why was it built?) that the capacity of the Coffer is equal (in English measures) to 128 pecks of wheat or 32 bushels of wheat or 4 quarters of wheat. Taylor also pointed out that in his day when a farmer speaks of 8 bushels of wheat as a quarter, they usually could not answer the question, "quarters of what?" Naturally it is the fourth part of some entire measure and is exactly equal to the measure of the Coffer.

The earliest measures of capacity, next to the Hebrew, are the

The *Handbook of United States Coins* by R. S. Yeoman

SILVER DOLLARS
1794 to Date

The silver dollar was authorized by Congress April 2, 1792. Weight and fineness were specified at 416 grains and 892.4 fine. The first issues appeared in 1794 and until 1804 all silver dollars had the value stamped on the edge: HUNDRED CENTS, ONE DOLLAR OR UNIT. After a lapse in coinage of the silver dollar covering the period 1804 to 1840, these coins had reeded edges and the value was placed on the reverse side.

The weight was changed by the law of January 18, 1837 to 412½ grains, fineness .900. The coinage was discontinued by the act of February 12, 1873 and reauthorized by the Act of February 28, 1878. The dollar was again discontinued after 1935 and since then only the copper-nickel pieces first authorized in 1971 have been coined for circulation.

HALF DOLLARS 1794 to Date

The half dollar, authorized by the Act of April 2, 1792, was not minted until December, 1794. The early types of this series have been extensively collected by die varieties, of which many exist for most dates. Valuations given below are in each case for the most common variety, and scarcer ones as listed by Beistle and Overton (see page 143, Bibliography) generally command higher prices.

The weight of the half-dollar was 208 grains and its fineness .8924 when first issued. This standard was not changed until 1837 when the law of January 18, 1837 specified 206¼ grains, .900 fine.

Arrows at the date in 1853 indicate the reduction of weight to 192 grains, in conformity with the Act of February 21, 1853. During that year only, rays were added to the field on the reverse side. Arrows remained in 1854 and 1855.

In 1873 the weight was raised by law to 192.9 grains and arrows were again placed at the date, to be removed in 1875.

QUARTER DOLLARS 1796 To Date

Authorized in 1792, this denomination was not issued until four years later. The first coinage, dated 1796, follows the pattern of the early half-dimes and dimes by the absence of a mark of value. In 1804 the value "25c" was added to the reverse. Figures were used until 1838 when the term "QUAR. DOL." appeared. It was not until 1892 that the value was spelled out entirely.

The first type weighed 104 grains which remained standard until modified to 103⅛ grains by the Act of January 18, 1837. As with the dime and half dime, the weight was reduced and arrows placed at the date in 1853, and rays were placed in the field of the reverse during that year only.

The law of 1873 also affected the quarter, for the weight was slightly increased and arrows again placed at the date.

Proofs of some dates prior to 1855 are known to exist, and all are rare.

Grecian, of which the linear foot is equal to 1.01 of the English, or 12.12 English inches. The cube of this foot is contained 40 times in the volume of the Coffer. The Roman measures of capacity are closely connected with the Greek, and in general assumed the same. The earlier Roman foot is equal to .972 of the English foot, or 11.665 English inches. Taking it as equal to 11.66 inches, the cube consists of 1585 inches, which cube is contained 45 times in the capacity of the Coffer.

Taylor also wrote "As the Pyramid Coffer contains 18,005,760 Troy grains, or 18,000,000 grains (omitting 5760 grains, equal to 1 pound) so it contains 3125 pounds Troy of 5700 grains. But this is the weight of water. If the coffer were filled with wheat, the weight would be only 2500 pounds, or one-fifth less. Accordingly, 10 pounds Troy water would occupy the space of 8 pounds Troy of wheat. The coffer was probably intended for a corn measure in the first instance, but it was also found that the same vessel which would hold 2500 pounds of wheat would hold 3125 pounds of water or wine. Hence, any vessel of capacity which would hold 10 pounds of 5760 grains (water or wine) was considered to hold 8 pounds of 7200 grains. (wheat) This was the original, in all probability, of our Avoirdupois pound." (The Great Pyramid: Why was it built? — pg. 146)

Taylor did considerable research on the Coffer and concluded that it was a standard of measures of capacity founded on measures of length and the origin of measures of weight for the Hebrews, Romans, Greeks and English. Taylor's computations were confirmed by Piazzi Smyth who added additional proportions in his work, "Our Inheritance in the Great Pyramid." (1867)

Not only is the coffer in the King's Chamber of the Great Pyramid a source of weights and measures, the King's Chamber itself can be shown to a source of weights for our American silver coinage. Our (U.S.) silver corresponds in grains to the measures of the King's Chamber in English inches. The silver "Dollar of the Founding Fathers" contains 412.5 grains, the exact length of the King's Chamber. The half-dollar contains 206.2 grains, the exact width of the King's Chamber. The silver quarter dollar contains the same number of grains as the number of inches of half the width of the King's Chamber or 103.1 grains.

There is an amazing relationship between the Coffer and the Sacred Ark of the Covenant of the Biblical Tabernacle. The cubic capacity of the Coffer is found to be equal to that of the Ark. The measure of the Molten Sea (the great brass bowl held up by 12

129

MOLTEN SEA

brass oxen) in Solomon's Temple is equal to exactly 50 times the capacity of the Coffer. These proportions are highly significant when one considers the fact that the Coffer (and the Great Pyramid) were constructed over a thousand years before the Bible was written. Thus, the builders of the Great Pyramid could not have used the Bible for the design of the Coffer or the King's Chamber.

The dimensions of the Ark of the Covenant were:

Length . . . . 2 cubits and a half = 62½ inches
Width   . . . . 1 cubit and a half = 37½ P. inches
Height . . . . 1 cubit and a half = 37½ P. inches

It is evident that these Biblical figures were the Ark's outside measurements, as the Mercy Seat, which formed its covering, was 2½ cubits by 1½ cubits, and if the measurements of the Ark were its internal measurements, the Mercy Seat would have dropped inside it, instead of covering it. Its vertical dimension is also spoken of as "height" not "depth," as it would if the measurements were internal.

The inter-relationship between the Coffer (and the King's Chamber) and the Ark of the Covenant can only be explained by the understanding and acceptance that in early times, God Himself imparted knowledge to certain individuals which was subsequently written in the Scriptures. How could Noah have built that Ark, if he had not been divinely instructed as to its fabrication? And might

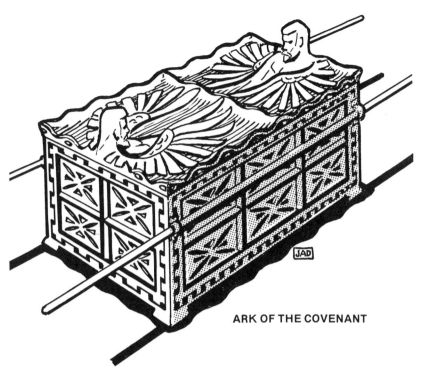

ARK OF THE COVENANT

the builder of the Great Pyramid have been equally instructed in the knowledge requisite to form the Coffin? Both of these works by the hand of man are based on "measures."

This same reasoning can only account for the equally amazing geometric structure of the Great Pyramid, the subject of the next chapter.

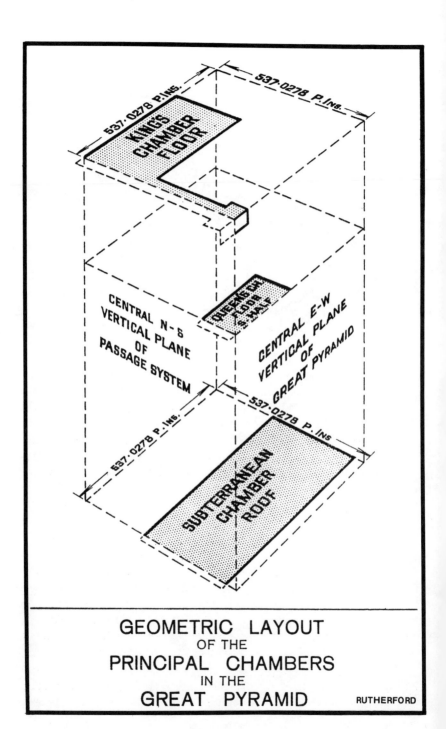

537.0278 P.INS.

537.0278 P.INS.

KING'S CHAMBER FLOOR

CENTRAL N-S VERTICAL PLANE OF PASSAGE SYSTEM

QUEEN'S CH. FLOOR & WALL

CENTRAL E-W VERTICAL PLANE OF GREAT PYRAMID

537.0278 P.INS.

537.0278 P.INS

SUBTERRANEAN CHAMBER ROOF

GEOMETRIC LAYOUT
OF THE
PRINCIPAL CHAMBERS
IN THE
GREAT PYRAMID

RUTHERFORD

CHAPTER 12.

GEOMETRIC CONSTRUCTION

In geometric form, the Great Pyramid is what is called a true pyramid. Its base is a perfect square. Each of its four sides form perfect equilateral triangles. These triangles slant evenly inward and upward from the base, until they meet at an apex situated perpendicularly over the center of its base where the two base-diagonals intersect. The last stone (the apex stone) laid in place is also a true pyramid in form. This unique feature of a cornerstone is found in no other form of a building.

To properly understand the Great Pyramid it must be noted that the whole structure, internally and externally, is geometric in conception and design. For this reason, the secrets of the Great Pyramid are ones to be solved, not by Egyptologists as such, but by the engineer, since it was erected on principles easily recognized and understood by the construction engineer.

Merely exploring the structure will reveal nothing as regards to its meaning. A knowledge of geometry and mathematics, therefore, combined with an understanding of their proper application, is essential to a correct understanding of the Great Pyramid and its true purpose. It is not by hieroglyphics nor by sculpture work, but by symbol, measure and angle, that the Great Pyramid of Giza, in the land of Egypt, yields its secrets.

Scientific directed surveys have furnished the actual geometric measurements of the Pyramid. From these measurements calculated data has been obtained which reveal the Great Pyramid to constitute a geometric representation, on a vast scale, of mathematical and astronomical knowledge not to be known, again, for over 4500 years. The remarkable manner in which this knowledge is geometrically expressed, relative to certain simple mathematical formulae, surpasses in every way, any similar undertaking of man.

It is worthy of special note that the entire geometric structure of the Great Pyramid is designed on the basis of π (pi) - 3.14159 - the mathematical ratio upon which the whole physical universe is designed, and the value of "y" - 365.242 - the number of days in earth's solar year. (the time interval in days between two successive vernal equinoxes in the earth's journey around the sun)

In mathematics, π (Pi - sixteenth letter of the Greek alphabet) is the ratio between the circumference of a circle and its diameter. (the straight line through its center) That is to say, the circum-

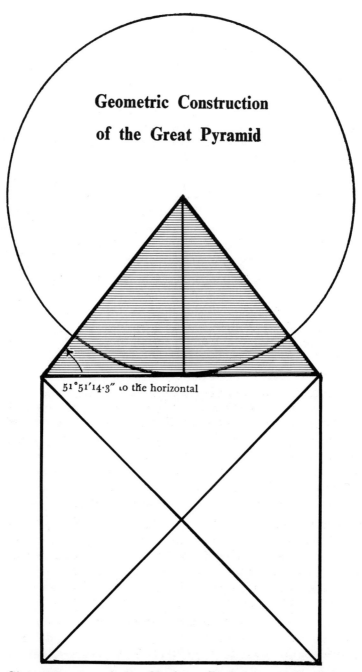

Geometric Construction
of the Great Pyramid

51°51'14·3" to the horizontal

Circumference of the Circle = Perimeter of the Square

ference of any size circle is always 3.14159 +, times its diameter. This sign has been adopted because of the fact that the ratio in question has never been ascertained to its finality. It has, however, been calculated to an exceedingly high degree of precision, namely, to over 5,000 decimal places. (To 30 places of decimals, π is 3.141592653589793238462643383280) In ancient arithmetic 22/7 (the best known approximations to π) was found sufficiently accurate - a number that lends itself to whole numbers and if greater accuracy be required, corrections can be applied.

The amazing fact that this geometric ratio π , which pervades the whole universe, from the vast solar systems to the tiniest atoms, also pervaded the Great Pyramid, was first revealed by the angle of the slope of the Pyramid's sides. This angle results in the Pyramid's vertical height bearing the same ratio to the perimeter of its base that the radius of a circle bears to the circumference. (See diagram, page 134)

In other words, if the height of the Pyramid to its apex is taken as the radius of a circle, the distance around the base of the Pyramid is found to be exactly equal to the circumference of that circle. The required angle of the slope of the Pyramid's sides to produce this result is consequently known as the pyramidic π angle and is 51° 51' 14.3". No other pyramid in the world is built at this exact angle.

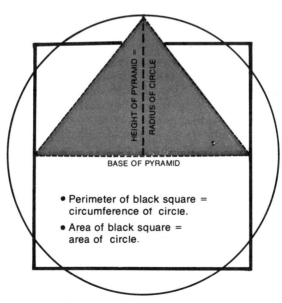

HEIGHT OF PYRAMID =
RADIUS OF CIRCLE

BASE OF PYRAMID

• Perimeter of black square = circumference of circle.
• Area of black square = area of circle.

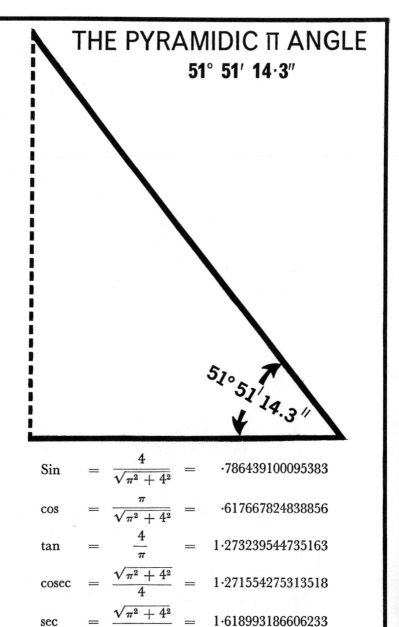

THE PYRAMIDIC π ANGLE
51° 51′ 14·3″

51° 51′ 14.3″

$$\text{Sin} \quad = \quad \frac{4}{\sqrt{\pi^2 + 4^2}} \quad = \quad ·786439100095383$$

$$\cos \quad = \quad \frac{\pi}{\sqrt{\pi^2 + 4^2}} \quad = \quad ·617667824838856$$

$$\tan \quad = \quad \frac{4}{\pi} \quad = \quad 1·273239544735163$$

$$\text{cosec} \quad = \quad \frac{\sqrt{\pi^2 + 4^2}}{4} \quad = \quad 1·271554275313518$$

$$\sec \quad = \quad \frac{\sqrt{\pi^2 + 4^2}}{\pi} \quad = \quad 1·618993186606233$$

$$\cot \quad = \quad \frac{\pi}{4} \quad = \quad ·785398163397448$$

ADAM RUTHERFORD

Although the squaring of a circle is considered an insoluble problem, if we use the incommensurable number of π , the Pyramid's design, for all practical purposes, accomplishes the squaring of the circle. In other words, a pyramid built with a slope of a 7 inch rise for every 11 inches of base practically solves the problem commonly called "squaring the circle." This ratio of the Great Pyramid's overall dimensions is duplicated in the King's Chamber. If the solid diagonal of the King's Chamber multiplied by 10 is taken as the side of a square, equal in area to the area of the right vertical section, such a pyramid would have the dimensions of this example.

The King's Chamber is also determined by the π proportions; the circuit of a side wall being equal to a circle described by the width as a radius. Thus the circuit of a side wall has its radius at right angles across the chamber, and its diameter the length of the side along the chamber. This means that if you draw a circle with the chamber width as a radius, or the chamber length as a diameter, the circumference of the circle would be the same length as twice the side of the chamber plus twice the height.

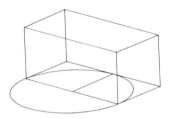

The proportions of the side, length and height of the King's Chamber are also duplicated in the horizontal measures of the niche in the Queen's Chamber. This duplication of proportions was evidently intended to insure that they would not be lost due to an subsidence or other earth movements. In such an event, we would be able to reconstruct where necessary; being certain what the measurements were intended to be and thus be able to read the meaning which they were designed to convey. In other words, when dealing with dimensions having a π ratio, if one measurement is known, the other two can be calculated. This was the case in computing two measurements in the King's Chamber that had been distorted due to subsidence.

Nearly all of the dimensions of the interior, (and the Architect's design of the exterior are expressible in terms of the length of the solar year. Some examples are:

(1) The square base of the Pyramid (four sides) equals 36,524,235 P. inches.

(2) Take the length of the King's Chamber as the diameter of a circle, then compute, by the best methods of modern science, the area of that circle. Throw that circle into a square shape — the length of a side of that square will be 365.2423 P. inches.

(3) Twice the length of the King's Chamber, (in Pyramid inches) taken in conjunction with the angle of the passages which lead up to it, also indicates the period of the earth's revolution around the sun. In other words, if the length of the King's Chamber (412.132 P. inches x 2) is marked off on the floor of the First Ascending Passage, and a right-angled triangle be formed drawing a perpendicular and base-line from the upper and lower extremities respectively of this portion of the floor, the perpendicular will be found to measure exactly the number of days in a solar year, or 365.2423 P. inches.

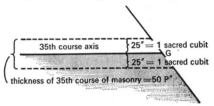

(4) In contrast to the other courses of masonry is the 35th course. It is 50 P. inches in thickness which is thicker than those courses above or below it. This course extends from the outside edge to the center vertical line, a distance of 3,652.432 P. inches. It is also 1162.6 P. inches above the base, and at this height its perimeter measures 1162.6 P. inches, so that a rectangle is defined as 3652.4 P. inches by 1162.6 P. inches. This rectangle defines the Ancient Egyptian unit of land area known as an "Aroura."

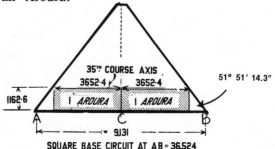

SQUARE BASE CIRCUIT AT AB = 36,524

138

(5) The height of each of the north and south walls in the Queen's Chamber, (182.62 P. inches) when multiplied by (3,14159) and doubled, equals 365.24.

The dimensions of the Ante-Chamber also relate to the solar year. Some examples are:

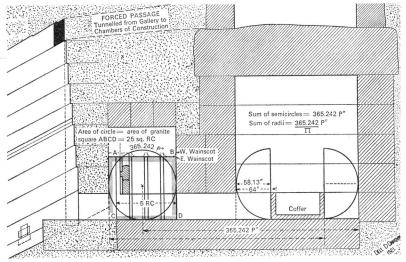

(1) The length of the Ante-Chamber (116.2603 P. inches) is equal to the diameter of a circle whose circumference is 365.24235 P. inches.

(2) From the center of the Ante-Chamber to the end wall of the King's Chamber is 365.242353 P. inches.

(3) From the same plane to the far end of the Coffer in the King's Chamber is 365.2423 P. inches.

(4) From the front wall of the Ante-Chamber to the back face of the Granite Leaf is 36.524 P. inches.

(5) Multiplying the length of the Ante-Chamber (116.2603 P. inches) by 25 Pyramid inches (a Sacred Cubit) and again by π (3.14159) equals the base side length of the Pyramid, (9131.03 P. inches) which is ¼ of 36,524,12 P. inches.

Although a longer list of clearly defined correlations could be quoted, the above should suffice to indicate that the geometric measurements can be seen, in all cases, as simple geometrical functions of the solar year circle, the latter being a circle whose circumference, in Pyramid inches, is 100 times the number of days in the solar year. There are other features, based on the Egyptian Royal Cubit (which is itself directly derived from the Sacred Cubit) that are based on the solar year circle of its derivatives.

It seems very likely that the aforementioned measurements for the Great Pyramid's external and internal arrangements should have been selected arbitrarily and yet reveal accidently such geometrical relationships. We can only logically infer that the design was definitely selected and erected to monumentalize these geometrical facts. This fact implies the possession of a knowledge of geometry, mathematics and astronomy, combined with the ability to express them in structural form, far in advance of contemporary knowledge of that time.

Archimedes (287-212 B.C.) is reported as being among the first of the ancients who made any approach toward the practical squaring of the circle, which is involved in the π (pi) ratio. By inscribing and circumscribing a polygon of ninety-six sides, he discovered that a circle of 4970 feet in diameter would have a circumference lying between 15,610 feet, and 15,620 feet. This was as near as that most ingenious mathematician and inventor of ancient times could arrive at it.

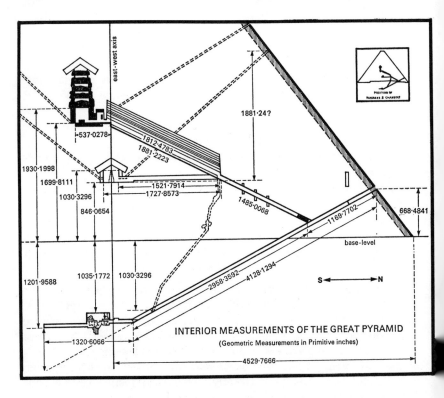

INTERIOR MEASUREMENTS OF THE GREAT PYRAMID
(Geometric Measurements in Primitive inches)

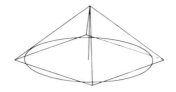

The Metrological View
of
The Great Pyramid

Dwelling like greatest things alone,
Nearest to heaven of earthly buildings, thou
 Dost lift thine ancient brow
In all the grandeur of immortal stone,
And, like the centuries' beacon, stand,—
 Upspringing as a tongue of fire—
To light the course of Time in Egypt's mystic land.
 'Tis not for poet to inquire
Why thou wast built and when?
 Whether, in monumental state,
So great thyself to tomb the great
 Beyond their fellow-men?
Or dost thou, in thy bodily magnitude,
 Not uninformed nor rude,
Declare the abstract ties which science finds,
 Seen by the light of geometric minds,
In fixed proportions, each allied to each?
Or dost thou still, in inferential speech,
 Reveal unto mankind the girth
 Of the vastly rounded earth;
And to the busy human race
 Bequeath a rule, to guide the range
 Of all the minor measurements of Space,
Which Traffic gets, and gives, in endless interchange?
Enduring pile! Thou art the link that binds
 The memories of reflective minds—
Vast mass of monumental rock sublime,
That to the present Age dost join the youth of Time.

Patrick Scott

SUMMARY

OF THE

TRIGONOMETRICAL RATIOS

OF THE

GREAT PYRAMID'S PRINCIPAL ANGLES

Casing

Sin	.786439100095383
Cos	.617667824838856
Tan	1.273239544735163
Cosec	1.271554275313518
Sec	1.618993186606233
Cot	.785398163397448

Arris

Sin	.669094599294229
Cos	.743177244804559
Tan	.900316316157106
Cosec	1.494556974536658
Sec	1.345574029608754
Cot	1.110720734539592

Passage

Sin	.443113462726379
Cos	.896465537068011
Tan	.494289456096249
Cosec	2.256758334191025
Sec	1.115491849547959
Cot	2.023106072093268

ADAM RUTHERFORD

CHAPTER 13.

MATHEMATICAL PROPORTIONS

Ancient Egypt had no difficulty in reckoning high numbers, and they possessed for integers a convenient decimal system. Each multiple of unity from 1 to 9 had a separate name, and also with the tens from 1 to 90. That is to say, they could divide by 10 up to 1 place of decimals, but no further. The only fractions used were 1/3, 2/3, 1/2, 1/4, 1/5, 1/6, etc. but there was no limit to the divisor. Addition and subtraction, doubling and halving, multiplying and dividing by 10, 2, and 5 were the methods adopted in solving mathematical problems.

The difficulty of multiplying and dividing without an algebraic and a decimal system was so great that the ancient Egyptians found it expedient to eliminate complicated fractions by approximations. In some cases, the most precise value for π (Pi) had to be disregarded, and exact equality of areas, circumferences, etc., had to be sacrificed, to secure the more important required results. However, where found in the design of the Great Pyramid, these approximations do not affect the geometrical and mathematical conclusions of whole numbers.

Although the Great Pyramid reveals an advanced knowledge of mathematics and kindred sciences, the ancient Egyptians were never able to duplicate the proportionate mathematic system of numbers used in the design of the Pyramid. Having been shown how to build the ideal pyramid, and with a perfect model before them, they could only copy it externally. However, all subsequent pyramids show a steadily deteriorating standard of construction.

An example of the symmetry of mathematical proportions in the Great Pyramid is found in the measurements of the King's Chamber and Ante-Chamber. Their dimensions show that:

(1) The width of the King's Chamber equals half of its length.
(2) The height of the King's Chamber, equals half of the diagonal of its floor.
(3) The length of the granite portion of the Ante-Chamber floor is equal to half the width of the King's Chamber.
(4) The length of the granite portion of the Ante-Chamber floor, multiplied by 5, (a special Pyramid number) equals the solid cubic diagonal of the King's Chamber.
(5) The length of the granite portion of the Ante-Chamber floor, multiplied by 50, (2 Sacred Cubits) equals the length of the

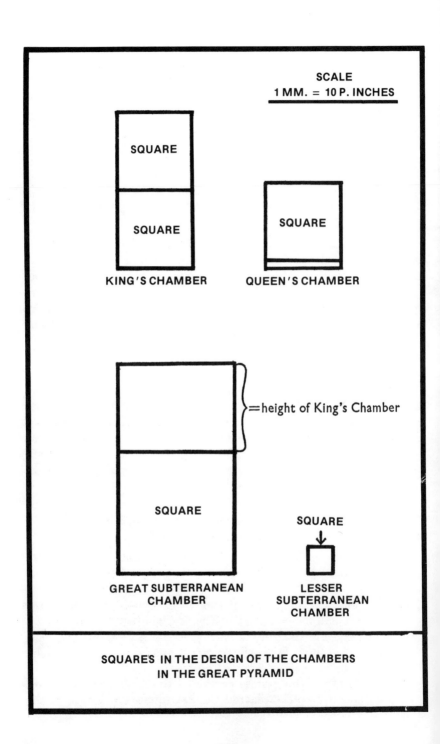

SCALE
1 MM. = 10 P. INCHES

SQUARE

SQUARE

KING'S CHAMBER

SQUARE

QUEEN'S CHAMBER

⎬ = height of King's Chamber

SQUARE

GREAT SUBTERRANEAN
CHAMBER

SQUARE
↓

LESSER
SUBTERRANEAN
CHAMBER

SQUARES IN THE DESIGN OF THE CHAMBERS
IN THE GREAT PYRAMID

side of a square, the area of which equals the area of a triangle of the shape and size of the Pyramid's right section.

(6) The length of the King's Chamber, multiplied by 25 (1 Sacred Cubit) equals an even 100 times the length of the Ante-Chamber's granite floor.

(7) If the length of the granite portion of the Ante-Chamber is multiplied by an even 100, and this length is taken to express the diameter of a circle, the arc of that circle will be found to equal the arc of the square base of the Pyramid.

(8) The height of the Ante-Chamber, multiplied by an even 100, equals the base side length, plus the vertical height, of the Pyramid.

(9) The Ante-Chamber length, multiplied by 50, equals the vertical height of the Pyramid.

The following mathematical proportions are found in the Queen's Chamber:

(1) The height of the north and south walls equals 365.24 and when this figure is multiplied by 25, the answer is 9,131 — the length of the Pyramid's base side.

(2) The height of the side walls bears the same proportion to the width of the Chamber as that width bears to the height of the King's Chamber — 182.62 : 205 : 205 : 230.1.

Another set of mathematical proportions is found in the Niche in the Queen's Chamber. In the horizontal measurements of the niche we find that:

(1) The top course is 1/10th of the King's Chamber width.
(2) The second course is 1/10th of the end wall diagonal.
(3) The third course is 1/10th of the side wall length.
(4) The fourth course is 1/10th of the solid diagonal.

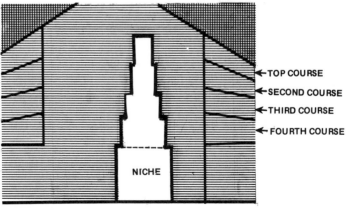

← TOP COURSE
← SECOND COURSE
← THIRD COURSE
← FOURTH COURSE

NICHE

These four measurements of the Niche corroborate the proportions of the King's Chamber and vice versa, affording a strong probability that these were the intended dimensions. In point of fact, the three top courses suffice to confirm all the proportions of the King's Chamber.

(5) The height of the Niche — 1185 P. inches when multiplied by (3.14159) and again by 10, gives 5,813 P. inches. (the approximate height of the Pyramid)

An interesting study of the proportionate sums of the squares of the King's Chamber was done by Mr. James Simpson of Edinburgh, Scotland. From the measurements of the King's Chamber, Mr. Simpson adopted what he thought the most probable numbers for the length, width and height, computed the several diagonals, and prepared the following theoretical numbers for the Chamber in Pyramid inches. (U = half of the width of the King's Chamber)

(Unit = 5 Royal Cubits)

Breadth	=	Unit	×	2	whose square is	4	Sum of squares of rect-
Height	=	,,	×	$\sqrt{5}$	,,	,,	,,	5	angular dimensions,
Length	=	,,	×	4	,,	,,	,,	16	
							25
End Diag.	=	,,	×	3	,,	,,	,,	9	Sum of squares of
Floor ,,	=	,,	×$\sqrt{20}$	,,	,,	,,	20	plane diagonals,
Side ,,	=	,,	×$\sqrt{21}$	,,	,,	,,	21	
							50
Solid ,,	=	,,	×	5	,,	,,	,,	25	Square of solid cubical diagonal 25

Sum of squares of all 7 dimensions 100

Although an examination shows that the Pyramid numerics are geometric, there is one arithmetical number that is prominent in the Pyramid, and that number is 5. The Sacred Cubit itself is comprised of 5 x 5 (25) inches and this inch is the 500,000,000 th part of the earth's axis of rotation. (polar axis) The number 5, and multiples, powers and geometrical proportions of it run through the Great Pyramid and its measure references. Some examples are as follows:

(1) The floor of the Queen's Chamber is 5 times 5 courses of masonry from the base upwards and its measures all answer to a standard of 5 x 5 inches.

(2) The King's Chamber floor is 10 x 5 courses from the base and its walls are composed of 20 x 5 stones, arranged in 5 horizontal courses.

(3) The Pyramid itself has 5 corners (four at the base and one at the apex) and hence it has 5 sides; four equal triangular sides and the square underside on which it stands.

(4) The name "pyramid" comes from the Coptic word "pyr," which means division and the word "met," which means ten, thus suggesting the number 5. The number 5, in the Bible, symbolizes "Grace" and is composed of 4, the number of this world (man) plus 1, the Divine Power. (God) — ("Number in Scripture" by Bullinger) Multiples of 5 were also the dimensions of Noah's Ark, the Wilderness Tabernacle and Solomon's Temple.

Great Pyramid of Giza

O, Sacred Pile, Divinely planned of old
By the Great Architect Who formed the Earth,
Thy truths, long hidden, thou dost now unfold
To those who truly seek to know thy worth.

Preserved, by God's decree, unto this day
Of science, almost deified by man;
When learning based on false theology
Obscures the true revealing of His plan——

Pillar of Light—shed forth thy quickening rays,
Shine o'er our path, for we would learn of thee;
Great Pyramid of Giza, guide our ways,
And grant us now the truth that makes us free.

Mary K. Kernohan

CONSTRUCTION OF THE GREAT PYRAMID'S BASE.

(Hollowing-in of core masonry GREATLY EXAGGERATED to show effect.)

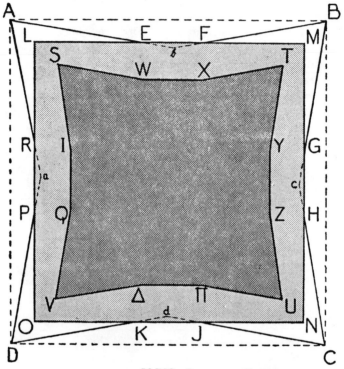

LMNO—Base as actually built.
SWXTYZUΠΔVQI—Base of core masonry.

AB = 365.242 Sacred Cubits = Number of days in the solar year.
AEFB = 365.256 ,, ,, = ,, ,, ,, sidereal year.
AbB = 365.259 ,, ,, = ,, ,, ,, anomalistic year.
The same arrangement holds good on all four sides of the Pyramid, hence the three complete circuits, ABCD, AEFBGHCJKDPR, AbBcCdDa also bear the same ratio to each other as the three astronomical years, i.e., 365.242 : 365.256 : 365.259.

Davidson

PLAN OF THE BASE OF THE PYRAMID
SHOWING THREE DIFFERENT WAYS OF MEASURING THE YEAR'S LENGTH

CHAPTER 14.

ASTRONOMICAL YEARS

The base circuit of the Great Pyramid contains still a greater wonder. As our Earth has three separate lengths of years, namely (1) the solar tropical year, (2) the sidereal year, and (3) the anomalistic year, so were the baselines and walls of the Great Pyramid constructed, with three different lengths of circumferences.

The measurements designing the three astronomical years were noted by Sir Flinders Petrie in his survey of the Pyramid. In the central portion of each face of the Pyramid there is a distinct hollowing of the core masonry. Hidden by the original straight planes of the exterior casing stones of the Pyramid, they would never have been revealed except for the removal of the casing stones. These different cycles have to do with the earth and its relationship to both the stars and the sun.

The Earth rotates on a plane inclined to the ecliptic. This motion from west to east every 24 hours gives us day and night and occurs at the rate of 1,000 miles per hour at the Equator. While spinning like a top, the earth is also racing in its orbit around the sun anticlockwise at the much higher rate of speed of 1,000 miles per minute. The tilt of the Earth's axis is the period where the sun appears to pass over the Earth 365.24235 times or days between the Vernal Equinoxes.

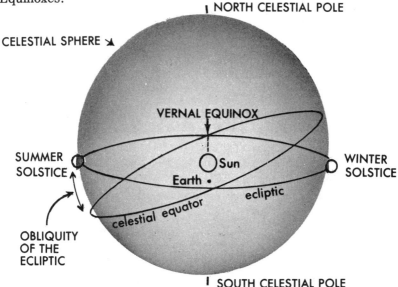

149

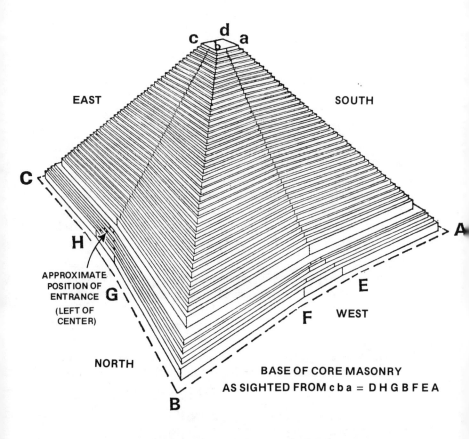

EAST

SOUTH

C

A

H

APPROXIMATE
POSITION OF
ENTRANCE G
(LEFT OF
CENTER)

E

F WEST

NORTH

BASE OF CORE MASONRY
AS SIGHTED FROM c b a = D H G B F E A

B

**HOLLOWING OF PYRAMID' SIDES EXAGGERATED
DEPTHS OF COURSE MAGNIFIED AND IN CONSEQUENCE
NUMBER OF COURSES REDUCED**

The sidereal year is the interval between the Earth's position at any time in the year, in relation to the fixed stars, and its return to that position. In other words, the star-heavens appear to pass over the Earth 365.25636 times during the circuit. This difference of about 20 minutes is due to the Earth's slow rotation clockwise, thus causing the solar tropical year to be shorter.

The anomalistic year is the interval between successive annual returns of the Earth to the point — defined as the perihelion — in its orbit nearest the sun. (Jan. 2-3) This requires 365.25986 days, or about five minutes longer than the sidereal year, due to the motion of the Earth's orbit.

This period of time varies, being greater or less depending on from what stage of its movement it is calculated. Modern science gives the cycle as approximately 26,000 years. It is noted that the sum of the two diagonals of the Pyramid's full designed base (12,913.27 pyramid inches) x 2 = 25,826.54, a figure considered by some scholars to represent the precessional cycle.

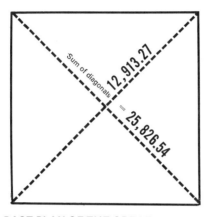

BASE PLAN OF THE GREAT PYRAMID

There are other remarkable examples of interlocking mathematical solar distances found in the design of the Pyramid, demonstrating the Architect to have preceded modern astronomers by over 4000 years.

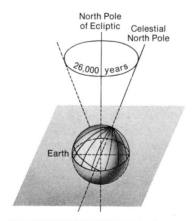

THE PRECESSION OF THE EQUINOXES

151

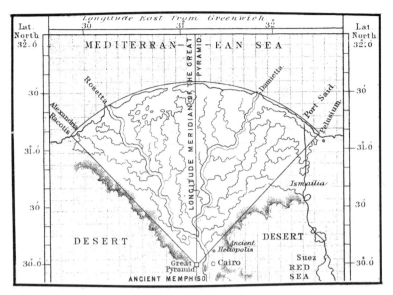

With regards to its astronomical position, it seems the builders intended to place the Pyramid as close as possible to latitude 30°, or, in other words, in that latitude where the true pole of the heavens is one-third of the way from the horizon to the point overhead (the zenith), and where the noon sun at true spring or autumn (when the sun rises almost exactly in the east, and sets almost exactly in the west) is two-thirds of the way from the horizon to the point overhead. Star observations, made from this position, would simplify many problems in the geometrical construction of the Pyramid.

That the Great Pyramid was constructed in accordance with astronomical observations of great accuracy is beyond doubt. And to achieve such exactness without modern scientific instruments is, seemingly, unbelievable.

By its vast hugeness mind and eye are dazed
And into silence awed. We stare and stand,
Striving in vain to grasp how it was raised —
To comprehend the skill by which 'twas planned.
Pigmies in mind and stature, stunned, amazed,
We stand and feel before that structure grand —
The mightiest Altar that has ever been,
Which cannot be imagined until seen.

Charles Casey

CHAPTER 15.

SCIENTIFIC FEATURES

Many features of the Great Pyramid exhibit design on the part of the Architect to embody relative scientific distance, weights and measurements in parts of the structure where they could not be overlooked. A few will be mentioned here, but only in briefest detail:

(1) The sun's distance from the Earth: For over 2,500 years man has struggled to solve this problem. The Greeks, in 500 B.C., judged the distance to be about ten miles, later guessing it to be more like 2,000 miles. In later centuries, man estimated it farther and farther away, until in the 16th century it had increased to 36,000,000 miles. The latest figures of modern astronomy give 92,900,000 miles as the sun's mean distance from the Earth. As there was absolutely no way of calculating this until our "space age," scientists were astounded to discover that built into the Great Pyramid's base plans was a figure approximating 92,000,000 miles.

This figure was arrived at by the discovery of the proper scale applied to the construction of the Pyramid. It was known that the four lines from the corner sockets to the apex of the Pyramid sloped inward 10 feet for every 9 feet of elevation. This suggested a possible equation. Multiplying the height of the Pyramid by 10, nine times, and reducing the result to miles, gave the astonishing result of 91,856,060 miles.

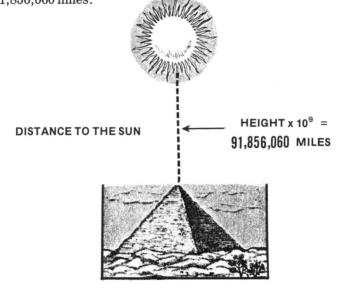

DISTANCE TO THE SUN

HEIGHT x 10^9 =
91,856,060 MILES

Two other simple equations produce approximately the same result; (1) Multiplying the number of the Earth's polar diameter, as expressed in inches, by twice the Pyramid's vertical height. (2) Multiplying the Pyramid's vertical height by the number, expressed in Pyramid inches, of twice the Earth's polar diameter.

(2) The mean density of the Earth: The true mean density or specific gravity of the Earth has also been an age-old problem. An average of prominent tests has placed it at 5,672 times the weight of water at 68 Fahrenheit. The Coffer in the King's Chamber appears to have been designed to show the mean density of the earth. Taking the cubic contents of the Coffer in Pyramid inches (71,250) and dividing it by the 10th part of 50 P. inches cubed (12,500) we arrive at a figure of 5.70, a figure closely aproximating the modern day average estimate.

cubic|contents|
71,250 inches

(3) The weight of the Earth: knowing the density of the Earth enabled physicists to ascertain its weight to be approximately 5,300,000,000,000,000,000,000 (U.S.A. — about six billion trillion) tons. The Earth's weight and the weight of the Great Pyramid were found to be proportionately related to one another. The Pyramid's weight of approximately 5,300,000 tons has been noted to be 1,000,000,000,000,000 (U.S.A. — one thousand trillionth) the weight of the Earth. Considering the many other scientific features incorporated in the design of the Great Pyramid, it is not unreasonable to assume that the Architect used this proportion to indicate the weight of the Earth.

(4) The volume of the Earth's crust above mean sea-level: The vast amount of surveying necessary to determine the average height of all the land on earth would have been an impossible task even a few hundred years ago. With the advent of aerial photography and the accumulation of data from continuing geological surveys, together with modern computers, an estimate is now given as approximately 455 feet. The top of the Pyramid, as the builders left it unfinished, is fully 454½ feet.

(5) The mean ocean level of the Earth: The mean ocean level was found to be approximately 193 feet 7 inches below the base line

of the Great Pyramid. Again, modern computers and the findings of modern oceanography were required to ascertain this figure. And again, the design of the Great Pyramid foretold this fact. It was found that taking twice the diameter (1,162.6″) of a circle having a circumference of 3,652.42″ (a circle related to the solar year and base circuit of the Pyramid) gave a result of 2325.2″, or just slightly over 193 feet 7 inches.

(6) The rotundity of the Earth: The rotundity, or curvature, of the earth was found recorded in the Great Pyramid by surveying the side baseline of the Pyramid. Due to the hollowed-in core masonry, (35.76 P. inches on each side) a curved line was produced. Computations were made to ascertain how long the radius would be that would produce a circle containing that curve. The resulting answer was that the radius would be approximately half the diameter of the Earth. This shows that the Great Pyramid, based upon the geometry of the year cycle is in harmony with the Earth's design.

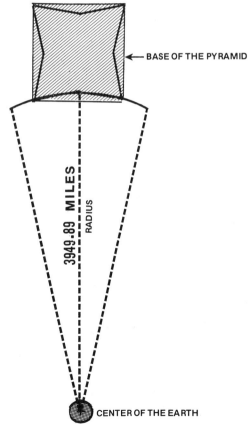

BASE OF THE PYRAMID

3949.89 MILES
RADIUS

CENTER OF THE EARTH

(7) The mean temperature of the Earth: As the Great Pyramid stands on the line which equally divided the surface of the northern hemisphere, there is a relationship between its climate and the mean temperature of all the Earth's surface. This temperature is about 68 degrees Fahrenheit. In the Pyramid this temperature is maintained permanently and unvarying in the King's Chamber. The two air channels, when cleaned of sand, were found to keep this chamber at the normal or mean temperature, which is exactly one-fifth of the distance between the freezing and boiling points of water. Scientists say that 68 degrees Fahrenheit is the ideal temperature for the existance of man. (To convert the 68 (degrees) into a "pyramidal" value, place zero - 0 and the boiling point of water at 250, and it is found that 68 equals the symbolical number of 50 Pyramid degrees)

(8) The Key to its own locations: The Great Pyramid's peculiar passage angle (26° 18' 9.7") tells its location more accurately than can a surveyor's sextant. An imaginary line extending from the Pyramid's entrance passage out into space, would cross the earth's axis of rotation at a distance precisely 7 earth diameters away from the center of the Earth. If the Pyramid were built even 100 feet away from its site, or if the passage angle were minutely different, or if the Earth were a fraction larger or smaller — this remarkable property would be lost.

Any of the above scientific relationships, if taken alone, would appear to be just coincidence. However, when considered together with the geometric, mathematical and astronomical relationships found in the construction of the Great Pyramid, it is more probable that they were purposely built into the Pyramid to express known knowledge.

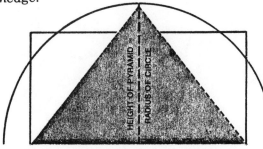

Now, the question can be asked, how did π (pi) and the Copernican system of astronomy come to be used in the Great Pyramid? — Built into its very structure as a constituted part of the immense mass, repeated over and over again in a variety of forms. and antedating, (so far as we know) by thousands of years, the knowledge that either such a mathematical quantity or astronomical system existed? How can all this science found in the Great Pyramid be accounted for? If it cannot be accounted for in any other way, is it unreasonable to ascribe to superhuman or Divine aid, what human aid was inadequate to accomplish?

The Divine Great Pyramid

When God of old devised this Plan,
As witness and a guide to man,
He based His symbols and His signs
On truly scientific lines;
For well He knew that in the end,
Would science and religion blend.

Thus for our benefit is shown,
The Bible symbolised in stone.
And if God's Holy Book you love,
And wish Jehovah's words to prove,
His myst'ries can be seen, long hid,
In The Divine Great Pyramid.

Amy Frances Cox

THE PARTHENON ON THE ACROPOLIS IN ATHENS

CHAPTER 16.

THE GOLDEN SECTION

Another phenomenon of the Great Pyramid is that it incorporates the proportion known as the "Golden Section" or "Golden Number." (Sometimes referred to as the "Golden Rule of Architecture") This proportion is based on the fact that the human eye recognizes that certain shapes of rectangles seem aesthetically more satisfactory than others. The rectangular shapes most pleasing to the eye seem to be those whose length bears to its width the ratio (V5 +1) 2, or 1.618+, the same ratio in fact, as the sum of both dimensions will then bear to the length alone.

$$\frac{n}{N} = \frac{N}{n+N}$$

The Egyptians, Cretans and the Greeks were familiar with the principles of the proportion that is today designated by the Greek letter ϕ (pronounced phi) and equals 1.618+. Such architectural masterpieces as the Parthenon on the Acropolis, at Athens, conform to it, but not with the high degree of mathematical precision to be found in the Pyramid of Giza, built over 2,000 years earlier. ϕ, like π, cannot be worked out arithmetically, but it can be easily obtained with nothing more than a compass and a straight-edge.

The Great Pyramid embodies a direct expression of the approximate relationship between the quantities of π (3.14159+) and ϕ (1.61803+). Approximation is, of course, inevitable, since both numbers are irrational. Other approximate expressions of the $\pi : \phi$ relationship are $\pi/4 = 1 \phi$ and $5/6 = \phi 2$. The appearance of the ϕ ratio is the consequence of the Architect's choice of a four-sided pyramid incorporating the π angle of 51° 51′ 14.3″ as its angle of slope.

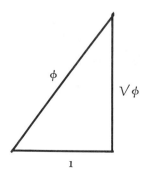

The Golden Section, when worked out, turns out to be the cosine of the angle of the Great Pyramid, expressed as correct to three decimal places, namely .618. In other words, the ratio that the distance from the center of the Pyramid's base out to each of the four sides bears to the oblique height of the Pyramid's faces is precisely the Architect's Golden Section or Number.

The Golden Section, or ϕ is obtained by dividing a line:

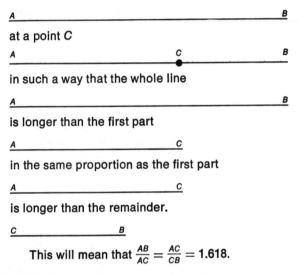

at a point C

in such a way that the whole line

is longer than the first part

in the same proportion as the first part

is longer than the remainder.

This will mean that $\frac{AB}{AC} = \frac{AC}{CB} = 1.618$.

In the Great Pyramid the rectangular floor of the King's Chamber (which consists of two equal squares, or a 1 x 2 rectangle) also serves to illustrate and to obtain the Golden Section:

If you split one of the two squares in half and swing the diagonal down to the base, the point where the diagonal touches the base will be ϕ or 1.618 in relation to the side of the square, which is 1: *

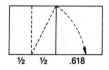

½   ½   .618

* Pythagoras' theorem will also show that the value of φ will be 1/2 + √5/2, or 1.618, and that φ — 1 will be .618.

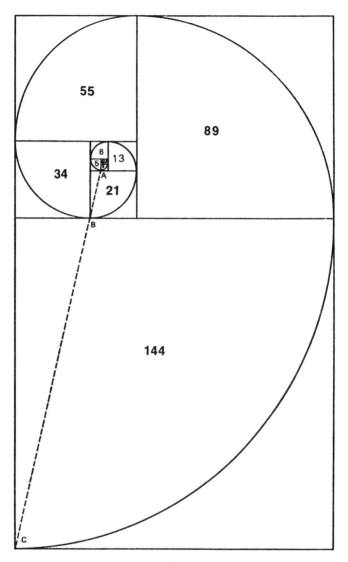

The above figure is the Logarithmic Spiral based on the Fibonacci
Series. The radius of each quarter-turn of the spiral is determined by
the length of side of the square in which it is inscribed, and the
value of this for each succeeding square is in turn determined by the
Fibonacci Series.

The Golden Section ϕ has several remarkable mathematical properties. For example, its square is equal to itself plus one, while its reciprocal equals itself minus one. Another intriguing feature is its relationship with the so-called "Fibonacci Series." The Fibonacci Series is the sequence of numbers in which each number is equal to the sum of the previous two: 1-2-3-5-8-13-21-34-55-89-144 etc. When plotted diagramatically, it provides the mathematical formula for the construction of a logarithmic spiral which is also found in nature. (Ex. the shell of the Nautilus — see diagram, pg. 161) This phenomenon is found in surprising frequency in patterns of plant growth, in flower-petal arrangements and fir-cone design.

The ratio between each member of the Fibonacci Series and its successor varies between one and infinity; but the further up the series one goes, the more the ratio tends to settle down toward a more-or-less constant figure. Investigation reveals that this constant figure is none other than ϕ or 1.61803+.

With the incorporation of the Golden Section ϕ the Great Pyramid provides an effective system for translating spherical areas into flat ones. Because of the Pyramid's structure it is possible to draw a rectangle (from the base of the Pyramid and twi·e its height) which will be equal in area to a circle on its height. This leads directly to being able to draw a rectangle or triangle equal to a spherical quadrant, resolving the main problem of the map maker with the same simplicity.

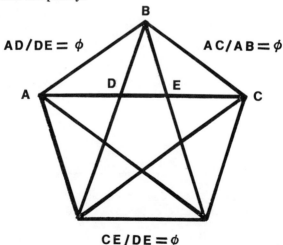

CHART SHOWING THE PENTAGON AND FIVE POINTED STAR

The following chart demonstrates the squaring of the circle of the Pyramid:

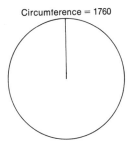

By adding three more lines, a mathematically correct cross section of the Pyramid is shown:

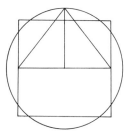

Then, by simply enclosing the diagram in another square and inserting the relationship as it exists in the Pyramid, a formula is obtained for readily translating sperical surfaces into flat ones of equal area.

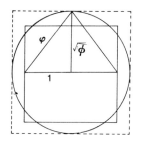

Next, by extending the two sides of the smaller square till they touch the sides of the larger square, we obtain a rectangle equal in area to the basic circle.

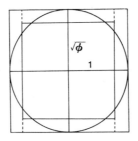

The area of the rectangle is its length times its width, or $2\sqrt{\phi}$ x 2 which is $4\sqrt{\phi}$.

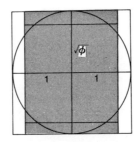

The area of the circle is πr^2 , or $\pi\phi$ in this case, the radius being $\sqrt{\phi}$. But since $\pi = \sqrt{4}$, the area is also $4\sqrt{\phi}$, the same as the rectangle.

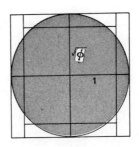

Therefore, the Great Pyramid demonstrates it is possible, with virtually no mathematics to draw a rectangle (from the base of the Pyramid and twice its height) which will be equal in area to a circle on its height. This leads directly to being able to draw a rectangle or triangle equal to a spherical quadrant. As the whole circle equals the whole rectangle, half the circle equals half the rectangle:

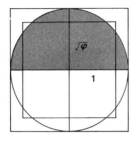 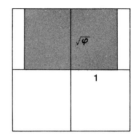

And half a flat circle is also mathematically equal in area to the spherical surface of a quadrant of 90 :

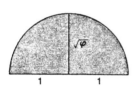 

Thus a rectangle of height   and a base of 2 is equal to a quadrant of height   and an arc of 2:

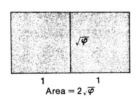 

As demonstrated by the Great Pyramid, it is possible to translate a spherical quadrant of 90 or longitude onto a flat Mercator surface of equal area or onto an undistorted triangle of exactly half that area. The Architect of the Great Pyramid not only squared the circle but effectively cubed the sphere.

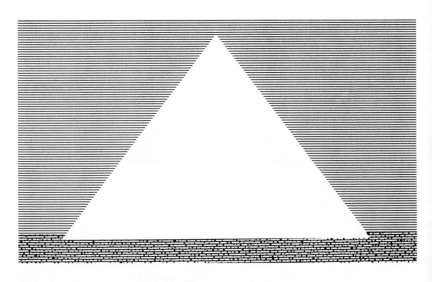

Behold this mighty beauteous wonder!
O Pyramid of God's own splendour.
O mighty glorious altar so dear,
Let us hear, let us know of thy secrets made clear.

What a glorious sight to behold;
What marvellous mysteries now unfold.
God's hidden plan revealed to man,
From ages past, at last made known.

Every stone, every inch of thy marvellous being
Are glories, are secrets our hearts are now seeing.
He drew His plan for all mankind
And left it there for us to find.

Thy casing stones of dazzling white
All shining with a heavenly light
Reflect the glories hid within
Reflect the beauty that is Him.

What glories, what secrets, what marvellous truths
Have you held for these many long years.
But now, praise to God, you speak loud and clear
As His Kingdom and glorious Reign nears.

                                        Dixielee Errico.

CHAPTER 17.

WHO WERE THE BUILDERS?

Manetho, the Egyptian priest and scribe, is quoted by Josephus and others, as saying, "We had formerly a king whose name was Timaus. In his time it came to pass, I know not how, that the Deity was displeased with us. And there came up from the East in a strange manner men of an ignoble race, who had the confidence to invade our country, and easily subdued it by their power without a battle. And when they had our leaders in their hands they demolished the temples of the gods." This King Timaus of Manetho may have referred to Cheops during whose reign the Great Pyramid was built.

Manetho continues, "All this nation was styled Hycsos, the Shepherd Kings. The first syllable, 'hyc,' according to the sacred dialect, denoted a king, and the 'sos' signified a shepherd according to the vulgar tongue; and of these is compounded the term Hycsos. Some say they were Arabians." Manetho wrote about 300 years before Christ and some authorities hold that Manetho mixed up the history of another set of shepherd kings of a much later dynasty. However, the ground of his story belongs to the period of Cheops and the Great Pyramid, for it was then that the events he relates occurred; the control of the reigning sovereigns by a shepherd prince, the temples closed, the gods destroyed and the people pressed into labor for the government.

Archbishop Ussher, the noted Church historian, in his chronology, refers to the migration of the Shepherd Kings from Arabia into Egypt. From Ussher and other authorities, it seems that some "Shepherd-Prince coming from Arabia or Palestine was enabled to exert such an amount of mental control over King Cheops as to induce the King to shut up the idolatrous temples and compel his subjects to labor in the erection of the Great Pyramid." Under this "Shepherd-Prince," Egypt's national religion was overturned in favor of the more simple worship of the One True God.

Upon completion of the Great Pyramid, ancient writings of the historians say that the "foreign" people withdrew and their departure was the cause of great rejoicing among the Egyptians. The restraint being removed, the people returned with fresh zest to their idolatrous practices.

Because chronology and the findings of archaeology have established the date of the start of the building of the Great Pyramid at 2623 B.C., many Egyptologists have disputed the Hyksos identity of the builders. They have labeled a much later date for the invasion of Egypt by the Hyksos and assigned a period of 1800 - 1500 B.C., as their domination of parts of Egypt. However, it is generally agreed that the beginnings of the Hyksos control of Egypt are obscure and that during the period of the Third and Fourth Dynasties, the Egyptians furnished the labor for the erection of several pyramids, culminating in the Great Pyramid.

Living in Arabia, at the time of the building of the Great Pyramid, were descendants of Seth, of whom Josephus wrote, "They were the inventors of the peculiar sort of wisdom which is concerned with the heavenly bodies and their order. And that their inventions might not be lost before they were sufficiently known... they made two pillars, the one of brick, the other of stone; they inscribed their discoveries on them both..." Josephus goes on to state that the pillar of stone "remains in the land of Siriad to this day." (A.D. 37-95) Siriad would indicate the Siriadic, or Sirius-worshipping land of Egypt, where Sirius was venerated as the star of Isis.

CANIS MAJOR (the Dog)

Herodotus, who made inquiries of the Egyptian priests regarding the builders of the Great Pyramid was also told the builders were strangers to Egypt and told of a particular individual who played an important part in the construction. The precise words recorded by Herodotus are: "They commonly call the pyramids after Philition, a shepherd who at that time fed his flocks about the place." (Rawlinson's Herodotus, vol. 2, pg. 176) Other ancient historians made reference to Philition, sometimes called "Philitis," indicating he came from Philistia. (Palestine)

Some authorities on the Great Pyramid have suggested that Philitis was none other than Melchizedek, King of Salem, to whom Abraham paid tithes. This thought is based on Manetho's statement that the "Arabians" (meaning the builders) when they left Egypt, instead of returning to Arabia, went to "that country now called Judea, and there built a city and named it Jerusalem." It is quite possible that Philitis was the founder and builder of Jerusalem and the original founder of the Divinely ordained order of the Melchizedek Priesthood, which was still in power in Jerusalem 500 years later, in Abraham's day. We note that Abraham paid reverence and tithes, and from Melchizedek he accepted blessings and communion; one who was called "priest of the Most High God." With reference to his character and office, the Bible calls him "Melchizedek," plainly a descriptive and not a proper name, he being first "King of Righteousness" and after that also "King of Salem." (Heb. 7:1,2) Thus, it is more likely Abraham paid tithes to a "descendant" of the Melchizedek Priesthood Dynasty.

JERUSALEM

It is significant that a conspicuous stranger to Egypt, possessed of flocks and herds, sojourned about the locality of the Great Pyramid for all the years it was being built. Then, centuries later, the Egyptian priests considered him its real originator and architect, Cheops merely furnishing the site, the workmen and materials.

If the ancient historians are correct that "Philition" or "Philitis" came from Arabia and of the people descended from Seth, then we may look to the Scriptures for his identification.

The greatest and mightiest population of ancient Arabia was mainly, if not exclusively, of pre-Abrahamic Shemitic stock. The Tribes which possessed it were mostly of the seed of Joktan, son of Eber, till the descendants of Abraham through Esau and Keturah and the descendants of Lot began to fill in from the northwest. These "Joktanites" were the true Arabians, and the superior people who planted their colonies in Eastern Africa, around the whole eastern coast of the Mediterranean and Jerah, from whom we have the name "Arabia, the land of Jerah."

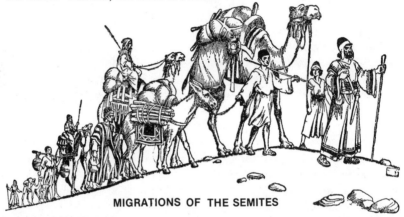

MIGRATIONS OF THE SEMITES

Joktan had thirteen sons; the eldest was Almodad, (Elmodad in the Septuagint Text, meaning "God is a friend") whose name in Hebrew means "the Measurer." Almodad is described in the Chaldaic Paraphrase of Johanthan as the inventor of Geometry and the Measurer of the Earth, and certainly the Great Pyramid was constructed according to a marvelous geometric design. Job, the youngest son of Joktan is also mentioned in connection with the building of the Great Pyramid. In the 38th chapter of the Book of Job, the Almighty speaks to Job as if he were the identical person who had laid the measures of the Pyramid, stretched the lines upon it, set its foundations in their sockets, and laid the corner stone.

In Job 38:4-7 we read *"Where wast thou when I laid the foundations of the earth? declare, if thou hast understanding. Who hath laid the measures thereof, if thou knowest? or who hath stretched the line upon it? Whereupon are the foundations* (Marg., sockets) *thereof fastened? or who laid the corner stone thereof: When the*

170

morning stars sang together, and all the sons of God shouted for joy?" It is obvious that if the creation of the earth is here alluded to, it is described under a type of something else, and not as the earth really was created. The same book of Job describes creation in the following words, *"He stretcheth out the north over the empty place, and hangeth the earth upon nothing."* (Job 26:7)

"In the beginning, God created the heavens and the earth."

The first parts of Job 38 might apply to the building of any ordinary house, but as successive practical features are enumerated, the building of a stone pyramid by careful measure, and on a previously prepared platform of rock, is the only known work that will fully correspond. The stretching of the line "upon" it, is more applicable to the inclined surface of a pyramid with an angle to the horizon of 51° 51′ 14.3″, than to the vertical walls of any ordinary house.

It appears the object of the passage in Job 38: is to convince Job of his incompetency to judge and understand God. The address seems to sound as if the Creator intended to say to him, "You laid the foundations of the great structure in Egypt, but where were you when I laid the foundation of the far greater pyramid of the earth? You laid the measures on the pyramid in Egypt, but who laid the measures on the earth and stretched the line upon it?" You fastened down in sockets the foundation of the pyramid in Egypt, but where-upon are the foundations of the earth fastened? You laid the corner stone amid songs and jubilations, but who laid the cornerstone of the earth when the celestial morning stars sang together, and all the heavenly sons of God shouted for joy?"

The image is unquestionably that of the Great Pyramid and is

171

suggestive that it was the builder of that pyramid who is thus addressed. However, the conversation between Job and God does not necessarily mean that Job was the chief builder, only that he completed some of the necessary layout. Other members of the Joktan family could have been involved. The second son of Joktan was called "Sheleph" and was represented by the Chaldaic paraphrase of Jonathan as "one who drew off the waters from the rivers." "Saleph" (Heb.) means "to draw out" or "to draw off." These terms could apply to "drawing off" the waters of the Nile.

About the time of the building of the Great Pyramid there existed a great man-made basin known as the Lake of Moeris, which served as a storage for water diverted from the Nile River during unusual flooding. Herodotus describes the lake as having a circumference equaling about 223 English miles and depth of about 300 feet. Herodotus wrote, "That water which is in the lake, is not native to the place, for the land is excessively dry; but it is conveyed by a trench from the Nile; six months it flows inward into the lake, (a distance of 10 miles) and six months outward into the Nile again." (Herodotus 11, 149)

In 1845, M. Linant de Bellefonds discovered the actual site of the lake. In earlier times it appeared to have been a natural basin, enlarged by digging, but reduced today in size to about 92 miles in circumference; its modern size and depth of only 25 English feet being due to deposits left everytime the waters of the Nile subsided. M. Linant also discovered parts of the trench that diverted water from the Nile into the lake and remnants of a lateral trench, or fosse, that would carry the side stream into the river again. By means of dikes, water was stored in the lake or allowed to run back into the river, exactly as alluded to by Herodotus.

M. Linant estimated that "the high water brought into the Lake Moeris by the Bahr Yousef (the canal) during a high inundation, was the twenty-eighth part of the total flow of the Nile. Therefore it can be imagined that, by directing so considerable a flow of the river, it was possible to prevent the damage sustained at that period from the superabundant overflow . . . Thus the Lake Moeris would fulfill the objective attributed to it by the historical traditions."

Modern engineers who have studied the Lake Moeris scheme say the greatness of the work is incredible for the period in which the project was built. A large labor force would have taken several years to complete and be directed by one highly knowledgeable in engineering and construction. Such a project would have been beneficial to the inhabitants of Egypt as well as for the builders of the Pyramid who were dependent on the Nile River for the conveyance of stone from the quarries. One can believe it was the work of Sheleph, the second son of Joktan, and done during the ten years of preparation work on the site of the Great Pyramid.

Peleg, the uncle of Almodad (Gen. 10:25-26) and the son of Eber, or Heber, (whose descendants became known as Hebrews) was also contemporary with the building of the Great Pyramid. We read of Peleg; "in his day was the earth divided." (Gen. 10:25; I Chron. 1:19) Since the Earth is incapable of separation from something else, we must conceive some division of the Earth which would not destroy its unity. A division effected geometrically, such as into degrees, minutes and seconds would be applicable to the expression, "was divided." The location of the Great Pyramid which divides the land surfaces of the world into equal parts — all the land east of the meridian on which the Pyramid stands being equal (within the limits of computation) to the west of it, is physical application of that expression.

Another personage whose name is often linked to the building of the Great Pyramid is Enoch, the seventh from Adam, (Jude 14) who lived 365 years, (Gen. 5:23) and perhaps to be more exact (since there are 365.242 days in a year — a prophetic 'day') 365.242 years, the value of the solar year. Ancient historians have referred to the Great Pyramid as the "Pillar of Enoch" and the circle formed in the Ante-Chamber as the "Enoch Circle." (described in Chapter 18) This "Enoch Circle" of 365.242353 units pervades the entire structure and constitutes the basis upon which the entire geometric design of the Great Pyramid is constructed.

The Apocryphal Book of Enoch, compiled about the 2nd century B.C., speaks of Enoch as having received from God a scientific revelation as well as a prophetic or spiritual one. Included in the revelation was information concerning the courses and times of the heavenly bodies. (stars and their cycles) From its Polar Star orientation to its defining the Precession of the equinoxes, the Great Pyramid is replete with astronomical features. And it is the symbolism of the Enoch Circle that reveals the prophetic revelations (covered in Chapter 20) of the Pyramid.

Since Enoch's "age" was from the 43rd to the 40th century B.C. he was no longer living on the Earth at the time of the building of the Great Pyramid. Scientific and prophetic information found in the Pyramid (attributed to Enoch) was most probably passed on from Enoch to his descendants, through Noah and his son Shem, and his descendants, the Joktan family. No doubt the Sacred Cubit was among the revelations from Enoch, and was employed by Noah in the building of the Ark. After its use in the Great Pyramid, this Cubit was employed by Moses in construction of the Wilderness Tabernacle, and later by King Solomon in the erection of the Temple at Jerusalem.

One other nominee for builder of the Great Pyramid is Shem, the eldest of the sons of Noah. Jewish tradition has it that Shem was Melchizedek, King of Salem, (also called Jerusalem) If so, he could have been the Shepherd Patriarch "Philition" of the Egyptian writers and the founder of the Melchizedek dynasty. The word "Philition" is a Greek word and appears to be compounded of "Philo" meaning "I love" and "ithus" meaning "upright," "just," or "equitable."

Based upon the Chronology of the Massoretic Text, Shem would have lived during the period of building of the Great Pyramid; however, modern chronology places him before the building of the Pyramid. It has been determined that the Massoretes systematically subtracted a hundred years from the times of each of the Patriarchs, in nearly every instance. The Septuagint, the Samaritan Text and in some instances Josephus' chronology, which all give the longer Chronology, have been found compatible with the Dead Sea Scrolls. The longer chronology places the Flood at 3145 B.C. Since Shem begat Arphaxad two years after the Flood and lived a further 500 years (Gen. 11:10-11) he would have died 502 years after the Flood, or 2643 B.C. This would be 20 years before the start of the building of the Pyramid. If this be the case, then Shem could have prepared the architectural design of the Great Pyramid before his death, and arranged to have it constructed by his immediate descendants.

The absolute identity of the builder or builders of the Great Pyramid remains one of its hidden secrets. No archaeological or historical evidence can be pointed to that would positively identify a single individual. Based on the evidence we have, we can conclude that we have a descendant of Shem (if not himself) as the builder. Whether Shem was living at the time of the building of the Pyramid is questionable but cannot be entirely ruled out. A little refinement of Chronology might place Shem in the time frame. However, it is most probable that Joktan, his thirteen sons and their uncle Peleg as a group constituted the builders.

CHAPTER 18.

WHO WAS THE ARCHITECT?

The Great Pyramid, which has stood at the border of the great Sahara Desert as a silent witness for more than 4,000 years, now speaks in modern scientific terms. Erected at a time when humanity had more crude ideas of this universe and even of our own Earth, this "witness" could not be understood before this present scientific age.

The perfect accuracy of all the various geodetic and astronomical statistics which man was unable to ascertain until modern times, after the development of trigonometrical knowledge and the invention of modern appliances, is evidence of Divine Revelation. The fact that the interior arrangements of the Pyramid are built up from the functions of " π " and "y" in Polar diameter inches is scientific evidence that He who designed the universe is the Architect of the Great Pyramid.

Notwithstanding the fact that no nation of antiquity on earth possessed the knowledge revealed by the design of the Great Pyramid or understood it, some may reject its Divine Inspiration. God seemingly anticipated man's need for additional evidential value of the Great Pyramid's Divine testimony and gave a line of proof which cannot be anticipated or counterfeited. God gave the test, which we are to apply, in Isaiah 46:9-10: *"I am God, and there is none like Me, declaring the end from the beginning, and from ancient times, the things that are not yet done..."* If it can be shown that the design of the Great Pyramid embodies a prophetic chronology, then we have the very evidence which God Himself has declared shall be proof that the design is from Him.

A suggestion for looking for this prophetic message in the Great Pyramid was revealed in the translation of an ancient Arabic writing, the Akbar Ezzeman MS., which states that the Great Pyramid contains "the wisdom and acquirements in the different arts and sciences... the sciences of arithmetic and geometry, that they might remain as records for the benefit of those who could afterwards comprehend them... the positions of the stars and their cycles; *together with the history and chronicle of the time past* (and) *of that which is to come."* Because the Pyramid dates from the dawn of history, such a chronology must be an anticipation of the future, recorded in stone centuries before fulfillment.

The factual evidence that the Great Pyramid does contain a prophetic message in chronology can be demonstrated from the actual passage lengths of the Pyramid, lengths proportionate to the respective ages which they represent. This remarkable discovery was made possible by a study of the geometric circle upon which the Great Pyramid is designed; the year circle, sometimes referred to as the "Enoch Circle." This circle, found by drawing a circle whose diameter equals the length of the Ante-Chamber in the Pyramid, produced a circumference of 365.242 P. inches.

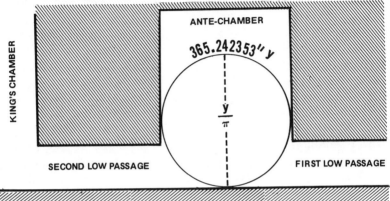

The circumference of 365.242 is not only the exact number of days in our Solar Year; it was also the number of years, expressed in decimals, that Enoch lived on earth, that is, 365 years, 88 days, 9 hours. Thus P. inches may be expressed in terms of years — 1 P. inch = 1 year. The origin of the scale of the Biblical chronological prophecy 1 day = 1 year is also traced back to the Enoch Circle in the Great Pyramid, which was built over 1000 years before the Bible was written.

In establishing a prophetic chronology it is necessary to have a starting point. Several unique factors determine this starting point in the Great Pyramid. Down the Descending Passage, at a distance of about 40 feet from the Entrance, there are found, on the side wall, straight knife-edge lines cut from roof to floor, one on each side and exactly opposite each other. Their appearance on the otherwise smooth walls of the passage certainly suggests that they are intended as a clear zero line, or "datum line" from which to take measurements. They are called the "Scored Lines."

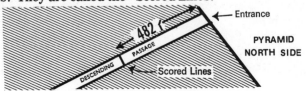

176

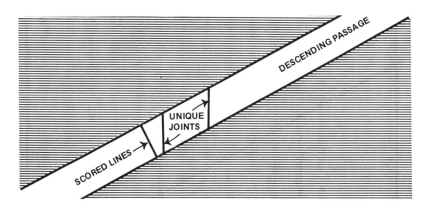

The possibility of the Scored Lines having astronomical bearings was raised by early investigators of the Pyramid because, it had been determined that the axis of the Descending Passage was exactly aligned with the Dragon Star, (Draconis) which was the Pole Star when the Pyramid was built. The determination of what date in history the Scored Lines represent was made by the famous astronomer, Sir John Herschel. (Astronomer Royal of Great Britain) His astronomical research revealed that these lines were in alignment with the star Alcyone of the Pleiades (the Seven Sisters) in the constellation of Taurus the Bull, at noon of the spring equinox (March 21st) of 2141 B.C. The years 2140 B.C. and 2142 B.C. were both found to be well outside the limits of error permissible, thus fixing 2141 B.C. as absolute.

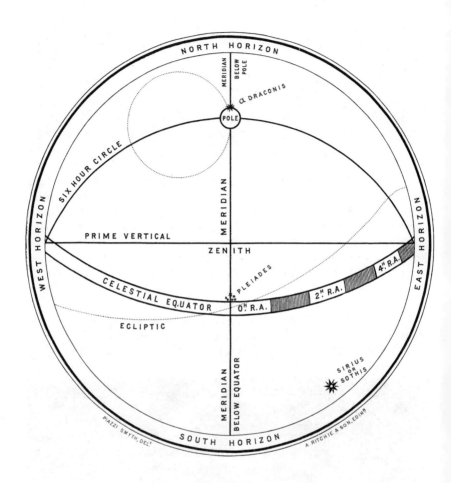

GROUND PLAN OF THE
CIRCLES OF THE HEAVENS ABOVE THE GREAT PYRAMID, AT ITS EPOCH
OF FOUNDATION, AT MIDNIGHT OF AUTUMNAL EQUINOX
2141 B.C.)
α DRACONIS ON MERIDIAN BELOW POLE, AT ENTRANCE PASSAGE ANGLE;
AND PLEIADES ON MERIDIAN ABOVE POLE IN 0ʰ R.A.;
OR COINCIDENTLY WITH VERNAL EQUINOX.

The Pleiades or Seven Sisters (stars) are referred to in the book of Job. (38:31) *"Canst thou bind the sweet influences of Pleiades, or loose the bands of Orion?"* They are also spoken of in Amos 5:8. *"Seek him that maketh the Seven Stars and Orion."* Alcyone is the principal star of the cluster — the others being Merope, Maia, Electra, Tayegeta, Sterope and Celaeno. The Pleiades appear to be the center of our Galaxy.

The premise is that measurements in P. (Pyramid) inches, backward or forward from the Scored Lines, represent the corresponding number of years before or after that astronomically fixed date of 2141 B.C. To test the accuracy of this startling premise one simply has to measure the passages and chambers up and down from the Scored Lines, counting one year for each P. inch and at every change of masonry, (beginning and end of every passage and chamber or change of direction) marking the date. The dates, being so far back in history, allow ample testing against known recorded historical events.

The Great Pyramid is not made of elastic, but of rigid stone, so the measurements cannot be stretched nor shortened. We can only take the dimensions of the passages, just as they were constructed by the ancient builders, and let the results take care of themselves. The scaler line itself however, is consistently the floor-line. As access into the Pyramid's interior is from the north only, progression in time is therefore represented by advancement southward. It is also important to know that although the dating is determined on the floor-lines of the passages, the respective dates are defined not only by specific points on the floors, but by vertical east-west planes in which these points lie. For example, the Vernal Equinox, 2141 B.C. is determined by the point at which the Scored Lines meet the floor of the Descending Passage, but also defined by the entire vertical alignment and east-west vertical plane of that point.

The distance measuring back up the Descending Passage from the Scored Lines is 482 P. inches, representing 482 years. Counting 482 years back from the datum line of 2141 B.C. brings us to the year 2623 B.C. This was the year that work on the construction of the Great Pyramid began. (See dia. page 180) The date 2623 B.C. was during the reign of Pharaoh Khufu. (Cheops)

Measuring 688 P. inches beyond the Scored Lines, down the Descending Passage, an aperture appears in the roof. This aperture is the entrance to the First Ascending passage, which leads into the Grand Gallery. Progressing 688 years from 2141 B.C. gives the date of 1453 B.C. This was the date of the Exodus of the Israelites from Egypt, and their receiving the Divine Law, through Moses, on Mt. Sinai. The institution of the Passover (the first feature of the Law) marked the beginning of the age commonly referred to as the "Dispensation of the Law," (Mosaic Law) a period of time from the Exodus and giving of the Law to man as a way to eternal life and ending at the Crucifixion of Jesus Christ.

Jesus Christ was the first man able to keep the Mosaic Law inviolate. He fulfilled it, thus ending that dispensation. This period has been considered by most Bible chronologists, as being 1485 years. As the date for the Exodus has been determined to be 1453 B.C. and that for the Crucifixion as Spring A.D. 33, the interval between the two dates is inflexible — 1485 years.

Measuring up the First Ascending Passage at the given scale of 1 P. inch to a year, we find the length is 1485 P. inches. Thus the end of the First Ascending Passage marks precisely the date of spring A.D. 33. (For the sake of any who may not be used to chronological reckoning, the rule for ascertaining the A.D. date required is to deduct the figures of the B.C. date from the total period and add 1. (1485 - 1453 + 1 = A.D. 33)

This period of time, being rigidly fixed as 1485 years, so far as the Pyramid evidence is concerned, clearly shows that the First Ascending Passage represents the Law Dispensation period. The Great Pyramid, built in the 27th century B.C., also clearly defined the precise dates of both the Exodus and the Crucifixion, long centuries before any of the Biblical prophecies concerning these events were written or fulfilled.

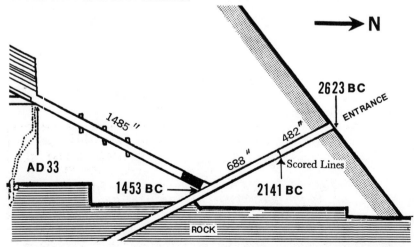

Another indication of Divine prophecy is found in the measurements of a geometric triangle formed between the point where the floor level of the Queen's Chamber intersects with the floor of the First Ascending Passage and the upper end of that passage. This triangle, known as the "Christ Triangle," has a base measurement of 30.043 P. inches and 33.512 P. inches for its hypotenuse.

Based on the prophetic scale of an inch representing a year in time, the north end of the base of the triangle falls upon the date September 29, 2 B.C. (the date of the birth of Christ — see Appendix A) The base length of 30.043 P. inches projected on the slope of the First Ascending Passage, and converted to years, marks the date October 14, A.D. 29, which is the date of His baptism, exactly 3½ years before His death (April 3, A.D. 33) on Calvary. After deducting the 30.043 P. inches from the hypotenuse of the triangle, the remainder is 3.469 P. inches or 3½ years.

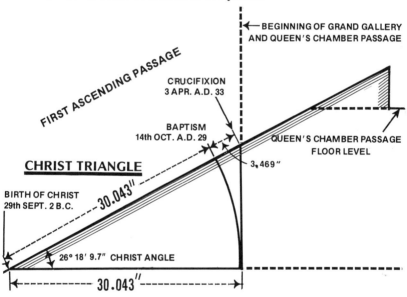

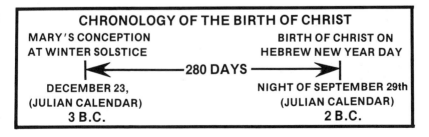

CHRONOLOGY OF THE BIRTH OF CHRIST

MARY'S CONCEPTION AT WINTER SOLSTICE		BIRTH OF CHRIST ON HEBREW NEW YEAR DAY
	←————— 280 DAYS ————→	
DECEMBER 23, (JULIAN CALENDAR) 3 B.C.		NIGHT OF SEPTEMBER 29th (JULIAN CALENDAR) 2 B.C.

JESUS' BAPTISM AND MINISTRY

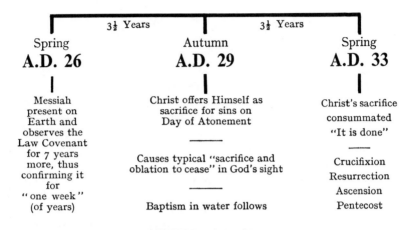

3½ Years	3½ Years	
Spring	Autumn	Spring
A.D. 26	**A.D. 29**	**A.D. 33**
Messiah present on Earth and observes the Law Covenant for 7 years more, thus confirming it for "one week" (of years)	Christ offers Himself as sacrifice for sins on Day of Atonement Causes typical "sacrifice and oblation to cease" in God's sight Baptism in water follows	Christ's sacrifice consummated "It is done" Crucifixion Resurrection Ascension Pentecost

The Bible in Stone

On the Land of Egypt's Border
Stands the Bible writ in stone,
Bringing chaos into order
Making God Almighty known.

Monument of ancient mystery
Puzzle of the young and old,
Now reveals the nations' history
As the dates and times unfold.

Through the ages somewhat hazy,
Hid from eyes of mortal man,
In the Pyramid of Gizeh
God reveals His mighty plan.

Praise and honour, glory, blessing
See His power almighty owned,
Everything to Him subservient,
Christ acknowledged, crowned, enthroned.

Mabel Christon

182

THE MESSIANIC ANGLE

OR

CHRIST ANGLE

26° 18′ 9·726″

IN THE

CHRIST TRIANGLE

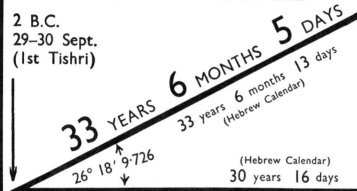

2 B.C.
29–30 Sept.
(1st Tishri)

33 YEARS 6 MONTHS 5 DAYS

33 years 6 months 13 days
(Hebrew Calendar)

26° 18′ 9·726

(Hebrew Calendar)
30 years 16 days

30 YEARS 15 DAYS

Sin	=	$\dfrac{\sqrt{\pi}}{4}$	=	·443113462726379
cos	=	$\dfrac{\sqrt{4^2 - \pi}}{4}$	=	·896465537068011
tan	=	$\dfrac{\sqrt{\pi}}{\sqrt{4^2 - \pi}}$	=	·494289456096249
cosec	=	$\dfrac{4}{\sqrt{\pi}}$	=	2·256758334191025
sec	=	$\dfrac{4}{\sqrt{4^2 - \pi}}$	=	1·115491849547959
cot	=	$\dfrac{\sqrt{4^2 - \pi}}{\sqrt{\pi}}$	=	2·023106072093268

ADAM RUTHERFORD

GEOMETRIC CONSTRUCTION
OF THE
CHRIST ANGLE

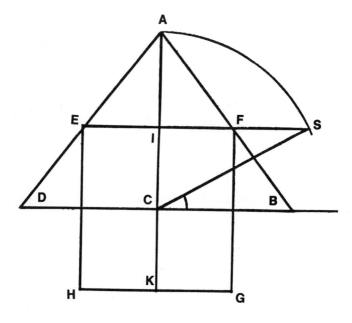

Let   **ABD** = Right Vertical Section of the Great Pyramid
      EFGH = Square of equal area to the △**ABD***
C is the centre of **BD** and also centre of square **EFGH**
    ∠**ABD** = Pyramidic π∠, 51° 51′ 14·3″
  With centre **C** and radius **AC** draw arc and produce **EF** to
meet the arc at **S**. Join **CS**.
        ∠**BCS is the Christ Angle, 26° 18′ 9·7″**

  * Note that the two top corners of the square, i.e., **E** and **F**, fall slightly outside
the triangle **ABD**.

ADAM RUTHERFORD

PROOF

BD $= y$ Sacred Cubits. $\therefore$ AC $= \dfrac{2y}{\pi}$ Sacred Cubits.

Area of $\triangle$ABD $= \dfrac{y}{2} \cdot \dfrac{2y}{\pi} = \dfrac{y^2}{\pi}$ square Sacred Cubits

$\therefore$ EF $= \sqrt{\dfrac{y^2}{\pi}} = \dfrac{y}{\sqrt{\pi}}$; IC $= \dfrac{EF}{2} = \dfrac{y}{2\sqrt{\pi}}$; CS $= \dfrac{2y}{\pi}$ Cubits

$\therefore$ sine $\angle$ISC $= \dfrac{IC}{CS} = \dfrac{y}{2\sqrt{\pi}} \div \dfrac{2y}{\pi} = \dfrac{y}{2\sqrt{\pi}} \cdot \dfrac{\pi}{2y} = \dfrac{\sqrt{\pi}}{4}$

$$\angle BCS = \angle ISC$$

$\therefore$ sine $\angle$BCS $= \dfrac{\sqrt{\pi}}{4} = \cdot443113462726$

$\cdot443113462726 =$ sine of the Christ Angle, 26° 18′ 9·7″

Q.E.D.

The Great Pyramid measurements given are those of the full design, not the contracted structure involving the displacement.

ADAM RUTHERFORD

185

GEOMETRIC CONSTRUCTION
OF THE
CHRIST ANGLE
26° 18′ 9·7″
ALTERNATIVE METHOD

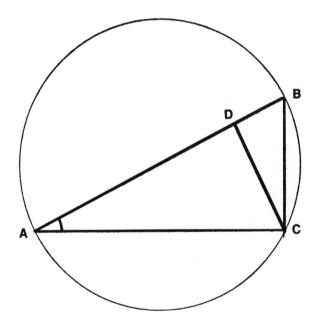

Let **AB** = Vertical height of the Great Pyramid
  BD = ⅛ of base side of the Pyramid
Construct semi-circle **ACB** with **AB** as diameter.
Draw **DC** at right-angles to **AB** and meeting the circumference
of the semi-circle at **C**
  Join **C** to **A** and **B**.
  ∠**BAC is the Christ Angle, 26° 18′ 9·7″**

ADAM RUTHERFORD

PROOF

$AB = \dfrac{2y}{\pi}$ Sacred Cubits: $BD = \dfrac{y}{8}$ Sacred Cubits

$\angle ABC$ is the complement of $\angle BAC$, $\therefore$ complement of $\angle BCD$

$\therefore \angle BAC = \angle BCD$

Sine $\angle BCD = \dfrac{BD}{BC}$; sine $\angle BAC = \dfrac{BC}{AB}$

$\therefore \dfrac{BD}{BC} = \dfrac{BC}{AB}$ $\therefore BC^2 = BD \cdot AB$

$BC^2 = \dfrac{y}{8} \cdot \dfrac{2y}{\pi} = \dfrac{y^2}{4\pi}$

$\therefore BC = \sqrt{\dfrac{y^2}{4\pi}} = \dfrac{y}{2\sqrt{\pi}}$

Sine $\angle BAC = \dfrac{BC}{AB} = \dfrac{y}{2\sqrt{\pi}} \div \dfrac{2y}{\pi}$

$\qquad = \dfrac{\pi y}{4\sqrt{\pi} \cdot y} = \dfrac{\sqrt{\pi}}{4.} = \cdot 443113462726$

$\cdot 443113462726 = $ sine of the Christ Angle, $26° 18' 9 \cdot 7''$

Q.E.D.

The Great Pyramid measurements given are those of the full design, not the contracted structure involving the displacement.

ADAM RUTHERFORD

GEOMETRIC CONSTRUCTION
OF THE
CHRIST ANGLE
26° 18′ 9·7″

ARURA METHOD

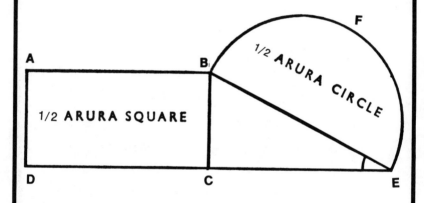

Let ABCD = ½ Arura Square

    AB = CD = side-length of Arura Square

    AD = BC = ½ side-length of Arura Square

    BFE = ½ Arura Circle with BE as diameter

Draw semi-circle BFE so that E falls on DC produced.

    ∠BEC is the **Christ Angle, 26° 18′ 9·7″**

PROOF

Area of Arura $= 10^4$ square Royal Cubits

$\therefore$ Diameter BE $= 2\sqrt{\dfrac{10^4}{\pi}}$ Royal Cubits

$$= \frac{2 \times 10^2}{\sqrt{\pi}} \text{ Royal Cubits}$$

sine $\angle \text{BEC} = \dfrac{\text{BC}}{\text{BE}} = \dfrac{50}{\dfrac{2 \times 10^2}{\sqrt{\pi}}}$

$$= \frac{50\sqrt{\pi}}{2 \times 10^2} = \frac{\sqrt{\pi}}{4} = \cdot443113462726$$

$\cdot443113462726 =$ sine of the Christ Angle, 26° 18′ 9·7″

Q.E.D.

ADAM RUTHERFORD

GEOMETRIC CONSTRUCTION
OF THE
CHRIST ANGLE
26° 18′ 9·7″

ROYAL CUBIT METHOD

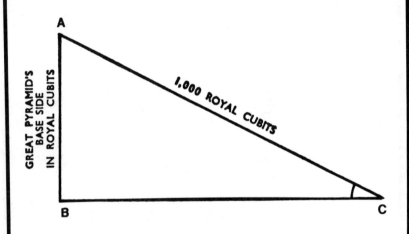

Let the vertical **AB** = base side of Gt. Pyramid in Royal Cubits
Construct right angle at **B**

Draw **AC** 1,000 Royal Cubits in length so that **C** meets the horizontal arm of the right angle, resulting in the formation of the △ ABC.

∠ACB is the Christ Angle, 26° 18′ 9·7″

ADAM RUTHERFORD

PROOF

$$AB = y \text{ Sacred Cubits} = \frac{10^3 \sqrt{\pi \cdot y}}{4y} \text{ Royal Cubits*}$$

$$= \frac{10^3 \sqrt{\pi}}{4} \text{ Royal Cubits}$$

$$\text{sine } \angle ACB = \frac{AB}{AC} = \frac{10^3 \sqrt{\pi}}{4} \div 1000$$

$$= \frac{10^3 \sqrt{\pi}}{4 \times 10^3} = \frac{\sqrt{\pi}}{4}$$

$$= \cdot 443113462726$$

$\cdot 443113462726 = $ sine of the Christ Angle, 26° 18′ 9·7″

Q.E.D.

The Great Pyramid measurements given are those of the full design, not the contracted structure involving the displacement

* 1 Sacred Cubit = $\dfrac{10^3 \sqrt{\pi}}{4y}$ Royal Cubits

ADAM RUTHERFORD

Continuing proof of prophetic chronology in the Great Pyramid is found by measuring the lofty passage (Grand Gallery) following after the First Ascending Passage. On applying the chronological test to the Grand Gallery, as we did to the previous passages, we again obtain an amazing result. We find its length to be 1881 1/3 P. inches. So, continuing consistently at the rate of 1 P. inch to a year, we ascertain that the end of the Grand Gallery marks the summer of A.D. 1914.

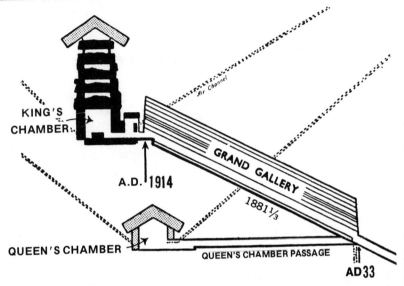

In the New Testament Our Lord prophesied about the "Times of the Gentiles" in Luke 21:24, which reads: *"Jerusalem shall be trodden down of the Gentiles, until the times of the Gentiles be fulfilled."* In accordance with this prophecy, Jerusalem was oppressed by one heathen power after another, all down through the centuries, from the first century of the Christian Era. In 1914 the last oppressor, Turkey, was challenged by Great Britain, and the ensuing World War I found Jerusalem delivered from the hands of its last oppressor.

It is interesting to note that the deliverance of Jerusalem, in December of 1917 by General Allenby of the British Army, was also precisely a prophetic "Seven Times" (2520 years) after 604 B.C., the date when Nebuchadnezzar (King of Babylon) captured the city of Jerusalem and led away that segment of the tribe of Judah captive into Babylon. Even the manner in which the city was delivered in 1917 was explicitly foretold by the Prophet Isaiah: *"As birds flying, so will the Lord of Hosts defend Jerusalem; defending, also He will deliver it; and passing over, He will preserve it."* (Isaiah 31:5)

British airplanes flew low at high speed, to and fro over the city, and frightened the Turks into surrender without firing a shot, and at the same time defending the city against Turkish planes.   In detailed fulfillment of Isaiah, the number 14 Bomber Squadron of the Royal Flying Corps (the old name for what is now the R.A.F.) took Jerusalem *"as flying birds"* and defended it, and passing over it, preserved it.   An indication of the Divine planning, in every detail, may be found in the motto, inscribed on the badge of the bomber squadron chosen for the task, which reads *"I spread my wings and keep my promise."*

A.D. 1914 is the ending of the "Seven Times" period of Daniel's prophecy in the Bible. (a time being 360 years x 7 = 2520 years) The fall of Assyria in 607 B.C. is the starting time and the termination is the beginning of the "time of trouble" with which this present age, and indeed the whole world order, is due to be replaced upon the inauguration of the New Order. (The beginning of this period overlapped the Mosaic Dispensation)   Both the Great Pyramid's chronograph and the Bible time-prophecies show the so-called "Times of the Gentiles" were due to run out in 1914.

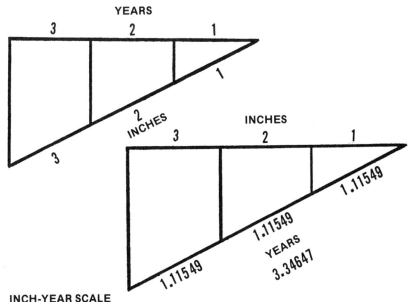

INCH-YEAR SCALE
PROJECTED ON TO THE HORIZONTAL AT ANGLE OF 26 18' 9.7"

193

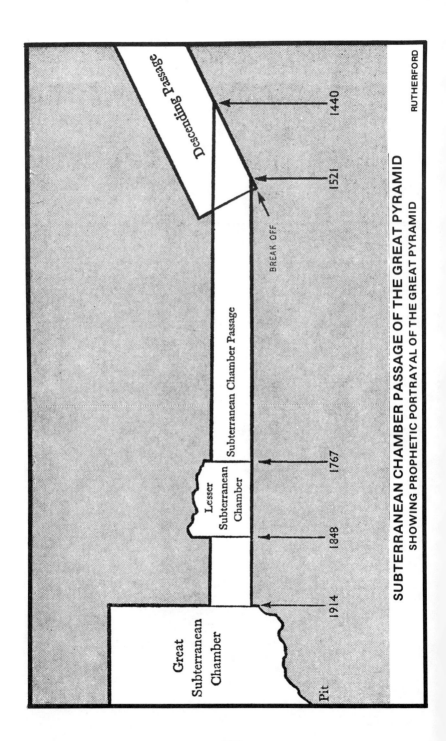

SUBTERRANEAN CHAMBER PASSAGE OF THE GREAT PYRAMID

SHOWING PROPHETIC PORTRAYAL OF THE GREAT PYRAMID

RUTHERFORD

Descending Passage

1440

1521

BREAK OFF

Subterranean Chamber Passage

1767

1848

Lesser Subterranean Chamber

1914

Great Subterranean Chamber

Pit

The verdict of time gives confirmation of the truth of the inch-year scale of chronological prophecy built into the design of the Great Pyramid, and added validity to the argument for its Divine Authorship. The Pyramid provides a witness to a great plan of an over-ruling Providence working His purpose in the affairs of men and nations. It gives evidence that the utterances of the Prophets of the Bible, the information supplied by chronological time-periods, are all factors built into the Great Pyramid.

The Bible proclaims, the Great Pyramid confirms — the God of the Bible is the God and Architect of the Great Pyramid and the God of history. *"By measure hath he measured the times, and by number hath he numbered the times; and he doeth not move nor stir them, until the said measure be fulfilled."* (II Esdras 4:37)

THE GREAT, THE MIGHTY GOD
THE LORD OF HOSTS
Great in counsel

and

mighty in work

who hath set signs and wonders

in the land of Egypt

even unto this day.

JEREMIAH 32: 18-20.

Great Pyramid of Gizeh

Long hast thou stood, Great Pyramid of Gizeh,
Hiding within thee secrets of our God,
Secrets that trace the end from the beginning,
Giving us hope for days that lie ahead.

God drew the plan that is enshrined within thee,
He gave the knowledge to the men who built,
That makes thee still, the greatest of earth's wonders,
Excelling far the wonders of our day.

In thee we see an infinite compassion,
Shewing a way whereby all men may come,
Through Christ our Lord to joy beyond expression,
When He shall reign, in justice, peace and love.

Eva I. Scott

CHAPTER 19.

BEYOND 1914

While students of the Great Pyramid generally agree that the Pyramid's Grand Gallery ends prophetically in 1914, the exact date varies. Adam Rutherford, one of the most outstanding interpreters of Pyramid Chronology, sets the date at June 22, 1914, about two months before the outbreak of World War I. David Davidson, another recognized authority on Pyramidology, determines the date at precisely Aug. 4, 1914. The discrepancy between the two dates can be accounted for by the fact that Davidson uses what he calls, the "Scalar Axis" of the Pyramid's Passage System — an imaginary line midway between the floor-line for his measurements. This method causes Davidson to assign the date of 2144 B.C. for the Scored Lines in the Descending Passage; 1486 B.C. for the Exodus, 4 B.C. for the Nativity and A.D. 30 as the date of the Crucifixion, all dates subsequently found in error.

Because most books on the Great Pyramid were written before Rutherford's research and publications, they will reflect Davidson's datings as continued on into the King's Chamber Passage. It should be pointed out that both Davidson and Rutherford depend on a scale change (in measurements) beyond the 1914 date at the end of the Grand Gallery. And both made predictions that failed to materialize.

In 1904 John Reeve of Toronto, Canada suggested that the year-inch scale of the 26° 18′ 9.7″ sloping Passage System of the Great Pyramid would end and an inch-month scale would begin to operate. His publication "History Fulfilling Prophecy," published in 1909, stated that the First Low Passage (52+″ in length) would equal 52 months, or 4 years and 4 months — representing a period of great trouble, "when judgement would be meted out against the enemies of Britain and the United States." It was only after it was observed that 52 such months exactly covered Britain's period in World War I (August 4, 1914 — November 11, 1918) that other students of the Great Pyramid accepted the inch-month scale. (using a prophetic month of 30 days)

At first, Davidson was hostile to Reeve's theory, but when it was observed that the length of the First Low Passage (52.0287 P. inches) so closely matched the 52 months of the War, he became interested in the possibility that a scale change did occur in 1914. By the application of a series of exploratory geometric measurements dealing with the Great Step and the sloping Passage angle, Davidson was able to come up with a method that caused his earlier set of measurements to intersect the beginning of the First Low Passage at the date of August 4-5, 1914. The following is a geometrical demonstration of Davidson's method:

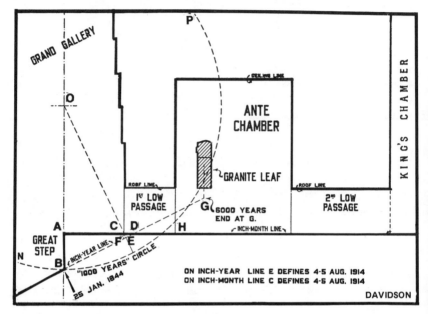

"Produce the face BA of the Great Step to such that the distance OB is the radius of a circle NBP of 1000 inch-years' circumference. Draw OCE perpendicular to BFED, the floor line of the Grand Gallery produced, and to intersect the latter at E. The distance BE is 70.5236972 inch-years, representing 25758.24925 days... Since the point B, at the foot of the Great Step, represents midnight between 25th and 26th January 1844, by Pyramid time, the point C represents 5.59 a.m. (Pyramid time) or 3.45 a.m. (Greenwich mean time) of the 5th August 1914."

Davidson, by projecting the inch-month scale into and through the King's Chamber Passage, predicted numerous events, climaxing August 19-20, 1953, a date reached by crossing the King's Chamber to the south wall. The measurements through the Second Low Passage approximated the beginning and end of the Great Depression, seemingly confirming Davidson's theory of the inch-month scale. Other writers, accepting the inch-month scale made many and varied predictions from measurements taken through the King's Chamber Passage system.

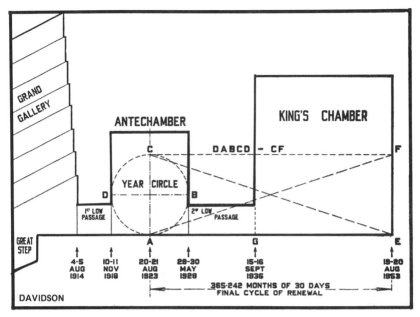

When Davidson's "Climax of the Ages" failed to materialize in 1953, students of the Great Pyramid's prophecy suggested alternate methods of measuring in the King's Chamber. Some changed the direction of measuring immediately upon entering the King's Chamber (to the right) When measurements reached the Coffer and the west wall beyond it, various events were predicted. When time passed beyond these dates, a hodgepodge of methods of measuring were produced, including measuring up the walls and circumambulating around the Chamber. To these measurements, events quite irrelevant were assigned in order to make out that their prognostications were fulfilled.

Rutherford, who originally accepted the inch-month scale, although offering June 22, 1914 as the beginning of the First Low Passage, changed his position after 1953. He suggested the inch-year scale continued on into the King's Chamber Passage. By applying this scale, the First Low Passage ended in 1966 and the limestone floor continued on an additional 13 inches into the Ante-Chamber before the floor changed to red granite. The added thirteen inches added thirteen years to 1966, bringing the limestone floor ending at 1979.

By theorizing that 1979 marked the beginning of the thousand year Millennium, Rutherford set that date (1979) at the beginning

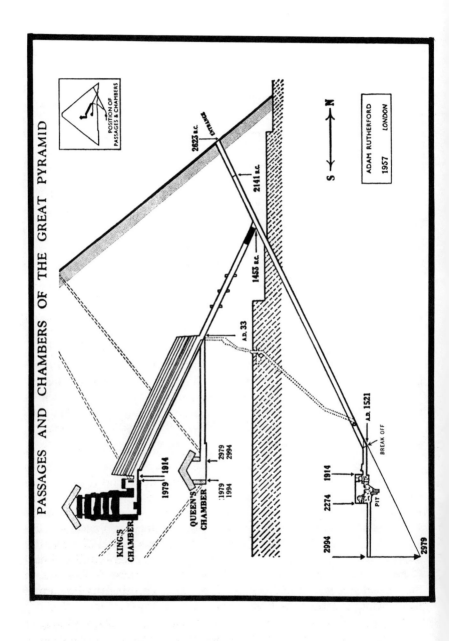

PASSAGES AND CHAMBERS OF THE GREAT PYRAMID

POSITION OF
PASSAGES & CHAMBERS

ENTRANCE
2623 B.C.
2141 B.C.
1453 B.C.
A.D. 33
A.D. 1521
BREAK OFF

KING'S CHAMBER
1979 1914
QUEEN'S CHAMBER
1979 2979
1994 2994
1979
1994

2994 2274 1914
PIT
2979

S ← → N

ADAM RUTHERFORD
1957   LONDON

200

of the Queen's Chamber. Because the Queen's Chamber was exactly 10 Royal Cubits in width, Rutherford further reasoned that if 10 Royal Cubits = one thousand years, then each one Royal Cubit = one century (100 years) and was the scale with which to measure the Queen's Chamber Passage. By applying this scale backwards from the Queen's Chamber to the beginning of that Passage at the Grand Gallery, it gave a beginning date of 5407 B.C. Based on the Old Testament Chronology of the Septuagint Text, that date very closely approximated the date of the fall of Adam. (Autumal Equinox of 5407 B.C.) Thus it appears that the entire Queen's Chamber Passage represents the record of mankind from the Fall of Adam to the Millennium.

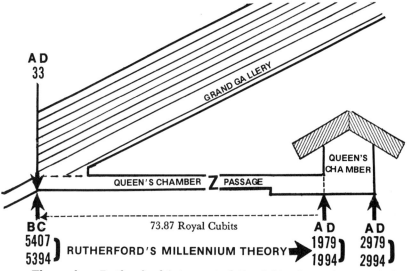

Then when Rutherford interpreted Daniel's three time periods (1335, 1290 and 2300) to all end in 1978-79, many scholars of the Great Pyramid accepted Rutherford's conclusions that Christ would set up His Kingdom on earth by 1979 and that measurements beyond the 1979 date in the Ante-Chamber did not apply to dates but only to symbolism. When one studies Rutherford's research it is found to be based on reasonable interpretation of Scripture and seemingly justified by archaeological evidence and Biblical chronology. Apparently, Dr. Rutherford's conclusion failed to materialize as others had before him. This failure, however, does not minimize his exhaustive research and writings on the Great Pyramid. His published works are considered a classic source of information on the Great Pyramid and will remain so for many years to come.

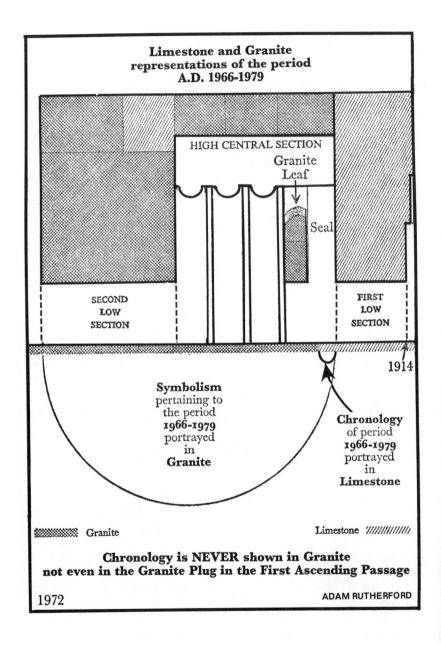

**Limestone and Granite
representations of the period
A.D. 1966-1979**

HIGH CENTRAL SECTION

Granite
Leaf

Seal

SECOND
LOW
SECTION

FIRST
LOW
SECTION

1914

Symbolism
pertaining to
the period
1966-1979
portrayed
in
Granite

Chronology
of period
1966-1979
portrayed
in
Limestone

Granite

Limestone

**Chronology is NEVER shown in Granite
not even in the Granite Plug in the First Ascending Passage**

1972

ADAM RUTHERFORD

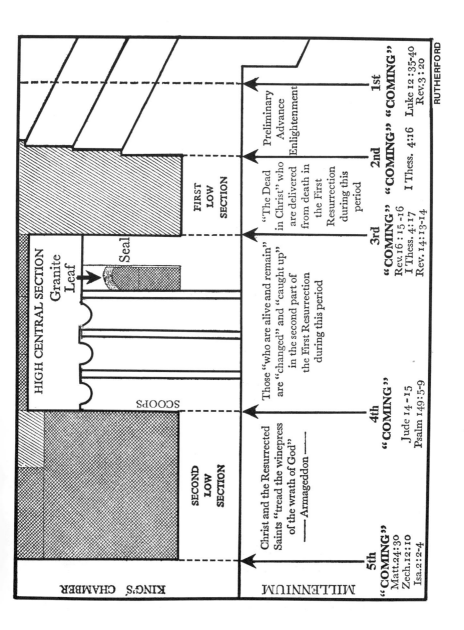

RUTHERFORD

1st "COMING"	Luke 12:35-40 Rev.3:20
Preliminary Advance Enlightenment	
2nd "COMING"	I Thess. 4:16
"The Dead in Christ" who are delivered from death in the First Resurrection during this period	
3rd "COMING"	Rev.16:15-16 I Thess. 4:17 Rev. 14:13-14
Those "who are alive and remain" are "changed" and "caught up" in the second part of the First Resurrection during this period	
4th "COMING"	Jude 14-15 Psalm 149:5-9
Christ and the Resurrected Saints "tread the winepress of the wrath of God" —— Armageddon ——	
5th "COMING"	Matt.24:30 Zech.12:10 Isa.2:2-4

FIRST LOW SECTION

HIGH CENTRAL SECTION — Granite Leaf — Seal

SCOOPS

SECOND LOW SECTION

KING'S CHAMBER

MILLENNIUM

203

It should be pointed out that if the interpretation of a future date by a student of the Great Pyramid does not turn out exactly as expected, this is no reason to begin to doubt the Divine nature of the Pyramid or lose faith in it. There is no justification for such an attitude. When time proves that a student of the Bible has not been quite correct in his interpretation of a future date in Scriptural prophecy, people as a rule do not begin to doubt the Bible because of him, but recognize the truth that the interpretation is either incorrect or at least requires some adjustment. As the Pyramid is the Bible in Stone, surely this is also the right attitude to take in regard to Pyramid interpretations.

The proof that the Great Pyramid is Divinely inspired and our implicit faith in its absolute accuracy do not depend on any man's interpretation of a future date therein. It is important for us to distinguish between what is absolutely conclusive in Pyramid interpretation. Pyramid chronological prophecy covering thousands of years on the inch-year scale has now been proved to the point of full demonstration. It is incontrovertibly established, and can be shown to anyone who cares to look. Even so, there are many today, even professing Christians, who shut their eyes and refuse to look, giving credence to the truth of the old saying, "there are none so blind as those who do not want to see."

The concurrent teaching of all precepts, promises, and prophecies relating to Scripture is that we are close to the end of this world order. And when the end of the present dispensation shall come has been an anxious question, among Christians, for nearly 2000 years. Inquiry and a desire to be informed about it is the natural fruit of faith in what has been foretold and promised. The Apostles themselves were concerned about knowing when the great events of the end of this world order are to be consummated. They often made inquiry with reference to this point.

The Scriptures clearly indicate that Christ shall return and reign on earth for a thousand years — a period known as the great Millennium. The Queen's Chamber (10 R. Cubits width) may well symbolize the Millennium. However, no man is to foreknow the "day and hour" of Christ's second return. In keeping with this pronouncement, the exact date of the beginning of the Queen's Chamber is still unknown and may remain unknown. However, the Scriptures make it the solemn duty of everyone to be in constant readiness and expectation for what must shortly come to pass, lest " that the day of the Lord so cometh as a thief in the night. " (I Thess. 5:2)

Christians look forward with joy to the time when Divine rulership is established on the earth (the Kingdom of God) promised and so long prayed for in the Apostles' Prayer (known as the Lord's Prayer) — *"Thy kingdom come. Thy will be done on earth as it is in Heaven."* An insight into that glorious era is found in Isaiah 35, which begins, *"The wilderness and the solitary place shall be glad for them; and the desert shall rejoice and blossom as the rose... And the ransomed of the Lord shall return, and come to Zion with songs and everlasting joy upon their heads; they shall obtain joy and gladness, and sorry and sighing shall flee away."*

Evidence that the manifestation of the Kingdom of God is close at hand is found in the writings of Daniel, who foretold that in the last days of this world order, *"many would travel"* and *"knowledge would be increased."* (Daniel 12:4) True to the prophecy, the advent of modern travelling facilities (including space travel — a thing entirely unknown in the history of the world hitherto) has been accompanied by an enormous increase in scientific knowledge, far surpassing all previous ages. The application of this increase of knowledge has resulted in the many wonderful inventions of our day.

In addition to the advanced knowledge, we have an unprecedented diffusion of this knowledge by means of free education and the circulation of books, magazines and newspapers by the millions at a very low cost. This condition has been intensified by means of radio and television. The purpose of all these inventions and modern conveniences may be discerned as approaching "The day of His preparation" for the Millennium. All these inventions and conveniences, if properly used and not abused, are great blessings to humanity. When Christ manifests Himself as King, no one will be allowed to use an invention to the hurt of his fellow man, or to take advantage of him thereby.

Thus, we see before our eyes, the grand and wonderful preparations the Almighty and Architect of the Great Pyramid is now making for the blessings, comfort and convenience of humanity when His Kingdom is established supreme in the very near future. We know it is very near, for the signs Christ gave us, of its nearness (Matthew 24, Luke 21) are before our eyes. He informed us, *"And when these things begin to come to pass, then look up, and lift up your heads; for your deliverance draweth nigh."* (Luke 21:28)

The Stone Witness

Beacon in desert land,
Placed there by God's command,
    Kept by His might;
Product of Master Mind,
Science and truth combined,
Grant now to all mankind
    Thy guiding light.

Herald of Gospel Age,
Christians' heritage
    Thy key to own;
We pray thy message grand
May o'er the world expand,
Sped forth by God's Own hand,
    And His alone.

Now in appointed time,
Clear as celestial chime,
    Thy truths make known;
Soon shall all error flee,
    True Christianity
All men shall find in thee,
    Bible in Stone.

Mary K. Kernohan

CHAPTER 20.

SYMBOLISM IN THE GREAT PYRAMID

Having established that the passage system and chambers of the Great Pyramid are chronological representations of prophecy, corroborating the Bible, one can postulate the symbolism of the Great Pyramid's chambers and passages in terms of the Christian Scriptures. Although all Christian writers on the Great Pyramid, in dealing with its symbolism, will express varying interpretations, based on their own religious persuasion, there is a general acceptance of the following six sections of the Pyramid's passage system:

(1) DESCENDING PASSAGE — a downward course representing the pathway of man, without hope of life after death. All are born in a dying condition, *"born in sin and shapen in iniquity,"* says the Bible.

(2) SUBTERRANEAN CHAMBER AND PIT — representing a state of death from which there is no awakening. This is the fate of the present evil world order, or the present evil institutions.

(3) PLUG — by blocking the upward passage to the chambers of "everlasting life" (symbolized by the air-channels) it represents the Law given by God to Moses — a Law no man could keep and thus gain eternal life.

(4) FIRST ASCENDING PASSAGE — representing the "Israelitish Age" or the "Mosaic Dispensation" in which man endeavored to gain eternal life by the works of the Law.

(5) WELL-SHAFT — this may represent Hades, a condition of death for mankind from which there is an awakening because the upper portion of the Well-Shaft enters the Grand Gallery at the very junction indicated by the Resurrection of Jesus Christ from the dead.

(6) GRAND GALLERY — represents the "Gospel Age" of Grace during which time the way of salvation for man is available.

■ ■ ■ ■ ■

(Note: there is no general consensus among students of the Pyramid as to the interpretation of the symbolism of the remaining six sections of the Pyramid's passage system. The following interpretations are suggested by Dr. Adam Rutherford)

(7) QUEEN'S CHAMBER PASSAGE — representing the complete period of world's history from the time of Adam to the beginning of the Millennial Reign of Christ.

(8) QUEEN'S CHAMBER — representing the "new earth" after the return of Christ as Lord of Lords and King of Kings. A place of eternal life for the Redeemed.

(9) FIRST LOW PASSAGE — represents the First Resurrection when the "dead in Christ" are delivered from death. It is written, *"the dead in Christ shall rise first..."*

(10) ANTE-CHAMBER — representing the second part of the First Resurrection wherein *"we who are alive and remain"* do not sleep in death, but at the moment of death experience the glorious resurrection of being *"changed in a moment, in the twinkling of an eye."*

(11) SECOND LOW PASSAGE — represents the period of time in which all the resurrected saints (overcomers) together, under the leadership of Christ Himself, *"tread the winepress of the wrath of God"* inflicting death on all evil systems and people in preparation for the Millennial rule of righteousness to follow.

(12) KING'S CHAMBER — represents the "New Heaven" where the executive body of Christ (the overcomers or saints) govern the Kingdom of Jesus Christ upon its establishment on earth during the Millennium.

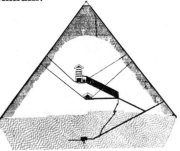

The foregoing symbolism fully agrees with the Bible. Adam willfully broke the Law of God (I. Tim. 2:14) and brought his descendants under sin and death. (represented by the Descending Passage to the Subterranean Chamber and Pit) The man, Jesus the Nazarene, (Matt. 2:23) kept the Law (represented by the Plug) and then voluntarily gave up His life as a sacrifice — the just for the unjust. (I Peter 3:18) Then, as it was not possible that He, the Innocent One, should be held in death, (Acts 2:24) God burst the bonds and raised His Beloved Son from Hades, the death-state. (represented by the Well-Shaft) Having risen as the last Adam, Jesus the Christ opened the way for the First Adam with all his family to eventually be raised from the death-state (I. Tim. 2:4-6) to everlasting life.

That way of salvation unto life everlasting is shown by the open mouth of the Well-Shaft entering the Grand Gallery (representing the Christian Dispensation). This agrees with the Bible that the only way to pass from death unto life is through belief in the atoning work of Christ through His death and Resurrection. *"If thou shalt confess with thy mouth the Lord Jesus, and shalt believe in thine heart that God raised him from the dead thou shalt be saved."* (Rom. 10:9) *"Behold the Lamb of God who taketh away the sin of the world,"* (John 1:29) *"Who gave himself a ransom for all, to be testified in due time."* (I Tim. 2:6)

The Grand Gallery, following after the First Ascending Passage, (and at the same slope) represents the age from Jesus' day onward, wherein Christ *"hath brought life and immortality to light through the Gospel."* (II. Tim. 1:10) While the First Ascending Passage, low and contracted, symbolized the bondage of the Law, the Grand Gallery, on the other hand, is exceptionally high, symbolizing the Gospel Age of Grace. *"By Grace are ye saved, through faith, and not of yourselves; it is the gift of God: not of works, lest any man should boast."* (Eph. 2:8-9)

In the Gospel Age the manner of worship was set aside and a new, purer and more spiritual form of worship established under the power of the Holy Spirit, whom Christ promised to send for a helper and comforter. Faith is as essential as before, perhaps more so than ever. But now, the faith is directed to an accomplished salvation, to a Redeemer in heaven and to a Savior who will descend from heaven at the appointed time. We no longer worship through the medium of sacrifices, types or shadows, that are earthy.

[Before proceeding with our study of the symbolism of the Great Pyramid's passages and chambers, it might be well to briefly consider *four* vitally important and significant implications bound up in the study of the Law and the Age of Grace.]

First, the Age of Grace does not mean that the Law is done away with. For Christ says, *"think not that I have come to destroy the law or the prophets, I am not come to destroy, but to fulfill. For verily I say unto you, till heaven and earth pass, one jot or one tittle in no way pass from the law, till all be fulfilled."* (Matt. 5:17-18) The Law was not made void by Christianity. *"Do we then make void the law through faith? God forbid: yea, we establish the law."* (Rom. 3:31) *"What then? shall we sin, because we are not under the law, but under grace? God forbid."* (Rom 6:14) *"For the wages of sin is death: but the gift of God is eternal life through Jesus Christ our Lord."* (Rom. 6:23)

Second, since death has not been destroyed (see I Cor. 15:25-26), it follows that "under grace" simply means that we, as Christians are free from the condemnation or "curse" of the law. Paul (an Israelite) wrote to Israelites in the dispersion in Galatia, *"When the fullness of the time was come, God sent forth his Son, made of a woman, made under the law, to redeem them that were under the law..."* (Gal. 4:4-5) Since the law was given only to Israel, the "them" to whom Paul speaks must be the Children of Israel who had come under the curse of the law through disobedience. This Redemption of Israel was collective and not personal, for the curse of the law came upon them collectively.

However, since every child of Adam is personally and individually born and every child of Adam dies individually and personally, it follows that every dying child of Adam must, individually and personally, be restored to life if he is to live again. In short, salvation unto everlasting life is a personal matter for each individual. Although Christ came to redeem His people Israel, he also became the "Saviour of the World." His "free gift of everlasting life" was offered to all the fallen children of Adam, Israelite and non-Israelite alike. *"As by one offence judgment came upon all men unto condemnation; even so by one righteousness the free gift came upon all men unto justification of life."* (Rom. 5:18)

Third, one of the purposes of the *"redemption from the curse of the law"* was that *"the blessing of Abraham might come on the nations through Jesus Christ."* (Gal. 3:14) *"Now to Abraham and his seed were the promises made. He saith not, And to seeds, as of many; but as of one, And to thy seed, which is Christ* (Messiah)." (Gal. 3:16) This can only mean that Christ was in Abraham, and it was this "seed," which is Christ, that was to be multiplied in a Family, or Race, which should become *"many nations,"* (Gen.17:5) whose seed was *"to multiply as the stars of heaven"* (Gen. 26:4) and *"be as the dust of the earth"* and *"spread abroad to the west, and to the east, and to the north, and to the south"* (Gen. 28:14) to carry the Gospel to all the world. (Gen. 28:14; Isa. 43:10; Micah 5:7)

When God caused Israel to be driven from the land of Palestine, He did not cast them away forever. Although they had been warned that, as a result of continued sinning they would be removed from their land (Lev. 26:15-43) and scattered throughout the nations of the earth, God made the definite statement that He would not cast them away forever. (Lev. 26:44; Deut. 4:26-31) Paul, in answer to the question, *"Hath God cast away His people?"* replied in no

210

uncertain terms, *"God hath not cast away His people."* (Rom. 11:1-2) The Epistle of James is addressed to the *"Twelve tribes scattered abroad."* Peter wrote to the *"strangers scattered,"* (I Peter 1:1) *"which in time past were not a people, but are now the people of God: which had not obtained mercy, but now have obtained mercy."* (I Peter 2:10)

Archaeological and historical research has discovered the so-called "Lost Tribes of Israel" escaped from Assyrian captivity and migrated westward, over the centuries, to become the Anglo-Saxon, Scandinavian, Germanic, Celtic and kindred nations of today. (Missing Links Discovered in Assyrian Tablets — Capt — see publications, page 264) Israel was divorced from the Mosaic Law and their identity temporarily lost to the history, but known to God. They were to be recovenanted, in Christ, to enjoy the Israel birthright in the "appointed land." (II Sam. 7:10) This was possible when Jesus the Christ, the Shepherd of His sheep, gave His life for His sheep on Calvary's Cross. *"He was wounded for our transgressions, He was bruised for our iniquities: the chastisement of our peace was upon Him; and with His stripes we are healed."* (Isa. 53:5)

Fourth, during this period of Grace, the High Calling to membership in the mystical Body of Christ (the Bridegroom) is offered to those who present themselves as a living sacrifice unto death, as defined in Romans 6:4; *"Therefore we are buried with him by Baptism into death."* The relatively small number of Christians who attain the "prize of the High Calling" are collectively called the "little flock" and individually called "Saints." Of these, Jesus said, *"Fear not, little flock; for it is your Father's pleasure to give you the kingdom."* (Luke 12:32)

It is the little flock (overcomers) who apparently constitutes the executive body (under Christ) that will govern the Kingdom of our Lord Jesus Christ upon its establishment on earth. *"To him who overcometh will I grant to sit with me on my throne, even as I also overcame, and am set down with my Father in his throne."* (Rev. 3:21) *"And he that overcometh, and keepeth my works unto the end, to him will I give power over the nations: And he shall rule them with a rod of iron: as the vessels of a potter shall they be broken to shivers: even as I received of my Father,"* (Rev. 2:26-27) *"Do you not know that the saints shall judge the world?"* (I Cor. 6:2)

From the above scriptures one can conclude that the little flock of overcomers will exercise top authority, with Christ, during the Millennium. An executive body, to be effective, must be relatively small and carefully selected for efficiency. The qualifications for holding such an office must of necessity be exceptionally high. It is the highest position ever offered to mankind. The examination requires that an applicant must be willing to give up certain things. The Bible reveals that everything must be sacrificed for the rest of one's life. Paul beseeched his brethren (Christians) to "present their bodies as a living sacrifice" and continues, *"And be not conformed to this world, but be ye transformed by the renewing of your mind,"* (Rom. 12:2) and states that in the case of the New Creation, *"old things are passed away; behold all things are become new."* (II Cor. 5:17)

Thus, we see that the Saints of the little flock (overcomers) are to have a separate and different resurrection from any other and with a different type of body. Paul, in I Corinthians 15: 40, speaking of resurrection, says, *"There are also celestial bodies and bodies terrestrial, but the glory of the celestial is one and the glory of the terrestrial is another."* Paul also declares in I Thessalonians 4: 16, those in Christ, that is the Saints (the little flock) shall rise first, hence the resurrection is called "the First Resurrection" in Revelation 20: 6 and those taking part in it are described as *"blessed and holy."* These saints are promised a glorious body like that of the Master. *"Beloved, now are we the sons of God and it doth not yet appear what we shall be: but we know that, when he shall appear,* (to them individually as part of the First Resurrection) *we shall be like him; for we shall see him as he is."* (I John 3:2)

Since the little flock of Saints are to have a Divine nature in the First Resurrection, it follows that they are also to receive immortality. Paul, in describing the First Resurrection says, *"As we have borne the image of the earthy, so shall we bear the image of the heavenly...For this corruptible must put on incorruption and this mortal must put on immortality."* (I Cor. 15:49, 53) ("immortal" is taken from the Greek word, "ashanasia," which means "deathlessness, a condition in which death cannot take place.")

It is necessary to understand that immortality and everlasting life are not the same thing, for immortality is much more. Mortal man can have life everlasting because God is faithful to maintain the necessary environment and food supply. However, immortality is eternal life irrespective of environment or condition; a condition shared only by Divinity. Such a condition constitutes an entirely new creation, higher than any of God's creation before. This is the promise to those Christians who were "buried with Him (in Christ) by baptism into death." — *"Planted in the likeness of his death."*

Paul wrote, *"If any man be in Christ he is a new creation."* (II Cor. 5:17)

Thus, it follows that the principal purpose of the present age (Gospel Age) which intervenes between the First Advent of Christ and the establishment of His kingdom on earth, is the preparation and testing of those who will be in charge of the world during the Millennial Age. The selection and the acceptance of the complete body (little flock) must be completed before the "restitution" of all things (the Millennial Age) can begin. We are most likely in the time when *"the whole creation groaneth and travailth together...waiting for the manifestation of the sons of God."* (Rom. 8:19,22) In this context the *"sons of God"* pertains to the saints, or *"little flock."*

Many theologians teach that the purpose of the Gospel Age is to convert the whole world. However, after nearly 2000 years of preaching Christianity, the world is in a greater state of apostasy than ever, just as the bible foretold, *"But evil men and seducers shall wax worse and worse, deceiving and being deceived."* (II Tim. 3:13) Today, the world is not converted. Non-Christians outnumber the Christians many times over and even much of the so-called Christianity taught is a conglomeration of creeds embracing doctrines which are often at odds with the teachings of Christ. Many of the practices of the largest professing Christian denominations would be condemned by Christ Himself.

Because the present world age is nearly ended and the world is far from being converted to Christianity, does it mean that God has failed? No, we know that God cannot fail, for He Himself said, *"So shall my word be that goeth forth out of my mouth: it shall not return unto me void, but it shall accomplish that which I please and it shall prosper in the thing whereto I sent it."* (Isa. 55:11) It is the will of God to convert the whole world to the truth of His Divine purposes. *"For the Earth shall be filled with the knowledge of the glory of the Lord as the waters cover the sea."* (Habakkuk 2:14) *"...the Most High whose Kingdom is an everlasting kingdom and all dominions shall serve and obey Him."* (Daniel 7:27) *"when Thy judgments are in the Earth, the inhabitants of the World will learn righteousness."* (Isa. 26:9)

From the preceding Scriptures it is evident that the Divinely appointed time for converting all humanity is in the next age when God establishes His long-awaited Kingdom with Jesus Christ and His little flock upon the throne. When Christ said, *"This Gospel of the Kingdom shall be preached in all the world for a witness unto all nations and then shall the end come."* (Matt. 24:14) he did not say that the Gospel would convert all nations but only that it would be proclaimed to them as a witness. That has been done. The Gospel has been proclaimed in every nation on earth and the Gospels printed in over a thousand languages. It is now obvious that the Gospel Age was for the election and training of the "little flock" with tests sufficient to produce and prove the high standard of character required.

The question may come to mind, where does the Church come into the picture during this Gospel Age? The English word "church" that occurs over a hundred times in the New Testament has several meanings: (1) a congregation of worshippers; (2) a building in which a congregation worships; (3) the organization of all congregations holding the same particular belief; (4) all such organizations collectively; and (5) the saints collectively. (the little flock)

It is the latter (5) meaning that is expressed in the Book of Revelation dealing with those worthy to be chosen, by Christ, to reign with Him. It is the resurrected Saints (overcomers) who are to be "co-heirs" and standing as "kings and priests" who shall *"live and reign with Him on earth for a thousand years."* (Compare Rev. 1:6; 5:10; 20:6) These Saints (overcomers) represent the true church and constitute the "Body of Christ" (the Bridegroom) in the Millennial Age. The Kingdom over which Christ and His Body will reign is the earthly Messianic House of Jacob. (the Bride of Christ) Although the Bride is represented today by the descendants of Jacob (Israel), it is not limited to Israel's descendants, but is open to the "strangers" (outside of Israel) who join themselves to the Lord. (accept Christianity) Those who do so are blessed with *"a name better than of sons and daughters."* (Isaiah 56)

* * *

At the upper end of the Grand Gallery we come to the "Great Step" from which the horizontal First Low Passage extends southward into and through the Ante-Chamber and Second Low Passage. Although Davidson and Rutherford differed as to the datings in the passage chronology, they are in complete agreement on the symbolism — the beginning of the end of this present World Order. The First Low Passage indicates a time of tribulation and chastisement of modern Israel, represented to a great extent by the British Commonwealth and the U.S.A.

While Davidson carries on measurements through the King's Chamber Passage system, Rutherford believes chronology ends at the end of the red granite that extends 13 inches into the

214

Ante-Chamber, and only symbolism can be applied from that date onward. To Rutherford, the First Low Passage represents the First Resurrection of the Saints (overcomers) as they pass from terrestrial to the celestial conditions and the Ante-Chamber symbolizes the completion of the Body of Christ as those "who are alive and remain" though still in the material flesh, and Resurrected as "new creatures in Christ." The Second Low Passage symbolizes the period called the "Time of Jacob's Trouble such as never was since there was a nation," otherwise called "the battle of that great day of God Almighty" or "Armageddon." (Rev. 16:14, 16-21; Daniel 12:1; Joel 1:15; 2:11; Jer. 25:33; Zeph. 3:8)

The Second Low Passage has exactly the same bore as the First Low Passage and they both represent death, but with two different aspects: The First Low Passage, all of limestone, represents the condition of dead Saints and the period of time during which they are gradually delivered from death. The Second Low Passage, all of granite, symbolizes all the resurrected Saints, under Christ, inflicting death on all the present worlds evil systems and people, and so cleansing and preparing the Earth for its Millennial Reign of righteousness.

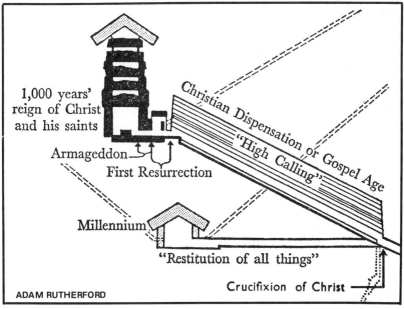

The King's Chamber symbolizes the Millennial Reign of Christ with His resurrected Saints. Satan's domain and the "kingdoms of this world" will be put away. War will be abolished and He *"will set my glory among the nations and all the nations shall see my judgment that I have executed and my hand that I have laid upon them. "* (Ezekiel 39:21) *"Behold the days come, saith the Lord that I will make a new covenant with the House of Israel and with the House of Judah...After those days saith the Lord, I will put my law in their inward parts and write it in their hearts; and will be their God and they shall be my people. And they shall teach no more every man his neighbor and every man his brother, saying, know the Lord; for they shall all know Me, from the least of them unto the greatest of them, saith the Lord: for I will forgive their iniquity and I will remember their sin no more. "* (Jer. 30:31-34)

During the Millennium, in the world we see the fulfillment of the prophecy, *"The kingdoms of this world are become the kingdoms of our Lord, and of his Christ; and he shall reign for ever and ever. "* (Rev. 11:15)

Thus, we see the design of the Great Pyramid's chambers and passage system clearly show a close parallel with the Scriptures. The next and final chapter, "The Chief Corner-Stone" reveals how the geometry of the chambers and the passages also parallel the Christian Gospel.

> *"Remember the former things of old: for I am God, and there is none else; I am God and there is none like me, declaring the end from the beginning, and from ancient times the things that are not yet done, saying, My counsel shall stand, and I will do all My pleasure: . . . Yea I have spoken it, I will also bring it to pass; I have purposed it, I will also do it."*
>
> —Isaiah 46 : 9–11.

CHAPTER 21.

THE CHIEF CORNER STONE

The greatest mystery and glory of the Great Pyramid is in the symbolism of its "crowning stone" known as the "Top-Stone ("Cap-Stone") which was rejected by the builders because of a constructural feature known as the "Displacement Factor." The problem was a deficiency in the perimeter of the Pyramid of 286.1 P. inches, which means that the Pyramid was built slightly smaller than the full design. According to the Pyramid's full geometric design each side should have been 9131 P. inches (9140 English inches) or a perimeter of 36524 P. inches. (4 x 9131) Actually, the perimeter of the Pyramid is 36238 P. inches, which is 286.1 P. inches less.

The dimensions of the full design of the Pyramid's base are revealed by the position of the outer sides of the south-west and south-east sockets. One of the purposes of these sockets was to enable the builders to fix the alignments of the Pyramid's two diagonals. However, in the case of the south-west socket this was not carried out. Instead, a chiselled line on the floor within the socket, running parallel to its western edge, was used for the purpose.

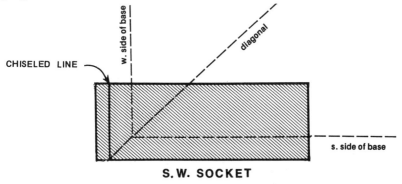

S. W. SOCKET

The outer edge of the chiseled line, at the south edge of the socket, was employed by the builders for establishing the position of the first diagonal (the N.E.-S.W. diagonal) of the Pyramid. This resulted in the sides of the Pyramid being contracted to the extent of 35.76 P. inches toward the center of the structure. This contraction, as geometrically ascertained, is more precisely 35.76277 P. inches and may be expressed as a negative or minus quantity which Dr. Adam Rutherford termed the "Contraction Factor."

To express the positive or plus quantity of the Displacement Factor, Dr. Rutherford used the term "Expansion Factor" (+ 35.76 P. inches). Both expressions can be seen in the top platform of the Pyramid as left by the builders. Each of the 203 courses of masonry has been drawn in to the extent of the Contraction Factor. (- 35.76 P. inches) In contrast, the amount to which the Top-Stone, if placed, would extend beyond the edges of the contracted summit platform would be the Expansion Factor. (+ 35.76 inches)

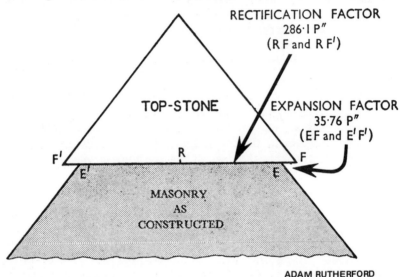

RECTIFICATION FACTOR
286·1 P″
(R F and R F')

TOP-STONE

EXPANSION FACTOR
35·76 P″
(E F and E' F')

F' R F
E' E

MASONRY
AS
CONSTRUCTED

ADAM RUTHERFORD

Because of the seeming error by the builders, in the alignment of the Pyramid's diagonal, it has been erroneously believed a "mistake" in their otherwise painstaking work. But, when one considers this "deficiency" of 286.1 P. inches is absolutely uniform, wherever it occurs, it is far more likely it exists for a very special and important reason. And, when considered together with the Sacred Scriptures, it can be neither a mistake nor accident but intentionally incorporated into the design by the Great Architect.

The Scriptures represent mankind of this planet in a condition of universal imperfection and therefore could be considered a negative or minus quantity represented in the Great Pyramid by the 286.1 P. inches displacement. This negative displacement pervaded the entire structure. The most conspicious example is the eccentricity of the position of the entrance to the Pyramid on its northern face. It is exactly 286.1 P. inches to the left or east of the N.-S. axis of the Pyramid.

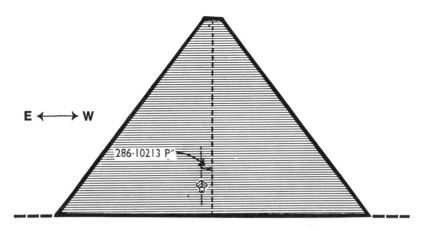

E ←——→ W

286·10213 P″

DISPLACEMENT OF THE PASSAGE SYSTEM OF THE GREAT PYRAMID

In symbolism, Biblical or Heraldry, the left or left-hand has a sinister significance in contrast to the right or right-hand which has an opposite meaning and signifies favor. For example, the Parable of the Sheep and the Goats. The sheep, on the right hand, are blessed, whereas the goats on the left hand are cursed. Furthermore, in Biblical symbology, an eastward direction or movement signifies going away from God or Divine favor. Hence, the fact that the Entrance and Descending Passage of the Pyramid are displaced to the left and east, intensifies the significance of the Displacement as being sinister. This confirms our interpretation (in the previous chapter) of the passage indicating the way to death without hope of everlasting life.

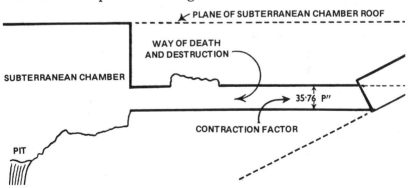

PLANE OF SUBTERRANEAN CHAMBER ROOF

WAY OF DEATH AND DESTRUCTION

SUBTERRANEAN CHAMBER

35·76 P″

CONTRACTION FACTOR

PIT

Further, the horizontal Subterranean Passage (at the end of the sloping Descending Passage) contracts to a height of 35.76 P. inches (Contraction Factor) before leading into the Pit, the symbol of death and destruction. However, just as the Scriptures offer a way of escape through the Redemption wrought by Jesus Christ, the Great Pyramid also shows a way of escape from death to everlasting life, symbolized by the two major chambers. (King and Queen Chambers) The center of the entrance to the Well Shaft lies exactly 286.1 P. inches (+ Displacement Factor) up from the end of the Descending Passage. By means of this passage the upper chambers (representing life by the air ducts) are accessible.

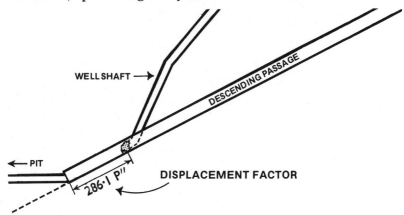

It is quite significant that the center of the top opening of the Well Shaft enters the Grand Gallery exactly 35.76 P. inches (Expansion Factor) from the beginning of the Grand Gallery — a point which marks the Crucifixion and Resurrection of Jesus Christ. It should also be noted that the Grand Gallery increased in height 286.1 P. inches (+ Displacement Factor) over the First Ascending Passage. Dr. Rutherford terms this expansion the "Rectification Factor" (see chart Page 221)

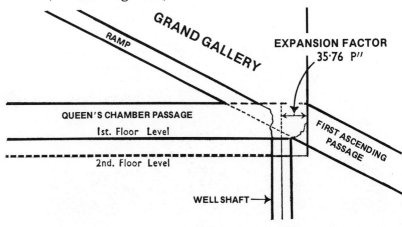

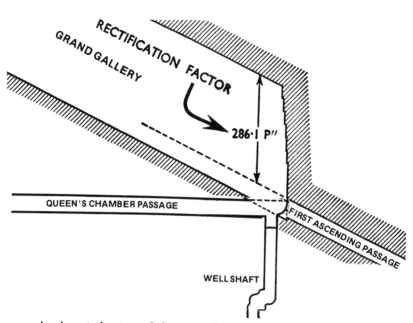

Again, at the top of the grand Gallery, we find the Expansion Factor in the height of the Great Step, which measures 35.76 P. inches. Although the Grand Gallery symbolizes the Gospel Age with Redemption offered through Jesus Christ, the world in general is still out of harmony with God's Plan for mankind. This is shown by the fact that the Grand Gallery and the King's Chamber Passage system is still 286.1 P. inches left of the N.-S. axis of the Pyramid. However, the center line of the King's Chamber Passage, when projected into the King's Chamber, is exactly 286.1 P. inches (+ Displacement Factor) from the center line of the open Coffer.

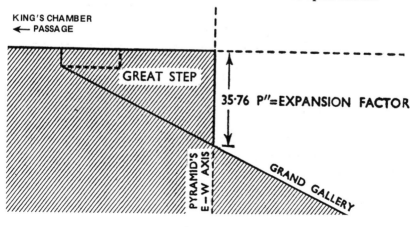

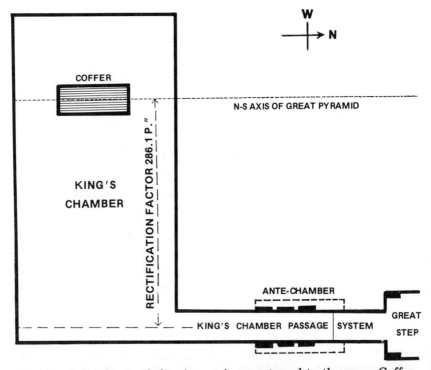

It will be observed that in moving westward to the open Coffer we have compensated for the minus Displacement Factor (- 286.1 P. inches) with a plus Displacement Factor (+ 286.1 P. inches) and at the open Coffer we are on the N.-S. axis of the Great Pyramid. What is clearly portrayed in the King's Chamber is that by the risen Christ this "displaced" world will be brought back into perfect tune with the Infinite Creator. This is further reiterated in the symbology of the Top-Stone which was not placed on the summit of the Pyramid.

Since all the courses of masonry in the Great Pyramid are short of the complete design to the extent of the Displacement Factor (286.1 P. inches) in the perimeter, it follows that the crowning platform was also 286.1 P. inches short in circuit. Actually, the circuit of the deficient square platform at this level height of 5448.736 P. inches was 2002.7 P. inches or 7 times the Displacement Factor. (7 x 286.1 = 2002.7) As the Top-Stone (the Chief Corner-Stone) was made to conform to the original (Divine) design, it would not fit and was subsequently "rejected" by the builders. Had it been placed in position, it would have overhung the edges of the platform all the way around.

But, if the Great Pyramid's form is to be perfected, the Chief Corner Stone must be placed and the whole mighty structure beneath brought into conformity with it. This means that all the four sides of the entire Pyramid must be filled out with masonry until all the sides come into exact alignment with the angles of the projecting perfect Top-Stone. The result of this would mean that the base perimeter of the Great Pyramid would be increased by 286.1 P. inches, or a total of 36524 P. inches. If this were done, the corners of the base of the Pyramid would fit exactly into the original setting-out dimensions cut into the foundation rock.

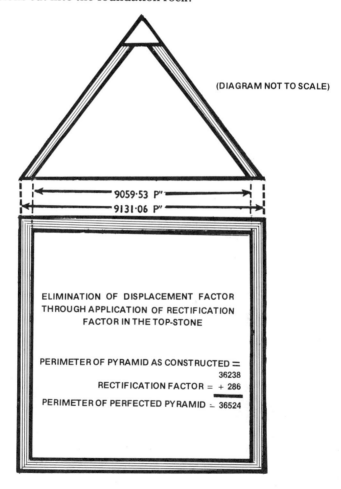

(DIAGRAM NOT TO SCALE)

9059·53 P"
9131·06 P"

ELIMINATION OF DISPLACEMENT FACTOR
THROUGH APPLICATION OF RECTIFICATION
FACTOR IN THE TOP-STONE

PERIMETER OF PYRAMID AS CONSTRUCTED = 36238
RECTIFICATION FACTOR = + 286
PERIMETER OF PERFECTED PYRAMID = 36524

"TOP-STONE" PLACED
AND RESULTANT PERFECTION OF THE GREAT PYRAMID

MATHEMATICAL REPRESENTATION
OF THE GREAT PYRAMID'S
SYMBOLIC FACTORS

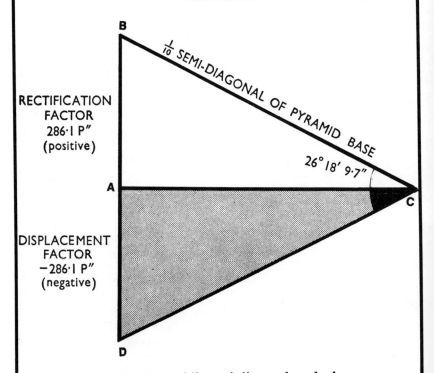

Let $BC = \frac{1}{10}$ Gt. Pyramid's semi-diagonal at the base
$\angle ACB$ = Christ Angle, 26° 18′ 9·7″ (ascending)
$\angle ACD$ = inverted Christ Angle = Antichrist Angle*
                                            (descending)

    AB = Rectification Factor
    AD = Displacement Factor

* The word "Antichrist" is used here in the broadest sense, embracing all that is not in harmony with the Divine will, and not just in the more limited prophetic sense in which Antichrist is portrayed in the N.T., although of course the latter is included.

ADAM RUTHERFORD

224

The Great Pyramid, in being expanded to fit the perfect Top-Stone, will have radiated out from the center to all the four cardinal points of the compass the exact Expansion Factor (+ 35.76 P. inches) and at the same time conform to the Rectification Factor (+ 286.1 P. inches) of the base of the Top Stone. This can be accomplished by the outer casing stones being laid at the uniform full thickness all the way around the base core. Then the reconstructed corners of the Pyramid's base will be increased outward an exact 35.76 P. inches (+ Expansion Factor) and be in perfect alignment with the great Chief Corner-Stone.

An allegorical parallel is found in the Scriptures: *"The stone which the builder's rejected, the same is become the head of the corner. This is the Lord's doing, it is marvellous in our eyes."* (Psalm 118:22-23) St. Paul, speaking of Jesus Christ, wrote: *"This is the stone which is set at nought of you builders, which is become the head of the corner."* This definition could possibly apply to a Pyramid, wherein all the four corners of the edifice converge in one stone at the top, which crowning stone is at once "the Head-Stone," "the Head of the Corner," and the "Chief Corner-Stone."

The Chief Corner-Stone is a fitting symbol of Jesus Christ because not only is it the most highly exalted stone but its form is a perfect model to which the whole building must conform. For a perfect pyramid all the many thousands of stones beneath must all be so placed that the entire structure comes into alignment with the sides and angles of the Chief Corner-Stone. In like manner, God has highly exalted Jesus *"that in all things he might have the pre-eminence"* and that ultimately *"in the dispensation of the fulness of times he might gather together in one all things in Christ both which are in heaven and which are on earth, even in him."* (Eph. 1:10)

In God's due time, at the Millennial Morning, *"He shall bring forth the head-stone thereof with shoutings, crying, Grace, grace unto it."* (Zech. 4:7) Then, under Messiah's glorious reign, Restitution work will bring the Earth to the condition originally designed by God. It will complete the Creation of Earth.

THE GREAT SEAL OF THE UNITED STATES

It is significant that the Reverse of the Great Seal of the United States has, for its leading feature, a Pyramid representing the Great Pyramid of Giza. Above the unfinished Pyramid is poised its "missing" apex-stone, which in this case is a triangle, and an "illuminated triangle" at that, with its apex dissolving in a blaze of light. This eternal symbol signifies a thing Divine. In the heart of the triangle is an open eye — the "All-Seeing Eye" of the Almighty God, and illustrates the prophetic words, *"Behold, he that keepeth Israel, shall neither slumber nor sleep."* (Psa. 121:4)

Above the Pyramid is written the Latin words, "Annuit Coeptis" meaning "He (God) has prospered our beginnings." (or "undertakings") Below the Pyramid are the Latin words, "Novus Ordo Seclorum," meaning, "A New Order of the Ages." On the base of the Pyramid are the Roman numerals 1776, referring to the date that the "New Order of the Ages (U.S.A.) was established. The two mottoes and the date clearly indicate that those responsible for the design of our Great Seal were cognizant of the Divine Providence that eternally watches over the welfare and destiny of our great nation.

226

The Pyramid shown on the Great Seal is very distinctly an "unfinished" Pyramid, whose apex, or cornerstone, is missing. The substitution for it is not a physical thing, but rather a "Divinely Illuminated Spiritual Stone." Its pattern, the Great Pyramid of Egypt was also left unfinished due to an error by the builders. This error is easily traceable in the construction of the Great Pyramid as it exists today and has from the time of erection.

Thus, both the Great Pyramid and the Great Seal of the United States of America, emblazon in the understanding mind the sublime "allegory of the builders' error" in that mystical "house not built with hands" but eternally in the heavens, is Jesus Christ. Jesus Christ, featured very prominent in the Scriptures as the "Great Light," is the "Stone that the builder's rejected." "Jesus said unto them: *Did ye never read in the Scriptures, 'The stone which the builder's rejected, the same is become the head of the corner' ...And whosoever shall fall on this stone shall be broken, but on whomsoever it shall fall, it will bring him to powder."* (Matt. 21:42-44)

Our Great Seal is symbolic of the coming reign of Christ over the earth, in fulfillment of the prophecy, *"The kingdoms of this world are become the kingdoms of our Lord, and of his Christ; and he shall reign for ever and ever.* (Rev. 11:25)

OBVERSE

227

SCRIPTURAL ALLUSIONS TO THE GREAT PYRAMID

Psa. 118:

22. *The stone which the builders refused is become the head stone of the corner.*

23. *This is the Lord's doing; it is marvellous in our eyes.*

Isa. 8:

14. *And he shall be for a sanctuary; for a stone of stumbling and for a rock of offence to both the houses of Israel, for a gin and for a snare to the inhabitants of Jerusalem.*

Isa. 28:

16. *Therefore thus saith the Lord God, Behold I lay in Zion for a foundation a stone, a tried stone, a precious corner stone, a sure foundation: he that believeth shall not make haste.*

Zech. 4:

7. *Who are thou, O great mountain? before Zerubbabel thou shalt become a plain; and he shall bring forth the head-stone thereof with shoutings, crying, Grace, grace unto it!*

Matt. 21:

42. *Jesus saith unto them, "Did ye never read in the scriptures, The stone which the builders rejected, the same is become the head of the corner; this is the Lord's doing, and it is marvellous in our eyes?"*

43. *"Therefore say I unto you, The kingdom of God shall be taken from you, and given to a nation bringing forth the fruits thereof."*

44. *"And whosoever shall fall on this stone shall be broken; but on whomsoever it shall fall, it will grind him to powder."*

Mark 12:

10. *"And have ye not read this scripture; The stone which the builders rejected is become the head of the corner."*

11. *"This was the Lord's doing, and it is marvellous in our eyes?"*

Acts 4:

10. *Be it known unto you all, and to all the people of Israel, that by the name of Jesus Christ of Nazareth, whom ye crucified, whom God raised from the dead, even by him doth this man stand here before you whole.*

11. *This is the stone which was set at nought of you builders, which is become the head of the corner.*

Rom. 9:

33. *As it is written, Behold, I lay in Zion a stumblingstone and a rock of offence; and whosoever believeth on him shall not be ashamed.*

APPENDEX A — THE BIRTH OF CHRIST

For many years the dates of the birth and Crucifixion of Christ have been matters of controversy. The birth of Christ must have been before the death of Herod the Great, King of Judea, for Herod, on hearing that a child had been born who was to become King of the Jews, ordered the massacre of all male children under the age of two years in Bethlehem. According to Josephus, Herod died shortly after an eclipse of the moon and not long before a Passover. (Antiq. xvii, vi. 4-167 and ix. 3-213) Since there was an eclipse of the moon on the night of (12/13) March 4, 4 B.C., which was exactly a month before the Passover, it has been widely held that Herod died in the spring of that year, and consequently Christ was born at least as early as 5 B.C.

Also, from the very outset, if Herod died in 4 B.C. then Jesus could not have been born that year, for the simple reason that Herod died very early in the year while Jesus was born in the latter part of the year, as reported in the Scriptures and by the early Church Fathers. It should also be pointed out that no ancient historian, ecclessiastical or secular, has given 4 B.C. as the date of Herod's death, or any date earlier than A.D. 1. The earliest church Fathers, while placing the birth of Jesus at varying dates, give no dates earlier than 2 B.C. and most place it that very year, which, it will be noted, is the precise date revealed by the Great Pyramid for the Nativity.

Within the possible limits for the date of the crucifixion, the 14th day of Nisan fell on a Friday only in the years A.D. 30 and 33, (Handbook of Biblical Chronology, Par. 458, Table 140 - J. Finegan) and of these two dates the general opinion has tended to favor the latter. But Luke 3: v. 23 says that Jesus was *"about thirty years of age"* when he began His ministry, and this could not have been earlier than A.D. 29 if we take A.D. 33 for the Crucifixion. Since Jesus may have been anything up to two years of age when Herod died, we find ourselves obliged either to accept Luke's statement with an undue degree of latitude, or to question the evidence for the date of Herod's death as early as 4 B.C.

Since Herod's death is related to a lunar eclipse, we have another eclipse to consider that fits into the time frame. On the evening of December 29, 1 B.C. an eclipse occurred that was visible in Jerusalem during the early evening. This eclipse was a total eclipse (7 digits) and took place three months before the Passover that commenced March 27, 1 A.D., whereas the 1 B.C. eclipse was a minor eclipse (4 digits) visible only from about 2 A.M. to 4 A.M. and took place only a month before Passover. A period of one month is not a realistic time for all the recorded events that took place between the eclipse and the Passover that year.

Further, many eclipses occurred during the lifetime of Josephus and yet Josephus recorded only the one related to Herod's death in his voluminous writings. It is more likely that Josephus would have reported that major eclipse (1 B.C.) rather than the small eclipse (4 B.C.) that happened at a time when nearly everyone was asleep in bed and never noticed it. This premise is strengthened by the fact that Josephus reported the eclipse as an astronomical happening which nearly everyone would have had knowledge of and associated with the "burning of Matthias."

Another way of calculating Herod's death is the duration of his reign. Josephus says that Herod reigned thirty-seven years from his appointment by the Roman Senate, or thirty-four years from the overthrow of Antigonus. To calculate the date of Herod's death from these figures, it is necessary to know what system of reckoning Josephus used. Under the system most commonly used in western Asia, called the "accession-year" system, the regnal years began to count from new year's day next after the king's accession, the foregoing fraction being termed his accession year. According to this system the last regnal year was numerically the same as the length of the reign.

The other method of reckoning a king's reign is the so-called "non-accession-year" system in which the accession year counted as the king's first year. Then all the subsequent years counted one year higher, and the length of the reign, again taken as numerically the same as the last year, appeared to be one year longer. (Mysterious Numbers of the Hebrew Kings-pp. 14f. - E.R. Thiele) The accession-year rule is clearly the more practical, since the interval between the two events separated by several reigns could be readily calculated by simply adding together the reigns of the intervening kings. Under the non-accession-year rule, straightforward addition would give an excess of one year for every reign involved.

A way of testing which system Josphus used is as follows: Both Josephus (Ant. xiii. vi. 7-213) and I Maccabees (I Macc. xiii, 41-42) records that Simon became high priest in 170 S.E. (140 B.C.) Another well established date in 63 B.C., when Pompey captured Jerusalem and reinstated Hyrcanus as high priest. The interval is seventy-nine years. During this period of time there were six priestly rulers whose reigns are given by Josephus. They are:

Simon........... 8 years (Ant. xiii. vii. 4 - 228)

Hyrcanus I.... 31 years (Ant. xiii. x. 7 - 299;   War I. ii. 8 - 68)

Aristobulus... 1 year (Ant. xiii. xi. 3 - 318;   War I. iii. 5 - 84)

A. Janneus.... 27 years (Ant. xiii. xv. 5 - 404;   War. iv. 8 - 106)

Alexandra..... 9 years (Ant. xiii. xvi. 6 - 430;   War I. v. 4 - 119)

Aristobulus... 3½ years (Ant. xiv. vi. 1 - 97)

   Total.......79½ years

If each of these reigns had been reckoned by the non-accession-year system, the total would have exceeded the actual period by six years, and the fact that it does not do so proves that Josephus used the accession-year system.   Following the above period Josephus adds that Hyrcanus II reigned twenty-four years and Antigonus three years and three months. (Ant. xx. x - 245-6) The two reigns totalled 27¼ years, which was the exact interval between the summer of 63 B.C. and the autumn of 36 B.C., when Herod captured Jerusalem.

Josephus says that Jerusalem was captured "on the solemnity of the fast," evidently meaning the Day of Atonement, 10 Tishri. Counting from his appointment in Rome, Herod began his first regnal reign in 38 B.C., either on 1 Nisan or 1 Tishri, and his 34th and last year in Nisan or Tishri 2 B.C.   In either case his death would have been at the end of January 1 B.C.   Thus Herod died a week or two after the eclipse of December 29, 1 B.C.

Josephus also reported that in the last weeks before Herod's death, the king "grew fierce and indulged the bitterest anger upon all occasions" and did "all things like a madman." (Ant. xvii. vi. i) In all probability Herod's order to slay all the male babies in Bethlehem occurred during this period.   Herod had been informed by the Magi, a week or two before, that the new-born king could be up to two years of age. According to Matthew (chapter 2) the Magi described Jesus as a "paidion," (a little lad or little child) whereas Luke's account of the birth of Jesus uses the word "brephos." (a new-born babe) This proves that Jesus must have been over one year of age but under two years. (Note: at the time of Jesus birth, a child's age started at conception so the term "over one year" is equivalent to "over three months" in modern times) Therefore, Herod fixed the age limits for the slaughter of the Innocents in accordance to the age of Jesus, the implication being that Jesus was born in the year 2 B.C.

Confirmation that Jesus was born in 2 B.C. can be found in Roman records. After the fall of the Roman monarchy, two magistrates, known as Consuls, were appointed as heads of the administration both in Rome itself and throughout the Provinces. When the Caesars came to power the Emperor himself was frequently elected to the position. This consulate office was held for one year and this arrangement began in A.U.C. 245. (509 B.C.) Two Consuls were elected that year; Lucius Junius Brutus and Lucius Tarquinius Collatinus. In A.C.U. 601 (153 B.C.) the Consuls elected for that year took office on January 1st and from that date onward they continued to do so annually on that day.

In Jesus' time the Romans had two usual methods of dating events. (1) by the year of reign of the Caesar or Emperor in power — (2) by naming the two Consuls in office for the particular year of the event in question. The latter method was similar to the ancient Assyrian practice of dating an event by naming the current "Limmu," (usually translated "Eponym") who likewise held office for one year only. The Greeks also used their annual "Archons" for dating purposes.

Epophasius (315 - 402 A.D.) Bishop of Constantia (or Salamis) states that Jesus was born in the 42nd year of Augustus and in the year when Octavius Augustus xiii and Silanus (Silvanus) were Consuls. (Haeres, LI 24, 1 Ed. Holl., pg. 293) Now the year in which these two Consuls were in office was 2 B.C., which also coincides with the 42nd year of Augustus' reign. In the Chronicle of Hippolytus, known as the "Chronicle Alexandrinum" or "Exerpta Latina Barbari" the Lord's birth is put in the same consulate period.

The following is the list of Consuls during the years around the time of the birth of Jesus:

B.C.	A.U.C.	CONSULS
5	749	Augusto xii et Sulla
4	750	Sabino et Rufo
3	751	Lentulo et Rufo
2	752	Augusto xiii et Silvano
1	753	Caesare et Paulo

The Great Pyramid itself, bears witness that Jesus was born in 2 B.C. This fact was first discovered by Dr. John Edgar who noticed that a "rhumb line" (not a great circle arc) drawn from the Great Pyramid at the passage angle (26° 18' 9.7") to the parallel of latitude on the north side goes over Bethlehem. The distance from the Great

Pyramid to Bethlehem, along the great circle arc, is 2139 Pyramid furlongs. (1 Pyramid furlong = 8000 Pyramid inches) If we start from the Pyramid's astronomically fixed datum year 2141 B.C. and apply the scale of a furlong to a year, we obtain not only the place where Jesus was born, (Bethlehem) but also the exact time when He was born, considering 2139 years after 2141 B.C. marks the date, 2 B.C.

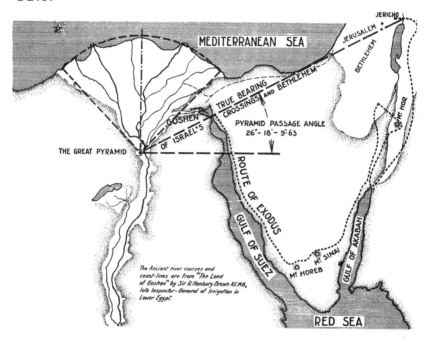

NILE QUADRANT AND BETHLEHEM TRIANGLE

It is also significant that the rhumb line describes the direct route that passes successively over Israel's crossing of the Red Sea (Sea of Reeds), through Bethlehem, and over Israel's crossing of the Jordan River. The two crossings define the beginning and ending of the children of Israel's "wandering," after coming out of Egypt.

Dr. Adam Rutherford, the late eminent Pyramidologist and Chronologist, produced one of the most scholarly studies on the birth of Christ. From the Gospels he has calculated the exact date and time of the birth of Jesus. The following extract is taken from Dr. Rutherford's Pyramidology Book II, published in 1962 by the Institute of Pyramidology of Great Britain:

────────────────────

Elizabeth and Mary

We have Scriptural data which enables us to fix the time of Jesus' birth within much narrower limits. The information supplied in the Bible in connection with the times of the conception of Elizabeth, the mother of John the Baptist and Mary, the mother of Jesus is of great chronological value. St. Luke 1:5, states that Zacharias (the father of John the Baptist) was a priest of the course of Abia. Verses 8-13 state that it was while Zacharias *"executed the priest's office before God in the order of his course."* that he was informed from above that his wife was to have a son who was to be named John. So in verses 23 and 24 of the same chapter it is recorded, *"And it came to pass, that, as soon as the days of his ministration were accomplished, he departed to his own house. And after those days his wife Elizabeth conceived and hid herself five months."* The next verses show that at the end of that time, i.e. at the beginning of Elizabeth's 6th month, the Annunciation to Mary the mother of Jesus took place, and so it is written: *"And in the sixth month the angel Gabriel was sent from God into a city of Galilee, named Nazareth, to a virgin espoused to a man whose name was Joseph, of the house of David, and the virgin's name was Mary ... And the angel said to her, Fear not, Mary; for thou hast found favour with God and behold thou shalt conceive...and bring forth a son, and shalt call his name Jesus."* (verses 26, 27, 30, 31) Then in the next chapter, verses 6 and 7 we read, *"And so it was, that, while they were there* [Bethlehem] *the days were accomplished that she should be delivered. And she brought forth her first-born son and wrapped him in swaddling clothes and laid him in a manger; because there was no room for them in the inn."* Fortunately, information is available whereby the precise date of the termination of Zacharias' period of service in the Temple, whereupon Elizabeth conceived, can be obtained, and from this, by means of the above details from St. Luke, we can ascertain the time of Jesus' birth.

Zacharias' Ministry

The priests were divided into 24 classes (I Chronicles 24:7-19), and it is known that each class officiated at the Temple in turn for a week. If we know the definite time at which any one of the classes or courses officiated it is a simple matter to trace the times of the succession of courses. The courses of priests changed duty with the changes of the week. The first day of the week of course began at the end of the Sabbath at sundown. From the Talmudical statements and Josephus we learn that the Temple at Jerusalem was destroyed by Titus on 5th August A.D. 70 and that the 1st course of priests (that of Jehoiarib) had just taken office. The previous evening was the end of the Sabbath: so that datum line for our calculation is Saturday (Sabbath) 4th August, A.D. 70. The period of service of the course of Jehoiarib, the 1st course of priests, was from the evening of the 4th August, A.D. 70 to the evening of the following Sabbath on 11th August. As we have seen, Jesus was born in the fall of 2 B.C. From St. Luke's Gospel quoted above we note that John the Baptist was only five months older than Jesus, so he also was born in 2 B.C., but earlier in the year, in the Spring, hence the conception nine months before would take place in the summer of the previous year, 3 B.C. Now this conception just followed the end of Zacharias' week of service in the Temple, i.e., with the end of the turn of duty of the course of Abia (Abijah), which was the 8th course. Reckoning from the above datum line, 4th August, A.D. 70 for the beginning of the week of duty of the 1st course, we find that the 8th course ended its turn and came off duty on 13th July, 3 B.C. Thus Zacharias returned home from the Temple at the end of the 2nd week of July, 3 B.C., and Elizabeth's conception therefore would be in that weekend (13th-14th July) and the birth of John the Baptists would take place about 40 weeks later, in the weekend of 19th-20th April, 2 B.C., precisely at the Passover of that year.

The account in St. Luke's Gospel shows that Elizabeth's 5 months hiding herself, beginning in the 3rd week of July, 3 B.C., had completely expired with the 3rd week of December and that it was into the beginning of the next week, i.e. the 4th week of December 3 B.C., that Mary's conception of Jesus took place (the precise day we shall show presently), for Luke 1:24-26 says that Elizabeth was already in her 6th month when Mary conceived. On her conception, Mary *"went...with haste"* (Luke 1:39) from Nazareth of Galilee to Ein Karim of Judea to visit her cousin Elizabeth, who was then, as we have seen, in the 1st week of her 6th month. Luke 1:56 states that Mary stayed in Elizabeth's home *"about three months,"* i.e., almost exactly 3 months, as we have seen from Luke's use of the word *about* in reference to time. Thus Mary stayed with Elizabeth until the 1st week of Elizabeth's 9th month, but returned to Nazareth before the babe John the Baptist was born, as the narrative of St. Luke shows.

The 40 weeks required from Mary's conception in the beginning of the 4th week of December, 3 B.C., till the birth of Jesus would thus bring us to the beginning of the 5th week of September, 2

B.C., as the due date for Jesus' birth; and the Monday of that week was September 29th in the evening of which the Hebrew New Year (1st Tishri) and Feast of Trumpets began.

Christ born on the Feast of Trumpets

In 2 B.C., the year of Christ's birth, the Hebrew New Year Day (Tishri 1st) began at sunset (6 p.m. for Calendar purposes) on September 29th and we know that Jesus was born at night, hence in the first hours of the New Year. Nearly 15 centuries before Jesus was born, God, through the Law of Moses, instituted this very day, Tishri 1st, as a holy day which He commanded to be observed year by year, and it was known as the Feast of Trumpets. All the holy days inaugurated by God through the Mosaic Law had a prophetic chronological significance in connection with Christ, either at His First Advent of His yet future work, the respective fulfillments taking place on the self-same days of the year. Because of John 1:14 *"The Word was made flesh and dwelt* (tabernacled) *among us"* the theory has been put forward that Christ was born during the Feast of Tabernacles, but this is only a play upon words, for the symbolism or prophetic meaning of that Feast has nothing to do with the birth of our Lord; it has to do with the yet-future as is clearly shown in Zechariah 14:16-21 *"And it shall come to pass that every one that is left of all the nations which came against Jerusalem shall even go up from year to year to worship the King, the Lord of Hosts, and to keep the feast of tabernacles."* The Day of Atonement had of course to do with our Lord's sacrifice, as we shall see later. The only other annual holy day in the fall of the year, Divinely instituted through the Mosaic Law, was the Feast of Trumpets on 1st Tishri, hence it is the only one left on which Christ could be born, and, as we should expect, the symbolism is fitting. It was a day of blowing of trumpets. (Numbers 29:1) Trumpets in symbol are associated with heralding and the proclamation of deliverance and liberty. At the birth of Jesus the angels heralded the great advent of the Messiah, in these words: *"Behold I bring you good tidings of great joy, which shall be to all people. For unto you is born this day, in the city of David, a Saviour who is Christ the Lord,"* which was immediately followed by the proclamation of the angelic hosts, *"Glory to God in the highest and on Earth peace, goodwill toward men."* The Feast of Trumpets being on New Year's Day was appropriately the initial festival of the year. So, at the present day the 1st of Tishri and the 29th of September are days of special significance on both the Hebrew and Christian Calendars respectively and, in both cases, have appropriate connection with the birth

236

of Jesus on the day that these two datings on the different calendars coincided, in the year 2 B.C.

The day on which Jesus was born was not only the first day of the year but was also the first day of a new Sabbatic Cycle of years the 77th Sabbatic Cycle since the reinstatement of the Sabbatic Cycles on the Jewish return from Babylonian Captivity. It is interesting to notice too that from that re-establishment of the Sabbatic Cycles in Tishri 534 B.C. till the birth of Christ in Tishri 2 B.C. was precisely a great Paschal Cycle of 532 years — the Paschal Cycle being the product of the number of years in the *Metonic* (Lunar or Minor) *Cycle* (19) and that in the *Solar* (or Major) *Cycle* (28), that is 19 X 28 or 532 years."

Thus it is clearly proved that our present Christmas Day is erroneous. This festival on December 25th was in existence long centuries before Jesus was born. It was a pagan festival, to which a Christian terminology has been applied and most of our Christmas customs (nice though some of them have become) are of pagan origin. It was the old Babylonian Feast of Bacchus, the drunken festival. In Rome, December 25th was the Feast of Saturn, and like the Babylonian feast from which it was derived, was also a feast of unrestricted drunkeness. What is perhaps our commonest Christmas custom, the Christmas Tree, was just as common in pagan Egypt and Rome, but in Egypt it was a palm tree while in Rome it was a fir tree. On this matter also, the *Companion Bible* has a very pertinent comment, which states: "The earliest allusion to December 25 as the date for the Nativity is found in the Stromata of Clement of Alexandria, about the beginning of the third century... That Christmas was a pagan festival long before the time of our Lord is beyond doubt... Among other things emanating from Egypt and Babylon, the various Festival Days of the old religions (the birthday of the Egyptian Horus or Osiris, December 25th) became gradually substituted for the (true) nativity of our blessed Saviour, viz., September 29th or Michaelmas Day."

From the date of Jesus' birth it is a simple matter to calculate the very day of the Annunciation to Mary over nine months before, for as our Lord was perfect in every way, the period of gestation before birth would be absolutely normal and perfect, namely 280 days. Now, 280 days before the Nativity on 29th September 2 B.C. brings us back to 23rd December, 3 B.C., which on the Julian Calendar then in use, was precisely the Winter Solstice. So, Jesus left the heavenly glory on celestial or astronomical time (the Winter Solstice), and 280 days later was born into the world on calendar time

237

(the Hebrew New Year Day) — see diagram on page 181.

The Law required 40 days to be fulfilled after birth, in the case of a male child, and then his presentation before the Lord was to be made. (Leviticus 12:2, 4, 6) As Jesus' 1st day was Tishri 1st, his 40th would be Marchesvan 10th and his presentation at the Temple at Jerusalem would be due the following day, Marchesvan 11th, i.e., November 9th in the year 2 B.C., and then *"when they had performed all things according to the Law of the Lord, they returned into Galilee, to their own city Nazareth"* and *"his parents went to Jerusalem every year at the feast of the Passover."* (Luke 2:39-41)

The first Passover after the birth of Jesus was that in the year 1 B.C., and between that one and the following Passover in A.D. 1, there occurred the visit of the Wise Men, the flight of the Holy Family to Egypt, the death of Herod the Great and the return of the Holy Family to Nazareth.

HEBREW AND BABYLONIAN MONTHS		
		Modern equivalent
Hebrew	*Babylonian*	*(approximately)*
1. Nisan	Nisanu	March–April
2. Iyar	Aiaru	April–May
3. Sivan	Simanu	May–June
4. Tammuz	Du'uzu	June–July
5. Ab	Abu	July–August
6. Elul	Ululu	August–September
7. Tishri	Tashritu	September–October
8. Marchesvan	Arahsamna	October–November
9. Kislev	Kislimu	November–December
10. Tebet	Tebetu	December–January
11. Shebat	Shabat	January–February
12. Adar	Addaru	February–March.
Ve-Adar	Arhu mahru sa	(Intercalary month)

Among the earliest forms of Egyptian writings was the "Book of the Coming Forth by Day." Long extracts from it are found copied onto the coffins and sarcophagi dating from the First Egyptian Dynasty to about 200 B.C. From the 5th and 6th Egyptian Dynasties the ancient writings are found on papyri as these writings came into general use. In time these transcripts received the name "Book of the Dead" from being found in the burial containers.

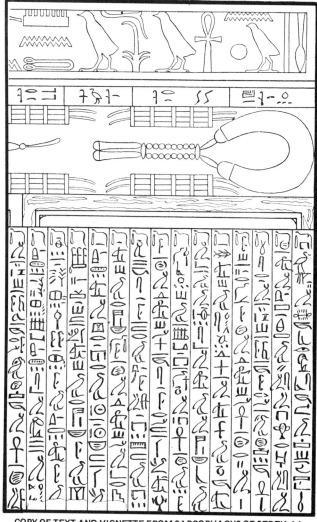

COPY OF TEXT AND VIGNETTE FROM SARCOPHAGUS OF SEBEK-AA

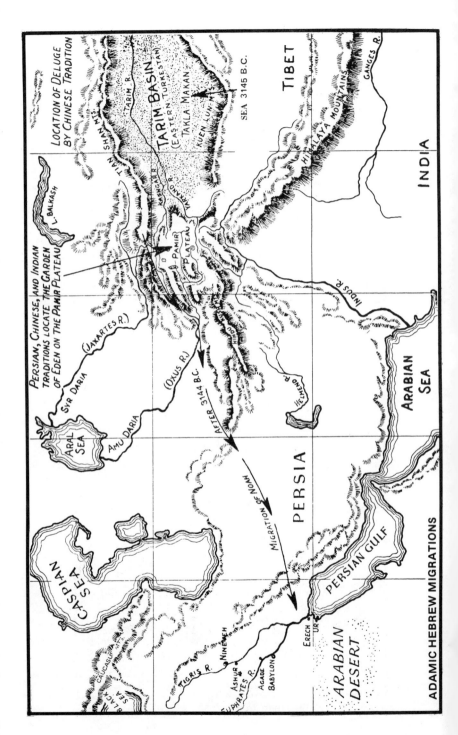

ADAMIC HEBREW MIGRATIONS

The ancient texts of the early Egyptians contain the religious beliefs, rituals and ceremonies designed to secure a happy after-life for the deceased, especially the Kings and Queens. It is also clear that the original semi-barbarous North African aborigines were not the authors of the writings that refer to an elaborate system of sepulture which they never practiced. Most of the beliefs found in the Book of the Dead were introduced into Egypt by some conquer-ing immigrants. Passages in the texts indicate that the aborigines, while adopting many of the beliefs and customs of the newcomers, never wholly gave up their own fantastic beliefs and imageries.

It is most likely the new immigrants were of Semitic stock. In the earliest Egyptian hieroglyphic inscriptions are found grammati-cal usages, verbal forms, idioms and pronouns which are identical with many of those in use in all the Semitic dialects. Conquest was followed by intermarriage and thus the historical Egyptians are a blend of the indigenous north-east African people and the immi-grants from the East, who, having settled in Egypt, were gradually absorbed into the native population. Later, purely Semitic colonies were established in Egypt. The writings in the Book of the Dead are a mirror in which are reflected most of the beliefs of the various peoples and races which came in to build up the Egyptians of history.

Among the texts of the Book of the Dead are found those that contain allusions to the interior features of the Great Pyramid, and to such an extent that the eminent Egyptologist, Sir Gaston Maspero (discoverer of the Pyramid Texts) declared "The Pyramids and the Book of the Dead reproduce the same original, the one in words, the other in stone." While that statement is somewhat imaginary and exaggerated, it did contain an element of truth. There are decided similarities between the mystical writings found in the Book of the Dead and the symbolism of the Great Pyramid.

This similarity leads one to surmise that the Book of the Dead and the symbolism of the Great Pyramid had a common origin. This is a logical conclusion because the early Pharaohs of Egypt (during whose times the Book of the Dead was originally composed) were most likely descendants of Enoch who had migrated from Central Asia,, probably from the Tarim Basin in Eastern Turkestan, where Noah's Flood occurred around 3145 B.C. (Septuagint chronology) Thus, they would have been cognizant of Enoch's wisdom and revelations from God concerning both science and prophecy, which were later incorporated into the building of the Great Pyramid by other descendants of Enoch through Noah and Seth.

COPY OF TEXT AND VIGNETTE FROM PAPYRUS OF ANI

Many of the texts from the Book of the Dead describe mystery initiations and picture them as if presented in the Great Pyramid itself. It must be realized, however, that even if the ritual did pertain to ceremonies involving the Pyramid's passages and chambers, it was not necessary for them to be enacted within the Pyramid itself. (We have a parallel today in Masonic rituals which are enacted as if the participants were in King Solomon's Temple.) Its interior arrangements would be long remembered by the workmen and witnesses after the Pyramid was sealed up when the structure was built. (except for the solitary passage leading down to the Subterranean Chamber) Thus it is not necessary to believe (or accept claims that are never proven) that there are secret passages existing, whereby the initiates could enter the upper recesses of the Great Pyramid, to account for the records of rituals continuing in initiations during the many centuries it was sealed.

As the religion of ancient Egypt lapsed into corruption and idolatry, the true meaning of the symbolism of the Pyramid's passages and chambers became lost. The Great Pyramid became the "House of Osiris," containing the "Secret Places of the Hidden God." There, the neophyte was initiated into the mysteries of Egypt. By stages the mysteries or secrets were revealed to the

Illuminate as he was pictured to pass through the passages of the Great Pyramid, finally passing through the "Passage of the Vail." (the King's Chamber Passage) When he entered the "Chamber of the Open Tomb," the final mystery was made known to him — the "Resurrection to Life Eternal."

In spite of the perversion woven around the ancient rituals, fragments of the ancient wisdom and knowledge of Divine things has been retained. The symbolism of the Pyramid's interior, expressed in the Book of the Dead, carries a heavy substratum of truth. (Chart on page 244 pictures the interior features of the Great Pyramid alluded to in the ancient Egyptian texts)

	(BOOK OF THE DEAD)
Descending Passage	The Descent
Subterranean Chamber	Chamber of Ordeal (or Chamber of Chaos)
Grotto	Well of Life
Stone That Concealed Plug	The Hidden Lintel
Plug	The Door of Ascent (or the Gate of Ascent)
First Ascending Passage	Hall of Truth in Darkness
Well Shaft Opening	Crossing of the Pure Roads of Life
Queen's Chamber Passage	Path of the Coming Forth of the Regenerated Soul
Queen's Chamber	Chamber of the New Birth or Regeneration (or Chamber of Second Birth)
Grand Gallery	Hall of Truth in Light (or Crossing of the Pure Waters of Life)
First Low Passage	Royal Arch of the Solstice
Antǝ-Chamber	Passage of the Vail (or Chamber of the Triple Vail)
King's Chamber	Chamber of the Open Tomb of Resurrection

Although much of the astonishing science of the Great Pyramid did survive the builders, a very great deal of it regretably did not. Among the cults of the Egyptian priesthood, a portion of the mathematical knowledge lived for hundreds of years. The wisdom the priests possessed was jealously preserved and guarded as a profound mystery which was later distorted. Eventually, through supression of learning, much of its true understanding was lost.

Many famous personages, such as Thales, Pythagoras, Plato, Democritus, Euclid, Archimedes, Eratosthenes and Hipparchus went to Egypt to seek and find wisdom in astronomy, geometry, philosophy and history. By skillful questioning, persistence and patience, they returned home with the wisdom the Egyptians had retained from their ancient records. Through those learned scholars, much of the ancient Egyptian wisdom was salvaged, preserved and passed on to succeeding generations.

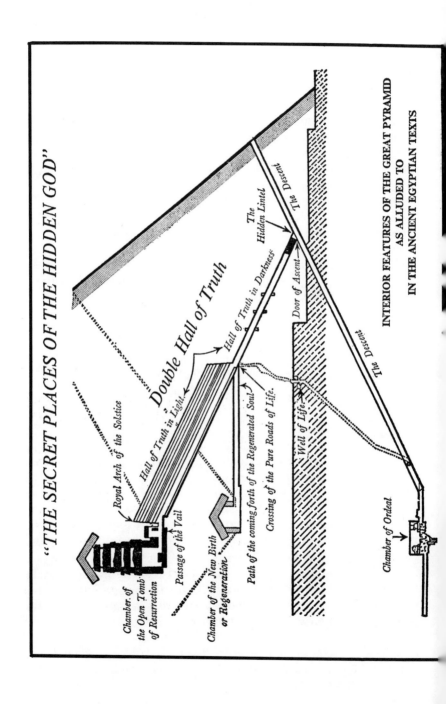

"THE SECRET PLACES OF THE HIDDEN GOD"

Double Hall of Truth

Royal Arch of the Solstice

Hall of Truth in Light.

Hall of Truth in Darkness.

The Hidden Lintel

The Descent

Door of Ascent.

The Descent

Chamber of the Open Tomb of Resurrection

Passage of the Vail

Chamber of the New Birth or Regeneration.

Path of the coming forth of the Regenerated Soul

Crossing of the Pure Roads of Life.

Well of Life.

Chamber of Ordeal.

INTERIOR FEATURES OF THE GREAT PYRAMID
AS ALLUDED TO
IN THE ANCIENT EGYPTIAN TEXTS

In Egypt, Moses undoubtedly gleaned much of the material for certain parts of Genesis as well as the foundation principles for some of what later came to him inspirationally. Moses is known to have been educated among the Egyptian priesthood, after having been adopted as a son by the daughter of Pharaoh. Every possible educational advantage would have been showered upon him. To some degree, Abraham may have received instruction from the Egyptian priesthood, for he, too, abode in Egypt for a time.

For over two thousand years, scholars from many nations visited Egypt, seeking the "ancient wisdom" of the Egyptian priesthood. Since the late 15th century A.D., scholars recognized the ancient knowledge of Egypt was more ancient, and therefore more superior, than that of the Greeks. Attention centered on the writings attributed to the mythical Hermes Trismegistus, which were believed to be of great antiquity. However, it was later proved that they were actually written in the first and second centuries A.D. (Proceedings of the Society of Antiquaries of Scotland – 1984)

The Mason craft of Britain claims a mythological history tracing its origins to ancient Egypt, though the place of Hermes as founder of architecture was here taken by Euclid — the basis of architecture lying in the mathematical sciences, which were therefore held to form a part of architecture. This belief is found in varying forms in different versions of the so-called "Old Charges" or "Old Constitutions." English copies survive from the late 14th century onwards. Traditions have the Scottish Masons possessing this belief as early as 1641 A.D.

The Masons claimed secrets of ancient Egyptian wisdom relating to their craft, and therefore to mathematics. These claims resulted in the revival of interest in classical architecture, giving it a dominant place among the crafts and mathematical sciences. This development was much advanced in Britain by John Dee's famous mathematical preface to Euclid, (1570) which hailed architecture as "a Science garnished with many doctrines, and divers Instructions: by whose judgment all works by other workmen finished, are judged." (Dee, 1975. table appended to preface) Such hints that Masons possessed "Egyptian" secrets led many to regard a Masonic lodge with interest, and whether seeking ancient secrets or practical knowledge, were eager to be admitted.

Many Egyptologists and investigators of the Great Pyramid are convinced that the Pyramid contains one or more secret and as yet undiscovered chambers. Piazzi Smyth suggested there will be found another chamber in the Great Pyramid "which will prove to be the very monument room of the whole monument." When a multitude of black diorite rock chips were discovered in the debris from the dressing of the stones used in the Pyramid, Smyth surmised that the undiscovered chamber might be lined with black diorite.

In the hope of finding previously undiscovered passages and chambers in the Great Pyramid several methods have been used and from time to time others will, probably, be tried. Sound waves and magnetism tests failed to produce satisfactory results. Cosmic ray probes, a system developed by Dr. Luis Alvarez (1968 Nobel Prize winner for physics) did prove to be successful although they failed to find any unknown chamber.

The Cosmic ray device operates much like an X-ray machine, except the rays are generated in outer space and not by the machine. A spark chamber, when placed in a chamber in a pyramid, will measure the strength and direction of cosmic ray particles, which constantly bombard the earth and pass through such massive stone structures as pyramids. By analyzing countless rays, over several weeks, those that have passed through empty areas are located, tunnels can be dug, directly, to the open area.

In 1968, under the direction of D. Lauren Yazolino, Alvarez's assistant, two million cosmic ray trajectories made in the Second Pyramid (Cephren) had been measured and run through a computer, in Cairo, for analysis. Results indicated the system was working satisfactorily. Re-analysis of the tapes, however, produced different patterns which caused Fr. Amr Goneid, another scientist affiliated with the project to be quoted as saying, "It defies all known laws of physics" and "some force beyond man's comprehension was brought to bear on the readings."

Further checks, at Berkeley, Calif. by Dr. Alvarez and Dr. Yazolino, showed the "mysterious readings" to be the result of the spark chamber running out of neon gas, and no other chambers than what is known to exist were found. Similar tests made later in the Great Pyramid also produced no indication of unknown chambers.

In 1974, a joint team from the Ain Shams University of Egypt and the Stanford Research Institute of California, U.S.A., carried out Electronmagnetic Sounder experiments at the Pyramids, again with the object of finding hidden chambers. This method, developed under the leadership of Professor Lambert T. Dolphin, utilized radio-wave propagation to detect chambers, instead of the cosmic ray method of Professor Alvarez.

The cosmic ray method was limited in that the detector, of necessity, must point in an upward direction and therefore cannot locate any chambers below its own position. The electromagnetic sounder method is not limited in this respect. It can be pointed in any direction, consequently in theory it should be more versatile.

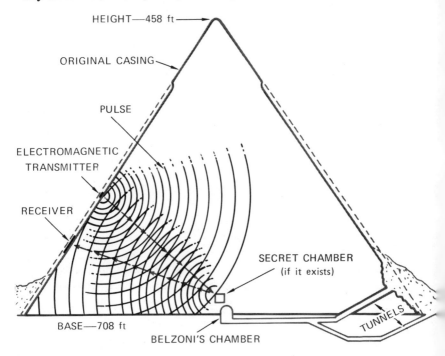

ELECTROMAGNETIC PROBING OF EGYPTIAN PYRAMIDS
Stanford Research Institute

The first test was to discover the actual in-situ losses in bedrock and in the core masonry of Chephren's Pyramid. Accordingly the apparatus was set up in the Lower Chamber and in "Belzoni's" Chamber, as well as half way up the North face of the pyramid. Much to everyone's surprise it was found that the energy loss in the bedrock was more than three times the expected level. In fact, no signals could be detected by the receiver over the 220 feet distance between the two chambers. Similarly no signals could be detected through the 270 feet of core masonry from Belzoni's chamber to the North face of the pyramid. Tests were then made at the Great Pyramid with the same negative results. Thus both pyramids were shown conclusively to have high radio-frequency losses.

The immediate question was, of course, why are the energy losses so high when tests made in the United States were successful for even greater distances. Although it was known that high moisture content in soil and rock produces high radio-frequency losses, the general knowledge that the climate of Egypt is dry (rainfall at Giza less than 1 inch per year) had ruled out any problems due to moisture. However, tests showed that this indeed was the root of the problem. In spite of the low annual rainfall and the warm climate, the average humidity level inside the pyramids was found to be 83 percent.

The reason given by the experimenters, for the high humidity, is the prevailing North wind at Giza, bringing with it the damp marine air from the Mediterranean Sea. It was also noted that the limestone bedrock and core masonry of the pyramids is quite porous (as far as rocks go) and there is a movement of water vapour from the ground water table, below the ground surface, up through the pyramids to the atmosphere, thus providing a high humidity in the structures.

It has been calculated that within the masonry of Chephren's pyramid, the total quantity of water and water vapour amounts to 100 million gallons. With this amount of moisture, the experiments have proved that this particular method of exploration using radio waves is, unfortunately, not suitable for testing the Giza Pyramids.

Under the name of "Psycho-phenomenon," investigations are continually in progress that are experimenting with models of the Great Pyramid to determine possible physical, chemical and biological process that may be going on inside that shape. Perhaps there exists an accumulation of electromagnetic waves, cosmic rays or some unknown "energy."

Some of the claims of what pyramid energy can do include: preservation of food, purification of water, razor blade sharpening, enhancement of meditation, shortening of healing time, increased concentration, improving personal relationships and affecting plant growth. One of the earliest investigators or pyramid energy, the late Verne L. Cameron of California, U.S.A., in 1953 noted the effect of cones and pyramids in stimulating plant growth.

Although no acceptable scientific evidence exists that proves the pyramid form is a generator of what is called "pyramid energy," there are many indications that the geometric form of a pyramid may have the ability to generate a "soft energy" which can energize or preserve life. It is speculated that the pyramid form traps some form of universal evergy that is attracted by the Earth's gravitational pull, converting it into a concentrated and useable "soft energy." In 1976 Ian Woods B.L.A. (pyramid design researcher) of Toronto, Canada, theorized pyramid energy is an "energy which affects life by encouraging the cells in animal, vegetable and mineral matter to resonate at a special frequency. In other words, the vibration of the pyramid causes the cells to match vibration with itself. This action has the ability to return organisms back to their 'natural vibration' and in so doing, energizes the cells of living organisms or preserves the cells of non-living organisms. Under the influence of pyramid energy then, an organism can realize a greater potential." (Pyramid Design — 1976)

The above theory is based on the hypothesis that all forms resonate energy and that a pyramid is a special form in that it resonates with a certain form of energy that can be beneficial for mankind. If this be true then perhaps the greatest potential of pyramid forms (energy?) will be found in the research being done with Pyramid Greenhouses. Current experimenters are reporting that the pyramid effect is causing plants to grow more quickly and vigorously and certain food plants to yield an increase of three times more than usual.

Experiments dealing with the reaction of solar energy in relationship to forms is currently being conducted by one research architect (Ralph L. Knowles) who recently performed a remarkable analysis of the solar energy flowing into Pueblos as a demonstration of what might be expected if such factors were considered in the design of buildings. He suggests that if the energy flows of an entire area were known, then it would be possible to design structures and urban layouts that would take advantage of them.

While such scientific investigations are being conducted, theories propounded by pseudo-scientific, science-fiction and sensational authors are constantly being published which do nothing more than hinder legitimate research.

APPENDIX D

THE GREAT PYRAMID AND THE CHEMICAL ELEMENTS

It appears the elements and their atomic weights are revealed by the mathematic statistics of the masonry courses of the Great Pyramid. It is known that the various elements are grouped according to their characteristics, or their properties. According to one scientific theory, the element Neon (Ne) No. 10 is the nucleus of all succeeding elements and the true starting point of the atomic development. By a mathematical process based upon the altitude of Course No. 10 of the Pyramid's masonry, we find the atomic weight of Uranium (U) No. 92 corresponds to the 92nd course of masonry above course No. 10.

The atomic weight is arrived at by taking the said altitude in Pyramid inches and moving the decimal point one place to the left, thus dividing by 10. Pyramid Course No. 92 is 2387 P. inches above Course No. 10, thus yielding 238.7 as the atomic weight of Uranium No. 92. According to the list of International Atomic Weights adopted, the atomic weight of Uranium is 238.07 and by the same method of computing, other elements in the same group show the following relationships:

ELEMENT	ATOMIC NO.	ATOMIC WEIGHT	COURSE NO. PYRAMID	HEIGHT ABOVE COURSE NO. 10	ONE TENTH HEIGHT
URANIUM (U)	92	238.07	92	2387 P."	238.7 P."
THORIUM (Th)	90	232.12	90	2320 P."	232.0 P."
RADIUM (Ra)	88	226.05	88	2259 P."	225.9 P."
RADON (Rn)	86	222.00	86	2214 P."	221.4 P."

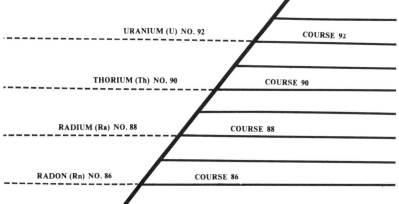

Another different but equally significant agreement between the atomic elements and the Pyramid course measurements is found by dividing the height (232.52050 Sacred Cubits) of the Pyramid in four equal parts. The quarter heights will fall on the following course numbers — 43, 95, 152, 215. (Apex) The heights being 58.37 Cubits, 115.80 Cubits, 174.16 Cubits, 232.52 Cubits. (Apex) The atomic weight of the following elements closely correspond to the four quarter heights:

ELEMENT	ATOMIC WEIGHT	NUMBER OF CUBITS ABOVE BASE	
THORIUM (Th)	232.12	232.52	(HEIGHT OF 4TH. QUARTER)
YTTERBIUM (Yb)	173.04	174.16	(HEIGHT OF 3RD. QUARTER)
TIN (Sn)	118.70	115.80	(HEIGHT OF 2ND. QUARTER)
NICKEL (Ni)	58.69	58.37	(HEIGHT OF 1ST. QUARTER)

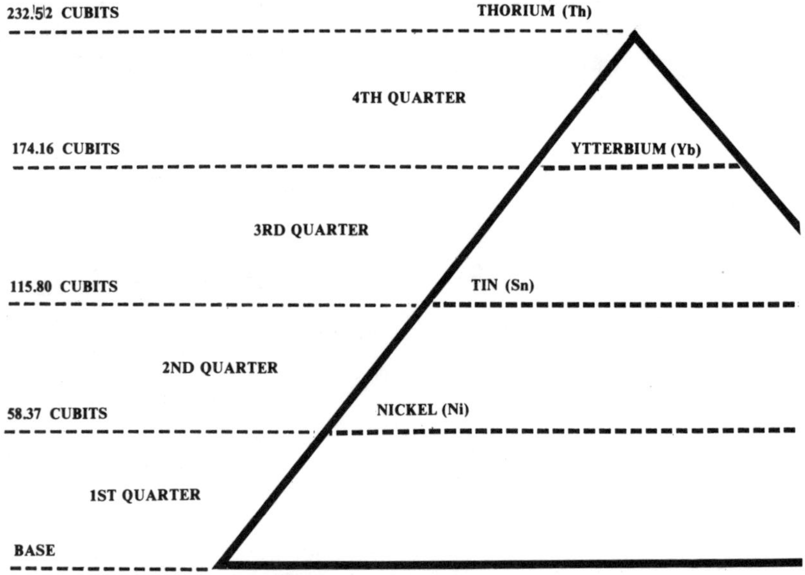

232.52 CUBITS   THORIUM (Th)

4TH QUARTER

174.16 CUBITS   YTTERBIUM (Yb)

3RD QUARTER

115.80 CUBITS   TIN (Sn)

2ND QUARTER

58.37 CUBITS   NICKEL (Ni)

1ST QUARTER

BASE

Considering the present dilapidated condition of the exterior masonry and the slight compression from the Pyramid's weight of nearly 6 million tons, the close agreement shown in the two charts is remarkable. The statistics shown on the charts are offered only as a yet undeveloped theory. However, from the comparisons discovered, this theory is worthy of further consideration and investigation by qualified authorities.

REFERENCES

A.R.G. - **THE TOWER OF EGYPT** - the types and chronology of the Great Pyramid - 1885? - Hazell Printers, London.

BUDGE - **THE BOOK OF THE DEAD** - 1960 - Routledge & Paul, London.

CHAPMAN - **THE GREAT PYRAMID** - 1896 - Virtue & Co., London.

CORBIN - **THE GREAT PYRAMID:** GOD'S WITNESS IN STONE - 1935 - Truth, Oklahoma, U.S.A.

DAVIDSON - **THE GREAT PYRAMID - ITS DIVINE MESSAGE** - 1946 - Williams & Norgate, London.

EDGAR - **THE GREAT PYRAMID: ITS SCIENTIFIC FEATURES** - 1924 - MacLure & MacDonald - Glasgow, Scotland.

EDGAR - **THE GREAT PYRAMID: ITS SPIRITUAL SYMBOLISM** - 1924 - MacLure & MacDonald - Glasgow, Scotland.

EDGAR - **GREAT PYRAMID PASSAGES** - in two volumes - 1923-1924 - Bone & Hulley, Glasgow, Scotland.

GARNIER - **THE GREAT PYRAMID: ITS BUILDER AND ITS PROPHECY** - 1912 - Robert Banks, London.

GRAY - **THE AUTHORSHIP AND MESSAGE OF THE GREAT PYRAMID** - 1953 - E. Steinmann, Cincinnati, Ohio, U.S.A.

GREAVES - **PYRAMIDOLGRAPHY, OR A DESCRIPTION OF THE PYRAMIDS OF EGYPT** - 1736 - J. Brindley, London.

HERBERT - **THE PROBLEM OF THE PYRAMID** - 1936 - Marshall Press, London.

HERODOTUS - **THE HISTORIES** - (various extracts)

HERSCHEL - **POPULAR LECTURES ON SCIENTIFIC SUBJECTS** - 1880 - W. H. Allen - London.

LEMESURIER - **THE GREAT PYRAMID DECODED** - 1977 - St. Martin's Press- New York, N.Y., U.S.A.

MARKS - **THE GREAT PYRAMID - ITS HISTORY AND TEACHINGS** - 1879 - Partridge & Co., London.

NICKLIN - **TESTIMONY IN STONE** - 1961 - Destiny - Mass. U.S.A.

PETRIE - **THE PYRAMIDS AND TEMPLES OF GIZEH** - 1883 - Field & Tuer, London.

PROCTOR - **THE GREAT PYRAMID** - 1883 - Chatton & Windus - London.

RIFFERT - **THE GREAT PYRAMID: PROOF OF GOD** - 1944-Destiny, Mass., U.S.A.

RUTHERFORD - **PYRAMIDOLOGY BOOK I** - The Divine Plan for our Planet- The Hidden Secret in the Great Pyramid - 1957 - Institute of Pyramidology - London.

RUTHERFORD - **PYRAMIDOLOGY BOOK II** - The Glory of Christ - as revealed by the Great Pyramid - 1962 - Institute of Pyramidology - London.

RUTHERFORD - **PYRAMIDOLOGY BOOK III** - Co-ordination of the Great Pyramid's Chronography, Bible Chronology and Archaeology - 1966 - Institute of Pyramidology - London.

RUTHERFORD - **PYRAMIDOLOGY BOOK IV** - The History of the Great
Pyramid - from the Glimmer of Pyramidographia to the Glories of Pyramidology - 1972 - Institute of Pyramidology - London.

SEISS - **MIRACLE IN STONE** - Or the Great Pyramid of Egypt - 1877-8 - Porter
& Coats - Philadelphia, Penn. U.S.A.

SMITH - **THE HOUSE OF GLORY** - 1939 - Wise - New York, N.Y., U.S.A.

SMYTH - **OUR INHERITANCE IN THE GREAT PYRAMID** - 1964 -
Staham & Co., London.

TAYLOR - **THE GREAT PYRAMID: WHY WAS IT BUILT?** - Longmans -
London.

TOMPKINS - **SECRETS OF THE GREAT PYRAMID** - 1971 - Harper & Row -
New York, N.Y. U.S.A.

TRACEY - **THE PILLAR OF WITNESS** - 1879 - W. H. Guest - London.

God's Witness of Stone

In a dry weary land; in a wilderness lone;
In a desert of sand, is the witness of stone,
So majestic the whole and so deep its design,
It convinces the soul of a Builder Divine.

Over four thousand years, it has stood in that place,
'Mid the sighs and the tears of the poor fallen race.
With its secret unknown some have gazed at this tower,
While Jehovah alone knew the depth of its power.

Now there's wonderful skill, that is seen all within;
Come! behold, if you will, the dark symbols of sin;
And then trace from "the fall" how the Lord doth atone,
Showing hope that's "for all" in this Bible of Stone.

'Tis a chart for the wise, giving signs for that day,
When mankind will arise and pursue the right way;
They'll read the glad story which before was unknown,
And God will have glory through the Witness of Stone!

(Anon.)

254

INDEX

C

Contents, Table of, 5

D

The Glory of The Great Pyramid

Behold this mighty beauteous wonder!
O Pyramid of God's own splendour.
O mighty glorious altar so dear,
Let us hear, let us know of thy secrets made clear.

What a glorious sight to behold;
What marvellous mysteries now unfold.
God's hidden plan revealed to man,
From ages past, at last made known.

Every stone, every inch of thy marvellous being
Are glories, are secrets our hearts are now seeing.
He drew His plan for all mankind
And left it there for us to find.

Thy casing stones of dazzling white
All shining with a heavenly light
Reflect the glories hid within
Reflect the beauty that is Him.

What glories, what secrets, what marvellous truths
Have you held for these many long years.
But now, praise to God, you speak loud and clear
As His Kingdom and glorious Reign nears.

Dixielee Errico.

PUBLISHER

ARTISAN SALES
P.O. BOX 1497 • THOUSAND OAKS
CALIF. 91360 U.S.A.

BOOKS BY E. RAYMOND CAPT

"JACOB'S PILLAR"
"OUR GREAT SEAL"
"THE GLORY OF THE STARS"
"KING SOLOMON'S TEMPLE"
"GREAT PYRAMID DECODED"
"STONEHENGE AND DRUIDISM"
"THE TRADITIONS OF GLASTONBURY"
"LOST CHAPTER OF ACTS OF THE APOSTLES"
"THE SCOTTISH DECLARATION OF INDEPENDENCE"
"MISSING LINKS DISCOVERED IN ASSYRIAN TABLETS"
"STUDY IN PYRAMIDOLOGY"

OTHER PUBLICATIONS

"STORIES OF LOST ISRAEL IN FOLKLORE"
"DAN THE PIONEER OF ISRAEL"
"COMING OF THE SAINTS"
"PREHISTORIC LONDON"
"ST. PAUL IN BRITAIN"
"STRANGE PARALLEL"
"BOOK OF JUBILEES"
"BOOK OF ENOCH"